Gender, Race, and Sudan's Exile Politics

Gender, Race, and Sudan's Exile Politics

Do We All Belong to This Country?

Nada Mustafa Ali

LEXINGTON BOOKS
Lanham • Boulder • New York • London

Published by Lexington Books
An imprint of The Rowman & Littlefield Publishing Group, Inc.
4501 Forbes Boulevard, Suite 200, Lanham, Maryland 20706
www.rowman.com

Unit A, Whitacre Mews, 26-34 Stannary Street, London SE11 4AB

British Library Cataloguing in Publication Information Available

Library of Congress Cataloging-in-Publication Data

Ali, Nada Mustafa, author.
Gender, race, and Sudan's exile politics : do we all belong to this country? / Nada Mustafa Ali.
pages cm
Includes bibliographical references and index.
ISBN 978-1-4985-0049-4 (cloth : alk. paper) -- ISBN 978-1-4985-0050-0 (electronic)
1. National Democratic Alliance (Sudan) 2. Opposition (Political science)--Sudan. 3. Sudan--Politics and government--1985- 4. Exiles--Political activity--Sudan. 5. Women--Political activity--Sudan. 6. Sudan--Race relations. I. Title.
JQ3981.A91A45 2015
323.1624--dc23

2015018658

∞ ™ The paper used in this publication meets the minimum requirements of American National Standard for Information Sciences Permanence of Paper for Printed Library Materials, ANSI/NISO Z39.48-1992.

Printed in the United States of America

In fond memory of my father Mustafa Mohamed Ali, and my sister Nagwa Mustafa Ali! May they rest in eternal peace! To my dear mother, Hyat Mohamed Nur, and to my dear daughter, Nagwa Nowara Kodi. And to the Vision of the New Sudan: Gendered!

A Luta Continua

Contents

Acknowledgments

I am thankful to many individuals and institutions whose collaboration and support have been crucial for the researching and writing of this book. I am grateful to Professor Paul Cammack for his diligent and valuable input during the research and writing of the doctoral thesis on which this book is based. I am also grateful to Nira Yuval-Davis and David Pool for their insightful comments. Nira Yuval-Davis' scholarship has been crucial to my research and teaching over the years.

I am indebted to the activists and politicians I interviewed in Egypt, Kenya, the United Kingdom, Sudan, and South Sudan over the past fifteen years for their time and insights. Special thanks to Dr. Al Shafie Khider, Soleiman Bakhiet, Daniel Kodi, Sarah Cleto Rial, Dr. Magda Mohamed Ahmed, Saida Pagaan, Deng Alor, the late Dr. Samson Kwaji, Dr. Pauline Riak, and Dr. Laketch Dirasse. I thank Abdullahi Annaim, Ibrahim El Nur, and the anonymous Middle East Award reviewers for constructive comments on my Cairo fieldwork plan. Premises of the Office of African Studies at the American University in Cairo, the Horn of Africa Centre for Democracy and Development (HACDAD), and the Sudanese Women's Association in Nairobi (SWAN) provided friendly and safe spaces for some of the interviews. I am thankful to the late Neimat, Captain Ahmed Yusif, and their kids who generously hosted me in Nairobi. Follow-up research in different parts of Sudan, and in South Sudan, was possible while on visits or while carrying out assignments in both countries. I am thankful to the institutions and individuals that made this possible.

I am very thankful to Lexington Books. Sabah Ghulamabi showed strong enthusiasm for this book from the very start. Kathryn Tafelski and Kayla Riddleberger provided stellar and prompt support. A reviewer for Lexington

Books offered insightful, encouraging, and generous feedback that has strengthened this manuscript.

I was able to share parts of the research on which this book is based in numerous fora. I thank the Small Arms Survey, John Ryle, and the Rift Valley Institute, Rev. Gloria White Hammond, Sarah Rial and friends at My Sister's Keeper, Jon Temin and the US Institute of Peace, Lilian Riziq and South Sudan Women's Empowerment Network, Friederike Bubenzer and the Institute for Justice and Reconciliation, Balghis Badri and friends at Ahfad University for Women, Fahima Hashim, Zeinab Al Sawi and friends at the Salmma Women's Center (sadly shut down by the government of Sudan in 2014), and Sami Salah, Abdalla Hilla, Huda Shafig, and friends at Gesr.

I am grateful to Atta El-Battahani who provided many of us with the tools to ask questions about gender, ethnicity, and social class as undergraduates during the second half of the 1980s, and who continues to provide guidance. I am also indebted to all my other professors at the Political Science Department at Khartoum University, especially Dr. Taisier Ali, Dr. Abdel Galil Al Makki, and Dr. Fatima Mahmoud. I also thank Abdelgaffar Mohamed Ahmed and Manzoul Assal. At AUC, I am grateful to the late Cynthia Nelson who encouraged me to think about feminisms. I am also indebted to Enid Hill and the late Cyrus Reed for valuable support. I thank Sondra Hale, Crolyn Fluehr-Lobban, Richard Lobban, Anita Fabos, and Suliman Baldo for continuous encouragement and support.

I developed many of my ideas on politicized Islam and women's rights while at the Cairo Institute for Human Rights Studies (CIHRS). I thank Omer Al-Garrai for inspiring conversations, and Bahey Eddin Hassan, founder of CIHRS, for the opportunity to design and carry out creative research. Being in Egypt during the 1990s was also an opportunity to engage the thriving women's movement in Egypt and in the Middle East and North Africa region.

I have learned so much from my students at various universities over the years. I am very thankful to Jonathan Bach, who invited me to develop and teach a course on gender and conflict in the Middle East and Africa at the New School, which was an ideal opportunity to think through and share some of the key themes of this book with students. At Clark University and the University of Massachusetts, Boston, I taught several courses, which allowed me to deepen my thinking about intersectionality and gender "mainstreaming." Many thanks to Anita Fabos, Denise Bebbington, Cynthia Enloe, Chris Bobel, and Elora Chaudhury.

Presenting this research at various institutions during the past decade offered important opportunities for getting feedback and for further learning. I am grateful to Douglas Johnson (Oxford University), Amir Idris (Fordham University), Ahmed Sikinga (Ohio State University), Amou Ajang (Columbia University), Balghis Badri (Ahfad University for Women), Khalid Kodi

(Boston College), Lilian Riziq (South Sudan Women's Empowerment Network), Sami Salah (Gesr), Ihsan Abdelaziz (The Women's NDA in Asmara and the Liberated areas and Sudan Voices), Fahima Hashim (Salmma Women's Center), Zeinab Al Sawi (Sudanese Women's Empowerment for Peace), Rev. Gloria White Hammond and Sarah Rial (My Sister's Keeper), the Brookings Institution and the Office of the Special Envoy on Sudan and South Sudan (USA), and SPLM/A office in Washington, DC, for opportunities to speak about the issues in this book. A research associateship at the Five College Women's Studies Research Center enabled me to update part of the literature and to share my research findings and get feedback from the Five College community.

Many generous friends and colleagues encouraged me over the years. I am grateful to Richard Lobban (who edited the book in which I published my first scholarly chapter in English), Abdallah Gallab, Hyder Ibrahim Ali, Abdullahi Ali Ibrahim (who edited the journal in which I published my first scholarly article in English), Salah Al Zein, Sarah Cleto Rial, Amir Idris and Jane Kani Edward, Bakry El Medni, Laura Beny, Khalid Kodi, Ahmed Al Zobeir, Amani Omer, El-Tayib Hassan, Entisar Abdalla, Susan Thomson, and Hind Ahmed.

A generous Overseas Research Students Award and a Manchester University merit studentship supported my PhD studies at Manchester University. I warmly thank both institutions. A generous Middle East Research Award enabled me to carry out the research in Cairo and Nairobi. Special thanks go to Mushira El Geziri and Seteny Shami. I also wish to thank the Gordon Memorial Trust for a writing grant.

The Center for Governance and Sustainability, and the Women's and Gender Studies Department at the University of Massachusetts, Boston, continue to provide an intellectually stimulating and supportive institutional home. Many thanks to Elora Chowdhury, A. El-Jack, Maria Ivanova, and Chris Bobel.

The views in this book do not necessarily reflect the views of any of the above individuals and institutions. Any errors are the responsibility of the author.

My greatest indebtedness is to my parents, Hayat M. Nur and the late Mustafa M. Ali, for their caring love, unlimited trust, and for their encouragement and cherishing of education and gender equality. I thank my brothers and sisters, Nazik, Khalid, Tarig (and Huda), and Nahla for their love, wits, and hard work. I thank my husband Khalid Kodi for his love and support. I am also grateful to the cute and smart Nagwa Nowara Kodi for the love, joy, and sunshine she brought into my life.

List of Abbreviations

ANC: African National Congress.
AUHIP: African Union High Implementation Panel.
BBSAW: Babiker Badri Scientific Association for Women.
CEDAW: Convention for the Elimination of All Forms of Discrimination Against Women.
CPA: Comprehensive Peace Agreement.
CPS: Communist Party of the Sudan.
DDF: Darfur Development Front.
DDR: Disarmament, Demobilization, and Reintegration.
DUP: Democratic Unionist Party.
EF: Eastern Front.
EPLF: Eritrean People's Liberation Front.
ESPA: Eastern Sudan Peace Agreement.
FEMNET: African Women's Development and Communication Network.
FGC/M: female genital cutting/mutilation.
FGR: The Feminist Group for Reconstructing Sudan.
FIB: Faisal Islamic Bank.
GAD: Gender and Development.
GOS: Government of Sudan.
GUBW: General Union of Beja Women.
HACDAD: Horn of Africa Centre for Democracy and Development.
HCC: High Coordinating Committee.
IGAD: Inter-government Authority on Development.
IWD: International Women's Day.
JEM: Justice and Equality Movement.
MDGs: Millennium Development Goals.

MSK: My Sister's Keeper.
NANS: National Alliance for National Salvation.
NCF: National Consensus Forces.
NCP: National Congress Party.
NDA: National Democratic Alliance.
NESWA: New Sudan Women's Association.
NIF: National Islamic Front.
NMGU: Nuba Mountains General Union.
NOB: Nuba Mountains Organization Abroad.
NSWF: New Sudan Women's Federation.
NUWEDA: Nuba Women's Education and Development Association.
OLS: Operation Lifeline Sudan.
PAIGC: Party for the Liberation of Guinea-Bissau and Cape Verde.
PCP: People's Congress Party.
PDF: Popular Defence Forces.
RFS: Rural Forces Solidarity.
RCC: Revolutionary Command Council.
SAC: Sudan African Congress.
SBS:Southhall Black Sisters.
SCDP: Sudan Cultural Digest Project, Cairo.
SCIC: Sudan Culture and Information Centre in Cairo.
SDFG: Sudan Democracy First Group.
SFDA: Sudan Federal Democratic Alliance.
SFDP: Sudan Federal Democratic Party.
SfP: Sisterhood for Peace.
SHRO: Sudan Human Rights Organization.
SLA/M: Sudan Liberation Army/Movement.
SMNL: Sudanese Movement for National Liberation.
SNA/SAF: Sudan National Alliance/Sudan Alliance Forces.
SNP: Sudan National Party.
SOAT: Sudanese Organization against Torture.
SOWAR: Solidarity for African Women's Rights.
SPLM/A: Sudan People's Liberation Movement/Army.
SPLM-N: Sudan People's Liberation Movement-North.
SRF: Sudan Revolutionary Front/Forces.
SSC: Sudan Studies Centre in Cairo.
SSU: Sudan Socialist Union.
SSWEN: South Sudan Women's Empowerment Network.
SuWEP: Sudanese Women's Empowerment for Peace.
SVTG: Sudan Victims of Torture Group.
SWA: Sudan Women's Alliance.
SWAN: Sudan Women's Association in Nairobi.
SWDA: Sudan Women's Democratic Alliance.

SWF: Sudan Women's Forum in Cairo.

SWGU: Sudanese Women's General Union.

SWRTC: Sudanese Women Research and Training Centre.

SWU: Sudanese Women's Union.

SWVP: Sudanese Women's Voice for Peace.

UNICEF: United Nations Children's Fund.

USW: Union of Sudanese Women.

UNHCR: United Nations High Commissioner for Refugees.

UNIFEM: United Nations Fund for Women and Development.

UNSC: United Nations Security Council.

UNSCR1325: United Nations Security Council 1325 on Women, Peace, and Security.

USAP: Union of Sudan African Parties.

WAF:Women Against Fundamentalism.

WODRANS: Widows, Orphans, and Disabled Rehabilitation Association for the New Sudan.

A Note on Transliteration

This book mostly uses the transliteration standards of the *International Journal of Middle Eastern Studies*. However, in the case of Arabic and Sudanese names, the author has at times used the form that the person uses in writing his or her name, or that is most common in Sudanese usage.

If an English term exists for the word, I use the English term, unless I want to discuss the translation of the word, as in the discussion of the term gender, for example. When used, all Arabic language technical terms have been italicized and fully transliterated, but without using diacritical marks (macrons and dots), except when I used *'ayn* and hamza, where I use an apostrophe.

I have avoided using Anglicized plurals on fully transliterated words as much as possible.

I have transliterated Sudanese colloquial terms consistently.

Chapter One

Introduction

Gender, Race, and Sudan's Exile Politics

Scholars of development and of women's, gender, and feminist studies in Africa, the Middle East, and beyond continue to query the relationship between women's and gender organizations, movements, and activisms on one hand, and nationalist and other political movements, processes, and projects on the other. Scholars also continue to interrogate transnational coalition building across difference, including racial difference, between women's organizations and movements that advocate for gender equality and women's human rights. With its histories of conflict, political oppression, social exclusion, and resistance, Sudan, South Sudan, and Sudan's exile politics and organizing offer important insights into our understanding of these questions.

This book examines the discourses and practices of the Sudanese opposition in exile from a gender perspective, using intersectional analysis that emphasizes the interplay of gender, race, social class, and regional location as aspects of identity and as power relationships. Taking the opposition movements organized under the umbrella of the National Democratic Alliance (NDA)[1] in exile in the 1990s and early 2000s as a point of reference, the book engages questions of women's participation, women's human rights, nationalism, and gender equality in contemporary Sudan and in Sudan's exile politics. The book discusses the socioeconomic and political factors that informed NDA discourses and practices, and the way diverse women's groups active in exile resisted, negotiated, or had been co-opted into these discourses and why.

The book further examines Sudanese and South Sudanese women's organizing in Kenya and Egypt in the 1990s and early 2000s. It engages current feminist debates on intersectionality, a theory, a methodology, and a policy tool that sheds light on the way gender, race, social class, sexuality, physical ability, and other aspects of identity constitute each other and shape women's and communities' experiences of oppression and resistance. I discuss how Sudan's ancient history, colonial encounters, and post-colonial politics shaped power relations based on these aspects of identity; how they contributed to Sudan's wars, political instability, and underdevelopment; and the impact on diverse women and men across Sudan and South Sudan.

Based on a multi-site ethnographic research in Egypt, Kenya, and Eritrea between 1998 and 1999, and on research and an examination of current activisms in Sudan, South Sudan, and among the diaspora of the two countries between 2010 and 2014, the book examines how narratives of gender and race continue to shape the major political questions in Sudan and South Sudan. These also continue to shape women's rights activism in the two countries, especially Sudan. I argue that understanding the dynamics of such relationships in the context of forced migration and exile can inform effective transnational coalition building around current challenges in and between the two countries.

While the book is based on rigorous field and desk research, and while it relies on Michel Foucault's discourse analysis and engages current feminist debates on integrating gender into policy and structures—difference, intersectionality, and transnational coalition building—the book also engages policy and activist debates on gender, conflict, women's participation, and women's human rights. I discuss these later in this chapter.

Sudan underwent exchanges between military regimes (1958–1964, 1969–1985, and 1989–present) and deformed democratic governments (1956–1958, 1965–1969, and 1986–1989). Predominantly male elites from central and Northern Sudan dominated these governments. The military coup that brought the National Islamic Front (NIF)—now National Congress Party (NCP)—to power in 1989 not only forced most political parties, trade unions, and activists in Sudan into either exile politics or underground activism in its early days, it has also urged Sudan's political forces and activists to rethink the very meaning of belonging and of the "Old" Sudan.

In the mid-1990s, this involved rethinking the relationship between religion and politics, a commitment to acknowledging Sudan's diversity, recognition of the need to restructure Sudan's economy and politics to ensure wider and more equitable participation of people from historically marginalized areas of Sudan, and a commitment to self-determination for the people of South Sudan.

The concept of "the New Sudan," which the late Dr. John Garang, founder of the Sudan People's Liberation Movement/Army (SPLM/A), coined in 1983, reflected this thinking. Garang defined New Sudan as the unity and territorial integrity of the Sudan, provided that this unity is based on restructuring Sudan politically, economically, and socially so as to ensure justice and equality for all Sudanese, regardless of religion, sex, or ethnicity (Garang 1998; Khalid 1990, 1992). By the mid-1990s, the New Sudan denoted a critique of Sudan's post-colonial order, a process, a location (the non-government-held areas), and a small coalition of opposition groups.[2]

The tenets of the New Sudan entered official opposition discourse during the Conference of Fundamental Issues, which the National Democratic Alliance (NDA) held in Asmara, Eritrea, in 1995. I argue in this book that while the resolutions of this conference (which were the result of several opposition meetings between 1991 and 1995) were a landmark for Sudan's opposition, the process of rethinking was largely gender-blind. I explore possibilities for integrating gender into New Sudan thinking and politics, including through dialogue or coalition building between women's organizations seeking to transform gender relations in Sudan, and New Sudan movements seeking to transform Sudan.

Using intersectional analysis, this book discusses race relations and politics in Sudan. Echoing Fanon's "white faces, black masks," anthropologist Sharif Harir, who was the vice president of the Sudan Federal Democratic Party and member of the NDA's executive office at the time of initial research, eloquently discussed structural racism in the Old Sudan in a lecture he gave in Cairo in 1998,

> Systems of internal colonialism are characterised by what we sociologists call *structural racism*. It is different from racism such as you saying to me for example, Sharif is from Western Sudan, *Gharrabi*, *Takruni* (local insult for people from Western Sudan) or call one of our Dinka brothers *Abid* (slang for slave/nigger). This is your and his business. I can decide to quarrel with you, beat you up, you beat me up, and it is over. This is insignificant. But structural racism is when those in the margins are excluded from decision-making within the state. When we formed resistance movements, our ruling elite said those were racist movements. These movements sought equality, but both military and democratic masters in the centre of power refused to recognise our grievances. The issue became one of human value and of identity: *Do we all belong to this country?* (Lecture at the Sudan Culture and Information Centre, attended and recorded by the author, Cairo, June 1998; emphasis mine)

Ushari Mahmoud develops this argument further. He argues that

> Within the New Sudan conceptual framework, cultural diversity, in and of itself, is irrelevant and politically unimportant. What matters is the system of injustice and inequality, which accompanies that diversity. Then, culture becomes not discrete categories in a diversity grid, but the practices generated by the interaction between the cultural makeup on the one hand, and the political, economic, and legal structures on the other hand. (Mahmoud 1993, 253)

This important discourse has informed some of the key peace agreements between the government of Sudan and opposition movements, especially the Comprehensive Peace Agreements. The same discourse was prominent in Sudan's 2010 elections, and in an expanding body of literature on Sudan's conflicts and identity, including literature on the New Sudan. With a few exceptions (for example, Ismail 1999), "much of the literature is silent on gender" (for example, Mahmoud 1993; Johnson 1998; and Deng 2010). I argue that the "New Sudan" as an emancipatory project that is concerned with racial/cultural and regional difference and the way it is turned into oppression (Anthias and Yuval-Davis 1992) in Sudan can inform the agendas of organizations and movements concerned with gender equality and women's human rights. These organizations, and gender and feminist theorizing, in turn, can inform the development of a vision where gender equality and women's human rights are central. Integrating a gender perspective into the programs of movements that seek transformation in Sudan can help these movements overcome some of the pitfalls that other nationalist and liberation movements in the Middle East and Africa encountered.

As discussed above, this book analyzes how exiled women's groups based in Egypt and Kenya at the time of initial field research accepted, negotiated, or resisted gendered opposition discourses. Given that these groups were diverse, I look at implications for coalition building both among women's groups, and between these groups and political parties with gender-sensitive agendas. Leaders of political movements organized under the NDA in the 1990s and early 2000s offer in-depth reflections on gender, marginalization, and visions for change.

Knowledge is socially and culturally constructed. My political and intellectual background is thus integral to the subject matter of and the analysis in this book. This entails self-reflexivity (Said 1994; Stanley 1993; Opie 1989; Harding 1987; Smith 1987), which is important in its own right, and so I do not seek to reproduce dominant gender, race, class, and other biases (Naples 2003, 3).

WHY THIS BOOK NOW?

The Political Argument

January 24, 2013

It is almost 10am. I had traveled from Boston to New York the night before, spent the night at a friend's house in Brooklyn, and was on my way to meet the chair of the Sudan People's Liberation Movement-North (SPLM-N) and head of the Sudan Revolutionary Front (SRF)[3] Malik Agar, Secretary General of the movement Yasir Arman, and SPLM's Humanitarian Affairs officer Nyrone Philip.

I see Agar, seated in the foyer of the United Nations Plaza Hotel. I am there to discuss the possibility of joining an initiative to draft a road map for future Sudan through a participatory process. Agar shows surprise that I was not a member in the SPLM-N. I tell him I strongly believe in the vision of the New Sudan. I then describe the various personal, political, and intellectual factors that had informed my decision not to be part of the movement. A key reason I highlight is the long-lasting destructive impact of armed conflict, especially on communities directly affected by war, and especially on women and girls. I share stories that women had told me less than a year earlier when I visited Damazin, capital of the Blue Nile State where until September 2011 Agar was governor.

I discuss the long-term impact of militarization[4] on Liberian and Rwandan women and communities and how political violence has resulted in devastating rape statistics in post-Apartheid South Africa. I tell him I know that South Kordofan and the Blue Nile states are already militarized, and that as a Northern Sudanese educated woman who spends most of the year in the United States, I did not have the right to determine whether or not people in the marginalized areas of Sudan should carry arms, but that during the last decade I realized it was better to use other means to achieve peace, social justice, gender equality, and transformation in Sudan.

Agar listens patiently, and then says, "I hear you, but [the government in Khartoum] has not given us any other choice. Look at me! I am in my sixties! I should be getting ready for retirement, and enjoying my grandchildren. Instead, I am out in the wilderness, making many sacrifices for [a better future for our people and country]." When others join us, we discuss visions for the future.

While current opposition movements are operating in a context that is different from that of the 1990s and early 2000s, like the NDA, these movements emphasize the need for a blueprint that would clearly identify their plans for the future.

The year 2015 is a year of multiple anniversaries and milestones that are directly relevant to the subject matter of this book. The year marks the twentieth anniversary of the Conference of Fundamental Issues and the Asmara Resolutions; the fifteenth anniversary of the NDA's second conference, which took place in Massawa, Eritrea, in 2000; and the tenth anniversary of the signing of the Comprehensive Peace Agreement (CPA) between the GOS and the SPLM/A.

Many consider the Asmara conference and its resolutions (discussed throughout this book) a landmark in Sudan's recent history. Current opposition networks, such as the Sudan Revolutionary Forces (SRF) and the National Consensus Forces, acknowledge the importance of the Asmara conference and resolutions, and have launched a similar process that resulted, at the time of writing, in *The Sudan Call* political declaration, which several movements and parties signed in Addis Ababa on December 3, 2014. It is important that current and future processes to unify Sudan's opposition learn from recent history. This might help movements address the shortcomings that accompanied the development and implementation of the Asmara 1995 resolutions, which involved a bargain that undermined women's human rights in favor of the unity of the NDA as discussed throughout this book.

The year 2015 also marks the fifteenth anniversary of the *United Nations Security Council Resolution 1325 on Women, Peace and Security*, the first UN Security Council (UNSC) resolution devoted to women's participation and gender equality in conflict, peace-building, and post-conflict situations. UNSCR1325 was the first resolution to acknowledge and address women's unequal participation in peace negotiations and in post-conflict reconstruction of war-affected countries. It stresses the importance of women's full participation in peace negotiations at all levels, and the need to integrate gender into post-conflict reconstruction efforts. The result of a major campaign in which some of the Sudanese women activists and organizations in exile took part, I remember sharing the initial slogan of the campaign that materialized in UNSCR1325: women's participation, from the village council to the level of the UN Security Council with women in areas held by the NDA in Eastern Sudan at the time.

The UNSC has since issued six follow-up resolutions,[5] involving the development of indicators to monitor progress on implementing resolution 1325; naming sexual violence in conflict as a war crime and mandating peacekeeping missions to protect women and children from sexual violence during conflict; and instructing the United Nations Secretary-General to appoint a special representative on sexual violence during armed conflict.

Despite shortcomings in implementation, these resolutions opened up spaces for further advocacy, as well as resources to promote women's participation, women's human rights, and efforts to achieve gender equality in conflict-affected countries like Sudan and South Sudan. Many countries have developed national action plans for implementing resolution 1325. South Sudan launched its national action plan on 1325 in November 2013.[6]

The year 2015 is the mid-point in the African Women's Decade, which the African Union launched in 2010. In 2003, feminists and women's rights activists from across the African continent, organized in the Solidarity for African Women's Rights (SOWAR), succeeded in persuading the African Union to adopt one of the most progressive international human rights documents: the Protocol to the African Charter on the Rights of Women in Africa. Sudan signed this protocol in 2008 but did not ratify it, and South Sudan had planned to sign and ratify it[7] before war re-erupted in the country in December 2013.

There is near consensus that commitment and action to achieve gender equality, women's human rights, and women's equal participation are important at the normative level (that is, working toward gender equality and women's human rights is important in its own right). There is also near consensus that women's participation, gender equality, and women's human rights are key to achieving key development goals. Yet a gender perspective and women's voices are often marginalized or absent from crucial political processes in countries like Sudan and South Sudan. Integrating a gender perspective into political and development processes was a key focus and outcome of the United Nations Fourth Conference on Women, which took place in Beijing.

The year further marks the twentieth anniversary of the United Nations Fourth Conference on Women, and *The Beijing Platform of Action*, which, among many other achievements, focused attention on the importance of *integrating gender* at all levels. My participation in some of the planning activities and meetings leading to the Beijing conference, and my participation in the conference have, to a great extent, influenced my advocacy with others around integrating gender into NDA activities in the decade that followed the Asmara and Beijing conferences.

Finally, 2015 also marks the deadline for many of the United Nation's Millennium Development Goals, and efforts are underway to ensure that the concerns of women and girls are central to the post-2015 agenda on sustainable development. The book engages some of these concerns and ways to address them in the case of Sudan.

The Personal Argument

May 11, 1998

I had just finished a two-hour interview with Azza, Secretary General of the Sudan Women's Union (SWU) and founder of the Sudanese Women Research and Training Centre (SWRTC) in Cairo, Egypt. I had started to write down her details and the date of the interview on the cover of the tape when Azza placed a pot of tea on the table in front of me, then said: "I now want to ask *you* a question!" She continued,

> I used to see you at events in [the premises of the] Sudan Human Rights Organization [in Cairo]. I also used to listen to you speak on women's rights. We have always seen you as someone who is active against *algabha* (the NIF) but through focusing on human rights and research. Then *suddenly*, we hear that [you] have joined a political party that seeks power. I have always wondered whatever had happened to you! (Interview with Azza Al Tigany, Secretary General of the SWU, Cairo, May 11, 1998)

Azza was one of many people who had asked me why I *joined* an opposition movement in the mid-1990s. My response to almost each person who had asked me this question started with recounting the story of Marwa (not her real name), a young Sudanese woman who jumped from a seven-story hotel in *el Ataba*, a busy, low-income market area in Cairo where Sudanese traders, visitors, and residents in Cairo live or meet. I had met Marwa only once prior to her death. An acquaintance who lived in the same hotel as Marwa invited me to visit this neighbor of hers who was ill and had recently lost a child.

Marwa looked frail but her eyes spoke of a strong spirit. She greeted us with a wide smile. While squeezing limes into two glasses through a colander and adding sugar, she narrated her story. She had arrived from Libya with her husband, who had decided to migrate to Libya because he was not able to find work in Sudan. He thought the reason for his unemployment was because of his membership in a major opposition party. With the money he made in Libya, Marwa's husband decided to return to Sudan to start a small business. Upon their arrival in Cairo, however, Marwa and her husband were robbed. Consequently, Marwa's husband worked as a laborer in the outskirts of Cairo to meet their daily living expenses. He was trying to contact members of his party to raise money so his family could return to Sudan. When Marwa's child died in a hospital in Cairo, Marwa said the hospital refused to release the body until they paid the outstanding healthcare fees.

Shortly afterward, my acquaintance's cousin told me over the phone that Marwa had jumped from the seventh floor of the hotel where she was staying. I went to the hotel in *el Ataba*. The scene of Marwa's body on the floor, covered with a white sheet, pinned to the floor with four bricks, in a foreign land, is still fresh in my mind, two decades later.[8] I was full of pain and anger. This incident, along with other experiences I discuss below, perhaps moved me in a way similar to what Mohammed Bouazizi's self-immolation ignited the protests that led to the overthrow of the regimes of Ben Ali, Mubarak, and Salih in Tunisia, Egypt, and Yemen respectively. Marwa's death convinced me at the time of the urgency and importance of organized collective action to bring about change and transformation in Sudan. It also transformed my relationship with the official opposition.

In my research, I was trying to understand and define my relationship to the project of the New Sudan. As a scholar, activist, and feminist, I was perhaps seeking histories I (and others) could "live with/by" and learn from "as well as utopian dreams of 'other worlds' for the future" (Andrijasevic, Hamilton, and Hemmings 2014, 1). In so doing, I wanted to avoid "the mythology of 'hygienic' research with its accompanying mystification of the researcher and the researched as objective instruments of data production" (Oakley 1981, 58), and to assert the recognition that personal involvement was "more than dangerous bias" (Oakley 1981, 58).

Born in Atbara, Sudan, I went to undergraduate school at the University of Khartoum (U of K) right after the 1985 *Intifada* (uprising) that overthrew a dictatorial regime that governed Sudan for sixteen years. Although it is a public university, the U of K is known for its high politicization and independence regardless of the nature of the government in power in Sudan. The strong university student union, at the time held by an alliance of student associations advocating for democracy, played an important role in the early days of the *Intifada*. Much of the pre-*Intifada* organizing took place at the university. An alliance of trade unions, the Trade Unions Alliance held some of its meetings in *Nadi Al Asatza* (the club of the faculty of the U of K). In that atmosphere, being a member of one of the student bodies associated with political parties in the university was part of being a student.[9] By the end of their preliminary year, many students would have joined one of the active student organizations on campus.

The Muslim Brothers student organization *Al Ittigah Al Islami* had introduced violence into the university campuses toward the end of the Numeiry years. It had expanded slowly within the student body. Other associations agreed on almost nothing but their hostility toward the Islamists and otherwise engaged in bickering. My involvement was limited to observation, voting during the Student Union's elections, and attending political rallies and intellectual debates.

I was active in the Political Science Student's Association,[10] the Disabled Students' and their Friends' Association,[11] and in my neighborhood's association at the university.[12] My interest in women's human rights and gender equality was confined to reading, research, and to celebrations of international women's day in March.

My exile had come about gradually. I arrived in Cairo (to complete my MA) in mid-1991, by which time the opposition was trying to establish its structures outside Sudan, I had no links to mainstream opposition movements. Like many women and men from my generation, until 1995, indeed until the Asmara 1995 Conference of Fundamental Issues, I did not have much hope in what the exiled opposition was doing. Political figures and parties whom many of us held responsible for the ascendance of the NIF to power dominated the post-1989 political scene in exile. Instead, I tried (with others) to address some of the immediate challenges that new Sudanese arrivals faced in Cairo, while thinking about long-term transformation through research. It was during that time that I started defining myself as a "third-world feminist" committed to the school of "standpoint epistemology."

I had read Mansour Khalid's book *John Garang Speaks* in the late 1980s in Khartoum, and became interested in the principles of the evolving New Sudan discourse. Nonetheless, I was only an observer throughout the process that led to the Asmara Conference of Fundamental Issues.

In 1994 I started to collaborate with the Cairo chapter of the Sudan Victims of Torture Group (SVTG), later renamed the Sudanese Organization against Torture (SOAT), and also engaged in projects on violence against women. I also became involved in the Egyptian human rights movement and the regional women's "movement" through my work at the Cairo Institute for Human Rights Studies.

It was probably the tormenting testimonies I came across through the SVTG, the stories of Southern Sudanese who came to Cairo from the war-affected areas, the conditions of the refugee community, and the challenges that women faced[13] which convinced me of the urgency and importance of transformational, collective action. In 1995 I founded the Feminist Group for Reconstructing Sudan with the help of several friends. At the time, the Sudan National Alliance/Alliance Forces was developing as a movement, drafting its programs, and reaching out to women's rights and peace activists. The founders of the SNA invited me to join the movement.[14] After reading the movement's limited literature available at the time, I put together a short document indicating my position on a number of issues that the documents did not address. Once the founders of the movement confirmed the points I raised reflected the ideas of the organization, I accepted the invitation and became a member.

The SNA held its First Preliminary Congress in Asmara, Eritrea, in August 1995. In addition to other basic documents, the conference adopted the *Sudan Women's Alliance* basic document, which I had drafted. The document outlined the key challenges to gender equality and women's human rights in Sudan at the time, and how SNA and SWA should address these challenges. My membership in the SNA was not officially disclosed until 1997, however. In that context, Azza's question regarding my political activism was valid.

One reason I became active in organized opposition was that at a personal level, the resolutions of the Asmara conference transformed my relationship with the "official" exiled opposition at large. The resolutions revealed a commitment (at least on paper) to the principles of the New Sudan, including a commitment to secularism (defined as the separation between the state and religion) and the recognition of the right to self-determination in the South—which several South Sudanese students were advocating at the time. Most importantly, the Asmara program emphasized the transformation of economic and political power relations in a way that would ensure justice and possibly the unity of Sudan. The whole process, however, was gendered as male. With the exception of Salwa Gibreel, wife of Southern Sudanese political veteran Bona Malwal, participation in the conference was exclusively male. As discussed throughout this book, the resolutions of the conference curtailed women's rights on religious basis.

Much of my activism during the second half of the 1990s and in the early 2000s focused on changing the clause devoted to women in the Asmara Resolutions, on integrating gender into the NDA's political programs, and on women's participation in the NDA. With other women activists, I was trying to redefine the political space before inhabiting it.

When I conceptualized the initial research for this book, the issue of women's human rights *within the NDA* was absent in public opposition discourse. The focus at the time was on women's lack of participation in the NDA. Moreover, most of those who later criticized the NDA's lack of commitment to women's human rights in the Asmara Resolutions thought of the NDA as a homogeneous unit and did not go beyond descriptive accounts of the NDA's position on women. I wanted to know why the diverse parties that comprised the NDA collectively decided not to commit to women's rights enshrined in international human rights conventions without reservation.

By the time I started the fieldwork in Cairo in early 1998, questions of commitment to women's human rights by the NDA and women's participation in the NDA had become prominent. That year saw intensive campaigning by several Sudanese women's groups in exile around this issue. During the fieldwork, I participated in public meetings and events, and reflected critically on these activities. I was involved in campaigns to ensure the NDA's unconditioned commitment to women's human rights. I attended some of the NDA leadership and executive office meetings in my capacity as a representative of the SNA in the NDA's executive office. However, I announced at an early stage that I was conducting research on the NDA's gendered politics. Interviewees who held views different to mine made sure to explain to me they disagreed with my views regarding the NDA's committing to CEDAW without reservations. Of course, that was a key concern for me, but was not the only concern. For, at the time, I also wanted to understand where gender figured in relation to the major political questions concerning the exiled opposition.

As a Northern Sudanese woman who has had access to education, difference and intersectionality, two concepts I discuss later in this introduction and in the next chapter, have shaped my research experiences and interaction with some of the interviewees. On one hand, many of the New Sudan leaders interviewed for this research appreciated my interest in their views. They considered me an ally and suggested that in the future I conduct research in the historically marginalized areas of East, West, and Southern Sudan. The chair of the SPLM office in Cairo introduced me in February 1998 to the predominantly Southern Sudanese women associated with the Cairo SPLM/ A office. On the other hand, I encountered difficulties in reaching out to some of the women I interviewed in Nairobi—the majority of whom came from Southern Sudan—given that I came from Northern Sudan. This experience was central to the questions I wanted to explore.

During the research, I was trying to learn whether women from various regions in Sudan could build strategic coalitions and work collectively despite our difficult and diverse histories of war and oppression, or whether it was "too late" for us to come together as Sudanese women.[15] This continues to be one of my key concerns, including in relation to ongoing conflicts in Darfur, Southern Kordofan, and the Blue Nile, and in relation to continued marginalization in these areas and in Eastern Sudan. It was the focus of a number of public lectures I gave in 2010, in the run-up to the South Sudan Referendum, which culminated in the secession of South Sudan in 2011, and other activities in and outside Sudan, South Sudan, and the United States. I discuss this further in the epilogue.

Before concluding this "soul-searching" (Harding 1987, 9), it is important to note that a key reason for this research is my desire to engage some of the current debates in political science, African studies, feminist studies, and Sudanese studies.

The Conceptual Argument

Writing about gender, politics, and social theory, Walby (1997) identified four approaches to the study of gender and politics. The first approach, argues Walby, renders gender irrelevant and/or briefly mentions women. The second approach exposes the analytical flaws that result from ignoring gender. The third approach focuses on the study of women's politics and activism to address neglect. The final approach, continues Walby, is *the complete theoretical integration of gender analysis into the "central questions of the discipline"* (1997, 137; emphasis mine).

Walby examines the first three approaches and argues that even the important third approach has its limitations in that at times the focus on "the politics that women do" conflates gender politics with women's activism. Gender politics, argues Walby, "should be defined not in terms of the gender of the actors (the politics that women do)," but according to "the nature of the transformations in gender relations that these political practices seek to achieve" (Walby 1997, 139). Using the latter approach allows feminist scholars to analyze patriarchal political practices as well as resistance to feminist political practices, as these, too, are considered gender politics (Walby 1997, 139).

Other researchers have argued that the tendency to focus exclusively on women's groups when approaching gender issues usually conceals the specificity of women's struggle within other subject positions that intersect with gender and that shape women's experiences of oppression. Such research focus runs the danger of subordinating other contradictions in sociopolitical power relations to gender (Vargas 1995) and of overlooking dominant problematic assumptions in literature in fields like development studies (Molyneux 1986, 220).

The arguments above should not undermine the important feminist scholarship that sought, since the 1970s, to redefine theories of knowledge that excluded women as knowers and knowledge-producers as a means to re-design the core questions of their disciplines and to restore the voices of diverse women into academia.

In chapter 2, I discuss intersectionality, a theory that Leslie McCall has described as the most significant "theoretical contribution that women's stud-ies" and a number of other related fields have made so far (McCall 2005, 1771). Intersectionality is a theory, methodology, and a political and policy tool that looks at how gender intersects with race, ethnicity, sexuality, physi-cal ability, and other aspects of identity and power relations, and how this shapes women's experiences, including experiences of oppression and resis-tance. Critical law theorist Kimberlé Crenshaw, who coined the term inter-sectionality based on research about discrimination against black women in the United States, wrote that her aim, in developing this concept, was

> To illustrate that many of the experiences Black women face are not subsumed within the traditional boundaries of race or gender discrimination as these boundaries are currently understood, and that the intersection of racism and sexism factors into Black women's lives in ways that cannot be captured wholly by looking at the race or gender dimensions of these experiences separ-ately. (1991, 1244)

Crenshaw mainly argued that at times black women in the United States experience discrimination as *black women* which is not the sum of racism and sexism (and in the case of Sudan, I would add marginalization), but as "Black women whose identity and social location are not simply derivative of White women's or Black men's lives" (Grzanka 2014, xv).

The debates on intersectionality are unfolding in exciting ways that are yet to inform Sudan studies, despite the theory's relevance to Sudan. In 2013, feminist and women's studies journal *Signs* devoted an issue to the theory. The Social Theory Forum in the USA has devoted its eleventh meeting in 2015 to a discussion of "New Perspectives in Intersectionality: Race, Gender, Class, and Sexuality." The theme for the journal *New Political Science*'s issue 4 (2015) is "Intersectionality for the Global Age." And the Pan-African electronic weekly *Pambazuka News* has devoted a special issue in 2015 to oppressions and intersectionality in Africa. In this book I engage this theory and ask whether possibilities for coalition building in light of difference and oppression in Sudan exist.

With this in mind, this book aims to offer a gender-specific analysis of some of the major questions in contemporary politics in Sudan. It examines both the way political movements organized under the umbrella of the NDA constructed fundamental issues from a gender perspective, and the way women organized and contested these constructions.

Although the issue of women and the NDA has been the subject of exten-sive public debates among the Sudanese in exile since 1995, with a few exceptions, this era of Sudanese politics is under-analyzed. Only in recent years have some authors published in Arabic on this era. Abdelaziz (2013) documents the exclusion of women from NDA's structures, and the role of the Sudanese Women's National Democratic Alliance in Eritrea and Eastern Sudan in advocating for better inclusion for women.

AN ETHNOGRAPHY OF SUDAN'S EXILE POLITICS

As mentioned above, this book is based on multi-site ethnographic research that took place in Egypt and Kenya in 1997–1998 and in 1999 respectively. It is also based on participant observation and a number of interviews in the United Kingdom and Eritrea between 1998 and 2003 and on research and participant observation in the United States, Sudan, and South Sudan between 2010 and 2014. In that sense, it analyzes history that is "just over our shoulder" (Romano and Potter 2012, 1) as well as current, evolving events and political and cultural discourses, which the same recent history (opposition politics in the 1990s and early 2000s) can complicate (Romano and Potter 2012, 4) and inform.

Ethnography is a form of (contextual) qualitative research, which encompasses several methods including interviewing, observation, and archival searches. Historically, ethnographic research originated in the colonial offices of the British Empire. The objective was to record and understand the cultures of subjugated nations. Hence scholars have criticized this methodology on political and sometimes moral grounds (Fielding 1993, 154; Hammersley 1995). Contemporary critical anthropologists, feminist philosophers, and other social scientists have also challenged the notion of the ethnographer "as any person, without gender, personality or historical location, who would objectively [. . .] produce the same findings" (Warren 1988, 51).

To avoid the pitfalls of conventional ethnographic research, I rely on the ideas of radical, feminist, and critical ethnographers regarding the nature of knowledge and the relationship between the researcher and his or her research subjects. My gender and discourse analysis seeks to not only document, but to challenge certain established views of politics, society, culture, masculinities, and femininities.

The research methods I used included documentary analysis, participant observation, key informant interviews, focus group discussions, and semi-structured, formal interviews with members of various opposition movements, women's organizations associated with the NDA, women at the grassroots level, and activists.

The documents I analyzed included leaflets, programs, position papers, press releases, newspaper articles, and reports, which the NDA, political parties organized under the NDA, and women's groups in exile produced, as well as mainstream Islamist media. I conducted twenty key informant interviews in Cairo, Nairobi, London, and Asmara. I also conducted over 100 in-depth, semi-structured interviews in Egypt (Cairo), Kenya (Nairobi), the United Kingdom (London), Sudan (Khartoum, Damazin, Port Sudan, and Kassala), and South Sudan (Juba and Wau). The majority of the interviews were in Arabic. I transcribed and translated relevant parts of these interviews. I quote the interviews I conducted in English verbatim, with minimal editing at times.

My focus on the opposition in exile was initially because of my limited access to Sudan at the time of initial research. It soon became clear that the opposition in exile deserved separate research. While the movements that constituted the NDA had overt or clandestine presence inside Sudan, six years after the NIF/NCP coup the exiled opposition had established key institutions in exile, especially in Eritrea, Kenya, and Egypt.

Until 2000, the headquarters of the NDA was in the former building of the Sudanese embassy in Eritrea. The opposition also had two radio stations in Eritrea. Armed opposition was based on the Sudanese/Eritrean borders and the Sudanese/Ethiopian borders at the time of initial research. Kenya hosted several SPLM/A offices. Egypt was a hub for both opposition parties[16] and Sudanese civil society organization, especially after the relationships between the governments of Egypt and Sudan worsened. The former accused the GOS of plotting to assassinate former Egyptian president Hosni Mubarak in 1995.

All opposition parties organized under the umbrella of the NDA had offices in Cairo. The premises of two opposition newspapers *Al-Khartoum* and *Al-Ittihad Al-Dawlia* were in Cairo. Both ran regular editorials, articles, and interviews with opposition leaders and reported on opposition activities.

Briefings, seminars, and meetings of the various NDA committees took place in the DUP Centre, the Umma Party Centre, and at the premises of the Union of Arab Lawyers, for which NDA Leadership Council member at the time of initial research and current head of the National Consensus Forces Farouq Abu Eisa was secretary general. The NDA leadership held regular meetings in Egypt, Eritrea, and elsewhere. NDA executive office members reported on the implementation of the resolutions of these meetings. In short, the NDA had the informal status of a government in exile.[17]

Other public activities took place on the premises of the Sudanese Studies Centre, Sudan Human Rights Organization (SHRO), and the Sudan Centre for Information and Culture. Cairo was also (and continues to be) host to a big number of Sudanese NGOs and communities (cf. Fabos 2010 and Edward 2007).[18] For a thorough analysis of construction of identity and difference by Northern Sudanese communities in Egypt in relation to Egyptians and to Egyptian government policy, which is beyond this book, see Fabos (2010).

Egypt, Kenya, Eritrea, and other countries in and outside the region hosted branches of Sudanese women's organizations that were particularly active in the mid-1990s and early 2000s, including in the run-up to and following the United Nations International Conference for Population and Development which took place in Cairo, Egypt, in 1994, and the United Nations Fourth World Conference on Women which took place in Beijing, China, in 1995.

In this book I focus on women's organizations whose programs reflected an awareness of gender inequality and that sought to transform unequal gender relations and ensure that women's human rights are safeguarded. I also examine organizations that engaged the NDA or some of its member parties, especially the SPLM/A, in various ways over women's participation, human rights, and gender equality. Collectively, these organizations resisted the policies and practices of mainstream NDA and New Sudan movements.

In Egypt, I focused on the activities of the Sudan Women Alliance (SWA), *Ma'an*, the Sudan Women's Union (SWU), and the former Sudan Women's Forum in Cairo (SWF). I also analyze the discourses of selected women's rights activists, and of the women's secretariats in NDA member parties. These organizations were predominantly Northern Sudanese.

In Kenya, I focused on women's organizations and movements dedicated to achieving gender equality, equal participation for women in the structures of the SPLM/A, and in the peace negotiations between the SPLM/A and the GOS which concluded in 2005 when the two parties signed the CPA (N. Ali 2005). These organizations included the Sudan Women's Association in Nairobi (SWAN), the New Sudan Women Federation (NSWF), Sudanese Women's Voice for Peace (SWVP), Widows, Orphans, and Disabled Rehabilitation Association for the New Sudan (WODRANS), and New Sudan Women's Association (NESWA). As these groups did not refer to their movements as feminist, I refer to them as "women's groups." I do not focus on organizations concerned with women's immediate needs.[19] I also do not discuss the Sudanese Women's Democratic Alliance in Eritrea and in the then non-government held areas in Eastern Sudan, the subject of Ihsan Abdelaziz's (2013) book *Nisaa fi Marma Al Bundoqya*.

A recurrent question that colleagues asked when I discussed my research questions with them was to what extent one could generate "accurate information from politicians some of whom might be used to manipulating information." Historians of politics in recent eras echo similar concerns. For example, Wilentz (2009) has questioned the reliability of interviews as a source for political historians who might "run the risk of being manipulated by informants" (cited in Romano and Potter 2012, 6). While Wilentz decided to forgo interviews in his (2009) book *The Age of Reagan*, my response to the above question often stressed that my interest was in the way the opposition's discourses and practices related to women's rights and gender equality.

I understand the interview process as "a discourse between speakers" (Mishler 1986, 33–34), constructed both by the researcher and the research subject(s), regardless of whether the latter were politicians.

Moreover, in this book I go beyond an examination of the diverse policy positions of political parties on gender and women's human rights. I analyze the statements of exiled opposition parties and movements and of members and leaders of opposition parties and women's organizations, using critical discourse analysis that draws broadly on Foucault's notion of discourse and discursive formations.

According to Foucault, "To analyse a discursive formation . . . is to deal with a group of verbal performances at the level of the statements and of the forms of positivity that characterize them" (1972, 125). Smith (1987, 214) modifies this argument by contending that discourses are not a matter of statements alone, but of actual ongoing practices and sites of practices. As such, I examine the relationship between verbal and written texts on one hand, and practices, social structure, and gender relations as mediated by class, race, and power, on the other.

Feminist theorists have mounted other critiques at Foucault's discourse theory. Some argued Foucault's theorizing did not translate easily into feminism (Morris 1979; Mills 1997). Others questioned the implications of his work and of the work of other post-structuralist thinkers who argue against "grand narratives" and "emancipatory projects" for feminist organizing to transform gender relations. Nonetheless, I believe Foucault's discourse theory, and Smith's modification, enable me to analyze the way opposition discourse constructed femininity, masculinity, and fundamental issues, as texts that reflected power relationships (Smith 1990, 163).

Foucault's discourse theory is also important in that it asserts the diffuse, heterogeneous, and productive nature of power. Oppression generates resistance, according to Foucault: "There are no relations of power without resistances. The latter are all the more real and effective because they're formed right at the point where relations of power are exercised" (Foucault 1980, 142). This helps illuminate not only the way Sudanese exiled opposition discourse constructed women and gender issues, but also the way women and women's groups reacted to these constructions.

Sudan's and South Sudan's exile politics offer important insights for our understanding of the relationship between women's organizations seeking gender equality and women's human rights on one hand, and nationalist and other political discourses and projects on the other—especially in relation to the current core problems facing both countries. This book shows how different and at times contradictory political discourses have used culture and religion to promote political and economic interests, to the disadvantage of women. These political groups prioritized unity of the Sudanese opposition at the expense of commitments to women's human rights and gender equality.

The politics and resistance discourses of Sudanese and South Sudanese women's organizations in exile, particularly in Egypt and Kenya in the 1990s and early 2000s, offer us the opportunity to interrogate the way intersections of gender, race, and other aspects of identity shape women's (and men's) experiences of oppression and resistance.

This introductory chapter discussed the key conceptual, political, policy, and personal factors that informed the writing of this book. The rest of this book is divided into five chapters and a conclusion. In chapter 2 I review relevant literature. I also discuss key concepts and relevant scholarly debates. I use insights from the literature on difference and intersectionality to analyze the "difference within" Sudanese and South Sudanese women's organizations active in exile in the 1990s and up to the present. I draw lessons on the politics of coalition building in Sudan, South Sudan, and elsewhere.

It is difficult to analyze the discourses and practices of the opposition in exile from a gender perspective without understanding the historical, socioeconomic, and political context within which these discourses and practices evolved. Chapter 3 explains how the mutually constitutive hierarchies of class, gender, race, culture, and region operate in contemporary Sudan. The chapter also highlights the development of women's organizing in Sudan and South Sudan. I discuss the impact of the politics of the 1980s on the nature of opposition politics in the 1990s and early 2000s. The chapter also discusses Islamism in contemporary Sudan, and the gender discourses and practices of the NIF/NCP.

Chapter 4 presents a critical discourse analysis of the individual and collective positions of the movements in the NDA on women's human rights and gender equality reflected in its texts and in the narratives of its leaders. Chapter 5 examines the discourses and practices of movements within the NDA that identified as New Sudan movements from a gender perspective. I highlight the key features of this discourse, and explore how it engaged gender, regional, cultural, racial, and socioeconomic differences as power relations. The chapter further explores prospects for coalition building with women's organizations and movements.

Chapter 6 asks whether women's organizations active in exile in the 1990s accepted, resisted, or had been co-opted into opposition discourses on gender. I use intersectional analysis to analyze the priorities, practices, and homogenizing tendencies of some of the women's organizations that were active in exile at the time of research. The conclusion sums up the discussion and highlights the key findings and arguments. I develop these arguments further in the epilogue.

I hope this book will enrich the fields of women's and gender studies, development studies, political science, history, African and Middle Eastern

Studies, and migration studies. I also hope that the book will inform policy debates on conflict, transformation, and post-conflict reconstruction in Sudan and South Sudan from a gender perspective.

NOTES

1. Founded in 1989, the National Democratic Alliance (NDA) was an umbrella of seventeen political parties, in addition to fifty-one trade unions, and independent "national characters." Opposition forces signed the initial Charter of the NDA in October 1989. The opposition amended the Charter in March 1990 (Hassan 1993), paving the way for the Sudan People's Liberation Movement/Army (SPLM/A) to join it. At the time of initial research, the alliance constituted a government in exile and operated from Egypt, Eritrea, and the United Kingdom. The NDA dissolved after the signing of the Comprehensive Peace Agreement between the Government of Sudan (GOS) and the SPLM/A in 2005. During the same year, member parties of the NDA, except movements representing the people of Eastern Sudan, signed an agreement in Cairo with the GOS, and its member parties became part of a government of National Unity that the ruling National Congress Party and the SPLM dominated. In October 2006, the two movements representing Eastern Sudan, the Beja Congress, and the Free Lions signed an agreement with the government in Asmara, Eritrea, and became part of the government. The government also signed a number of separate agreements with Darfuri movements that emerged since 2003, and that were not part of the NDA. This book focuses on movements organized under the NDA. For literature on the conflict in Darfur and Darfuri movements, see Johnson (2003), Hassan and Ray (2009), Flint and de Waal (2008), and El-Tom (2011, 2013). For literature about the Sudan Revolutionary Front (SRF), which the Sudan People's Liberation Movement-North formed, along with a number of Darfuri movements following the independence of South Sudan and the re-eruption of war in Southern Kordofan and Blue Nile states, see McCutchen (2014) and Gramizzi and Tubiana (2013). Most of these studies do not use gender analysis, however.

2. In addition to the Sudan People's Liberation Movement (SPLM), several small movements within the NDA identified as "New Sudan forces" in the 1990s and early 2000s. These included the Sudan National Alliance/Sudan Alliance Forces (SNA/SAF), the Sudan Federal Democratic Alliance (SFDA), the Beja Congress, and the Sudan National Party (SNP).

3. Founded in November 2011, the SRF is an umbrella organization that unites the SPLM–N, three Darfuri movements, factions of the Beja Congress, and members of the Umma Party and Democratic Unionist Party serving in their personal capacity. Movements comprising the SRF fought several battles in Darfur and South Kordofan. In 2013, the SRF launched an attack in Abu Karshola and Um Ruwaba (McCutchen 2014, 5). These movements signed a "New Dawn Charter" in Kampala in early 2013 with representatives of the National Consensus Forces. In November 2014, the SRF, the National Consensus Forces, and the Umma Party signed the *Sudan Call Declaration*. The declaration emphasized the need to establish a state that respects citizenship and democracy in Sudan. Some of the civil society organizations and activists, including women's organizations, later endorsed the declaration. While the Sudan Revolutionary Front is of political and scholarly interest to me, a comprehensive analysis of the SRF is beyond the boundaries of this book.

4. Militarization is a process through which a worldview that promotes militaristic values of discipline, hierarchy, and obedience predominates across arenas of social life. Military solutions to problems become the commonsensical, inevitable, and effective response in a context of impending threat, insecurity, and danger (Mendez and Naples 2014, 13; Enloe 2007). This often reinforces gender, race, and other hierarchies. Movements in conflict-affected settings often utilize traditional constructions of gender to justify its military action. Women who are empowered and involved in the military unsettle dominant gender norms, but also end up reinforcing "gendered and sexualized notions of womanhood" (Enloe 2007; Mendez and Naples 2014, 13).

5. These include Security Council resolutions 1820 (2008), 1888 (2009), 1889 (2009), 1960 (2010), 2106 (2013), and 2122 (2013). For the text of these resolutions see UN Women (n.d.), http://www.un.org/en/peacekeeping/issues/women/wps.shtml.

6. Sudan is planning a national action plan for implementing UNSR 1325. Interview with the Disarmament, Demobilization, and Reintegration (DDR) Gender Officer at UNDP, Khartoum, Sudan, June 2014. Meeting with the Director of Planning at Sudan's DDR Commission, June 2014.

7. Interview with officials at South Sudan's Ministry of Gender in July 2010 and October 2013. Also see N. Ali (2011).

8. Paradoxically, I called the Sudanese embassy in Egypt, who then arranged to receive Marwa's body and contacted Marwa's family.

9. Despite curtailed public spending because of austerity measures that the Numeiry government introduced in the early 1980s toward the end of the Numeiry era, university education was based on a system where students paid nominal annual fees, depending on their parents' financial ability. The university provided free lodging and food. Students from remote regions of Sudan received a travel allowance at the end of each school year. This created a lot of space for student activism.

10. I served as the secretary for social affairs in 1988. The association organized intellectual and cultural events and exhibits, and addressed women's issues, the Eritrean struggle, and South African politics.

11. The association addressed the practical needs of students with disabilities. These included facilitating access to buildings and to the main library, fundraising to cover medical rehabilitation expenses, and sensitizing the university students on disability.

12. The association organized summer courses for high school students and cultural activities.

13. I narrated Marwa's story earlier in this chapter. In 1994, the Egyptian police flooded Southern Sudanese women protesting in front of the UNHCR office in Cairo with water; in December 2005, the Egyptian Riot Police violently evicted Sudanese (mostly Darfuris) who had camped in Mustafa Mahmoud Square in Cairo's affluent area of Mohandesseen where the UNHCR had an office. Over twenty Sudanese were killed in the process. In 2014, Sudanese artist Mohamed Bahnas died of cold and hunger on the streets of Cairo. Some of the interviewees reflect on living in Cairo later in this book.

14. To the best of my knowledge, there were no women in the movement at the time. The director of one of the Sudanese centers in Egypt told me that members of SNA/SAF wanted my contact details. Friends (who were members in other political parties and who were related to one of the founders of the movement) also said I should get in touch with the founder of SNA/SAF. When I first spoke on the phone with the founder of SNA, he mentioned the name of a leading Sudanese human rights activist with whom I discussed the group I was forming (FGR Sudan), so I thought the meeting was to discuss FGR Sudan. I joined the movement at the same time as another woman who was also based in Cairo. She resigned a few months later, however.

15. I spent much time during the summer of 1998 discussing this issue with a Southern Sudanese friend and member of the SWA, who was being criticized by Southern Sudanese women members in the SPLM/A for joining a predominantly northern organization. Later we decided to widen the discussion and invite a number of friends (from the North and the South) to a bi-weekly meeting where we discussed "issues that divide us" (Deng 1989). The issues we raised and debated could have enriched the discussion on difference in this book. I did not include those discussions in this book, however, because some of the Southern Sudanese women asked my friend whether that initiative was guided by an interest to understand the issues that divide us or whether it was part of my research. I believe that my desire to understand "the issues that divide" us drove the meetings and influenced this research.

16. These included a number of smaller political parties that were not members in the NDA, which I do not cover in this book.

17. Over the years, opposition activities became transnational as parties and movements forced into exile moved between countries in the regions of East and North Africa and the Great Lakes—depending on geopolitical alliances of the GOS or the opposition with countries

in the region. Chad constituted a haven for Darfuri movement for several years after the eruption of war in Darfur in 2003. Since 2011, Uganda has become the key location for the SRF. Mainstream political parties are currently organized in the Sudan-based alliance of "the Forces of National Consensus." A number of youth and women's organizations such as *Girifna* (we are fed up), *al-Tagyeer al-An* (change now), and *La Liqahr al-Nisa'* (no to women's oppression) are also openly opposing the government. A detailed consideration of these parties and movements is also beyond the contours of this book.

18. In 1998–1999, large numbers of the Sudanese in Egypt moved to Europe, Australia, and North America via United Nations Higher Commission for Refugees (UNHCR) resettlement programs.

19. Alvarez's (1990) study of Brazil suggests that organizations that support women's practical interests can be politicized. I consider these groups' work as important and have discussed some of its aspects in my research on women's strategies for survival during crisis in an urban poor setting in Sudan (N. Ali 1993, 1998).

Chapter Two

Gender and Intersectionality in Sudan and South Sudan

When I joined Operation Lifeline Sudan (OLS) in late 1995 nobody knew what gender was about: gender could have been an animal. Gender could have been a spare part of a vehicle or something. But everybody now knows what gender is or at least understands that gender has something to do with either women or men or to do with women and men together. For me it just made a difference because I was a lone voice in late 1995 and most of 1996. Today you find a lot of indigenous women's groups, but also you see the difference in the [non-government held areas in Southern Sudan] where even men at the village level, for example the chief, say, upon seeing us: ohhh [*sic*], you are the gender people. Fine it may be in a negative tone, but it is a start. They now acknowledge that this social relationship exists.
(Nadi Albino, Southern Sudanese activist and Gender and Development Project Officer, OLS, UNICEF, Southern Sudan at the time of interview. KII, Nairobi: March 17, 1999; emphasis mine.)

GENDER, INTERSECTIONALITY, AND SUDAN STUDIES

As in other countries in the Middle East and Africa, gender, intersectionality, and other "buzzwords and fuzz words" (Cornwall and Eade 2010) in development and feminist discourse remain sites of political contest, including in Sudan, South Sudan, and among Sudanese and South Sudanese Diaspora and exiled communities and movements. Consider these instances.

In 2011 several universities, non-governmental organizations (NGOs), and United Nations (UN) agencies in Sudan sought to inform a constitution-making process which the Government of Sudan (GOS) launched in 2011. These actors published three booklets to inform the constitution-building process. The booklets were entitled: *Sudanese Women's Issues in the Interim*

23

Constitution; *A Proposed Constitution that Takes Gender into Account*; and *The Status of Women in the Next Constitution: Gender and Good Governance*.

Following the launch of the booklets at the University of Khartoum's Institute of Development Studies, *Al-Intibaha*, an Islamist daily newspaper—better known for its enthusiasm for the secession of South Sudan and for its racist discourse and fierce criticism of armed opposition movements representing marginalized areas of Sudan—ran a series of six articles entitled "What is Gender? Is it heresy, decadence or promiscuity? The University of Khartoum as an example!" The author, Saad Ahmed Saad, hurled insults at the participants in this project, UN agencies, the University of Khartoum, and Ahfad University for Women. Reportedly trained in the Netherlands, Saad argued that focusing attention on gender, which for him meant "the third sex" [lesbian, gay, bisexual, transsexual, intersex, and queer communities (LGBTIQs)], was a Western conspiracy against Islam and against Sudan as a nation. As a respectful academic institution, argued the author, the University of Khartoum should have refrained from supporting such a scheme, which he deemed more relevant to Ahfad University for Women. In such a context, charges of "jargonitis" are the least of worries for scholars, practitioners, and activists seeking gender equality.

Similarly, an article about the conflict that escalated in South Sudan in December 2013 stated that Salva Kiir dismissed Rebecca Nyandeng De Mabior, who was "his advisor on gender and human rights" (Silverstein 2015). The author continued, "That's not a joke. Obviously, some Western consultant got paid ~$100 million for coming up with titles for government officials in the newly created nation" (Silverstein 2015). These comments show that even within Western circles (which are not homogeneous), a concern with gender and human rights in "a hellhole" (Silverstein 2015) like independent South Sudan can be at best a joke and at worst a product of Western profiteering.

Over a decade earlier, a Northern Sudanese self-identified feminist based in North America at the time commented on something I posted on the Internet by writing "Her training seems to be in women studies as evidenced by the overly frequent presence of the word 'gender' and other 'academic' jargon in her writings." The discussion was on secularism—an equally perplexing term in the context of Sudanese politics, but its "relevance" was never questioned in that discussion (posted on sudanese@list.msu.edu, January 3, 2000).

What these narratives and Albino's narrative above tell us is that it is difficult to think about gender in terms of a binary opposition that divides Sudanese and South Sudanese women, and women in other countries in the Global South (see, for example, Narayan 1997) into a feminist, middle-class, urban-based movement working to establish legitimacy for concerns with gender equality within politics and society on one hand, and rural, "grass-roots," "anti-feminist" women and organizations in war-affected areas that question a concern with gender on other. Nadi Albino's narrative—reflecting on the gradual opening up to gender awareness—is grounded in her work experience in war-affected villages in Southern Sudan, where illiteracy is high, and where there was virtually no access to computers or the Internet at the time of research. On the other hand, other narratives were uttered in Khartoum and in "the West." The narrative that discounted "gender" as academic (read irrelevant) was uttered on the cyberspace. This is not to argue that women's organizations and activists in conflict-affected and post-conflict settings all believe that a concern with gender should be a priority (see N. Ali 2011).

This is also not to argue for an uncritical or depoliticized use of the terms "gender" or "gender activism." Ugandan scholar and activist Sylvia Tamale has criticized women's rights practitioners who call themselves "gender activists" to avoid using "the F word: Feminism" (2006, 39).

There is no consensus on the translation of gender into Arabic, my first language, and the language or lingua franca of most of the interviewees for this research. Feminist researchers and writers in Middle Eastern and African countries where Arabic is the official language have coined the phrases *alnu'* and *alnu' alijtimaii* which literally translate into the "kind" or "social kind" respectively. Others found the translation inaccurate and preferred to use the term *gender* until a better translation is found.[1]

I define gender as the sociocultural and political of sexual difference. It is the roles, responsibilities, and traits that societies allocate to men and women. Gender is also a tool of analysis and a power relationship. It is part of an intersecting web of power relations that are based on the mutually constituting categories of class, race (which I believe is a sociocultural construct and a resistance discourse),[2] and sexuality, among others. Like Anthias and Yuval-Davis (1993, 9), I believe that in the context of Sudan's and South Sudan's contemporary politics and society, we should not consider racism and sexism as relations between the sexes or races respectively. These are rooted in social, economic, and political structures, institutions, and power relations, in the dominant culture, and in dominant ideologies.

The Beijing conference was a platform where diverse women's groups and other stakeholders discussed gender and the importance of integrating gender into political and development visions and projects. Two years after the Beijing conference, the Economic and Social Council defined "gender mainstreaming" as

> [t]he process of assessing the implications for women and men of any planned action, including legislation, policies or programs, in any area and at all levels. It is a strategy for making the concerns and experiences of women as well as of

men an integral part of the design, implementation, monitoring and evaluation
of policies and programs in all political, economic and societal spheres, so that
women and men benefit equally, and inequality is not perpetuated. *The ulti-
mate goal of mainstreaming is to achieve gender equality.* (ECOSOC, 1997)

Molyneux has argued that the articulation of gender interests is linked to
processes of identity formation and to the historical, socioeconomic, and
political context (Molyneux 1998, 233). This is particularly important in the
case of Sudan, where what constitutes "women's interests" and women's
priorities is also connected to processes of exclusion and belonging along
race, regional location, culture, and politics. As such, achieving gender
equality in countries like Sudan involves the transformation of sexist, racist,
classist, ableist, and homophobic neopatriarchal structures and institutions,
and a commitment to women's rights enshrined in international human rights
conventions, such as CEDAW (which Sudan has not signed, and which
South Sudan ratified on September 3, 2014) and the *Protocol to the African
Charter on Human and Peoples' Rights on the Rights of Women in Africa*
(the African Women's Rights Protocol), which Sudan signed in 2008. As of
March 2015, Sudan has not ratified the African Women's Rights Protocol.
These two conventions constitute a useful basis for articulating claims for
gender equality and women's human rights claims.

Another concept that is relevant to the discussion in this book is the
concept of globalization. Sudan's opposition politics of the 1990s and early
2000s and Sudan's current opposition politics evolved in "a historical moment characterized by global political, economic and cultural interconnec-
tions" (Mendez and Naples 2014, 2), and by "heightened mobility of increased numbers of populations" (ibid., 6). Nonetheless, "the free flow of
capital across national borders that is so central to neoliberal globalization
has been accompanied by the systematic and oppressive social control of
populations through the militarization of national, territorial borders and the
increasingly restrictive migration regime" (Mendez and Naples 2014, 6).
Sudan's position in this global milieu has affected the way political parties
and women's organizations articulated their priorities and conducted exile
politics. An elaborate discussion about gender and globalization is acutely
relevant to, but is beyond, this book, however.[3]

Where does gender fit in relation to Sudan studies? Despite a rise in
interest in women's and gender studies in Sudan, many of the key texts in
Sudan studies have traditionally paid little or no attention to women and
gender. With a few exceptions of books that include chapters on women and
gender (cf. Spaulding and Beswick 2000; Hassan and Ray 2009) and until
recently, most of the standard texts on government and politics in Sudan, for
example Abdul Rahim (1986), Woodward (1990, 1991), Niblock (1987), and
Harir and Tvedt (1997) seldom mentioned women's roles in politics and

society. This mainly reflects the androcentric nature of the fields of political science and history within which some of this scholarship emerged (Walby 1997; Enloe 1989; Lerner 1987). Niblock (1987) briefly analyzes Numeiry's (1969–1985) policies toward women, but gender is not integrated into the analysis.

Sudanese and Sudanist feminist scholars have criticized studies that ignore women's role in Sudan's history. Tomader Khalid (1995), for example, highlighted the lack of attention to gender in Yousif Fadl Hassan's history of modern Sudan. Women are more visible in texts that document Sudan's social history such as *Tabagat wad Def Alla* (Badri 1985). The content of the latter book deserves an analysis from a critical gender perspective, however.

Literature on South Sudanese women is even more limited (Beswick 2000, 93). Beswick argues that part of the limited existing literature on South Sudanese women was flawed. She cites the example of a study that argued that Nuer women were forced into assertive roles because men of the tribe were "lazy" (Beswick 2000, 93). Beswick reconstructs parts of this invisible history by offering a pioneering account of women's leadership in South Sudan between 1700 and 1994.

El Bakri and Kameir (1990) and Ibrahim and El Bakri (1991) argue that women's studies in the Sudan passed through two main phases. In the first phase (from Sudan's independence in 1956 to the first half of the 1970s), the focus was on development and technological advancement, without reference to women's roles in development and production (El Bakri and Kameir 1990, 161). The second phase witnessed a rising interest in women's and gender studies that coincided with the United Nations' international women's year (1975) and the International Women's Decade (1975–1985). Most of this research responded to requests by international agencies and was not necessarily concerned with advancing women's studies scholarship in Sudan (El Bakri and Kameir 1990, 162; see also Ibrahim and El Bakri 1991 and Hale 1996). It is interesting that during this period, according to Ibrahim and El Bakri (1991, 2), studies commissioned by international organizations mainly focused on Darfur and Kordofan in Western Sudan, where most of the projects of these organizations were.

Ibrahim and El Bakri (1991, 2) argued that in the late 1980s and early 1990s, women's studies in Sudan started to become more institutionalized. A number of departments at the University of Khartoum, the University of Gezira, and Ahfad University for Women started to offer courses in women's studies. Women's studies in Sudan have since progressed. In addition to the gender and development unit in the University of Khartoum's Centre for Development and Research Studies, Ahfad University for Women has established a regional Institute for Gender Studies. Preparations for the Beijing conference at the regional level also spurred interest in women's and gender studies and research. The late 1990s and the early 2000s have witnessed an increased interest in women's and gender studies, and the proliferation of graduate research as well as published material on women and gender in Sudan.

Early studies on "the position of women in Sudan" documented women's daily experiences and reflected on women's experiences but did not account for the structures and power relations that shaped women's positions and experiences in Sudan. Ismail (1982) documented the daily experiences of middle-class housewives in urban Sudan. In *Sisters Under the Sun*, Hall and Ismail (1981), described the social and political activities of women in different regions in Sudan, but lacked an analysis of power relationships that shaped these experiences.

Susan Kenyon's (2004) *Five Women of Sennar*[4] provides a sophisticated account of the social, economic, and cultural dynamics in the town of Sennar from the perspectives of five women who live in the town, using oral history. Kenyon's (2009) account of the life of Zainab, an allegedly former female slave who was also a healer in Sennar, shed light on the roles women played in establishing the colonial town of Sennar in the nineteenth century.

A number of studies discuss the impact of Islamism and of shari'a laws on Sudanese societies and on gender relations in Sudan (Nageeb 2004; Ali 2010; Fadlalla 2011; Fluehr-Lobban 2012). Several scholars have examined the impact of Sudan's conflict and displacement on women in South Sudan (Jok 1997a, 1997b, and 1998; Abdel Halim 1998). Abdel Halim maintains that in the war-affected zones, women's bodies constitute sites of contention between the government and the opposition. Jok examines violence against women in both the public and private spheres, and women's attempts to resist confining their roles to reproduction. Other studies document the role of women in peace building (Badri and Abdel Sadiq 1997; Verwijk 2012).

The signing of the Comprehensive Peace Agreement (CPA) between the Sudan People's Liberation Movement and the government of Sudan, and the subsequent independence of South Sudan, have, among other factors, contributed to a rising interest in research on women and gender in South Sudan. Some of this literature addressed the experiences of South Sudan's "lost girls" in Kakuma camp in Kenya and in countries of resettlement, including experiences of education and marriage (Grabska 2010; El-Jack 2010). Grabska's *Gender, Home and Identity* focuses particularly on the lives of seventeen Nuer families that were displaced to Sudan, Kenya, and elsewhere in East Africa during the war in South Sudan. Grabska analyzes the gender and age relations upon the return of these families to their areas in South Sudan.

When I started my research for this book, research on Sudanese exiled women's movements was limited. In addition to my own papers and publications over the last decade (cf. Ali 1999, 2000, 2003, and 2005), several other Sudan scholars have since written about women's social, economic, and political roles in displaced communities and in exile and diaspora (Hale 2001b; Abusharaf 2002).

Important research has focused on women, gender, and politics in Sudan (Hale 1996; El Bakry 1995; El Bakry and Kameir 1990; Ahmed 1997; Abdel Halim 2009) or on the "Women's Movement" (Badri 1985). Hale's *Gender Politics in Sudan* (1996, 2006) discusses gender and the state in contemporary Northern Sudan, with a focus on the Islamist movement and the Communist Party of the Sudan (CPS). She analyzes the ideologies of the two movements and investigates how they position women in culture to serve their political aims and to achieve cultural and political hegemony. The book investigates ways women use Islam to define their identity and improve their conditions, but also explores challenges arising from the control of state power by the NIF.

Another comparative study is Abdel Halim's (2009) account of the approaches of the Sudanese Women's Union and the Republican Sisters toward access to justice in Sudan. Abdel Halim argues that the Republican Sisters' experience proved that a religious group could advocate for a reinterpretation of Islamic norms. Recent studies have focused on political Islam in Sudan and women's responses to it (Tønnessen 2011; Tønnessen and Kjøstvedt Granås 2010).

Tomadur Khalid (1995) and Niblock (1987) investigate the relationship between the Numeiry's regime and the women's movement. Tomadur Khalid examined the relation between the Union of Sudanese Women (USW) and the Sudan Socialist Union (SSU), both created by Numeiry. The USW, argues Khalid, was a case of a ruling-party controlled women's organization in the context of rising Islamism.

In addition to Hale's (1996) influential study, very few studies have addressed the nature of gendered political processes that occurred in the 1980s, particularly after the 1985 uprising that overthrew the Numeiry regime.

Other research that examines the post-1989 era addresses the Islamist women's movement in the Sudan and the politics of Islamism (Tønnessen 2011). N. Ali (1995) looks at the way a secular women's organization has resisted the NIF's negative constructions of women and the way the regime subordinated women through its policies. Anis (2001 and 2002) analyzes the resistance waged by secular women's groups inside Sudan against the NIF's policies. She also addresses the NDA's stand on women and identifies the problems that might result from the organization's conservative stand.

One of the early accounts of organizing among Sudanese women is *The Women's Movement in Sudan* (Badri 1985). The book documented the development of the women's movement in Northern Sudan. It included short biographies of some of the Northern Sudanese women pioneers. Beswick (2000) criticizes Badri's book as a flawed representation of Southern Sudanese women (see above).

In *Transforming Displaced Women in Sudan: Politics and the Body in a Squatter Settlement*, Abusharaf uses urgent anthropology and feminist ethnography to document the experiences of displaced women who lived in the outskirts of Khartoum. Karin Willimse's (2007) *One Foot in Heaven* examines gender and Islam in Darfur.

A number of books analyze the experiences of Sudanese or South Sudanese women and communities in the diaspora, especially in the United States. In *Wanderings: Sudanese Migrants and Exiles in North America*, Abusharaf (2002) documents the experiences of diverse Sudanese communities in the United States and Canada. She uses conversations, interviews, and participant observation at social and religious events to explore reasons for migration and ways Sudanese cope with exile.

Similarly, Abdel Halim's (2006) *Sudanese Women in the United States: The Double Problem of Gender and Culture* examines the experiences of Sudanese women in the United States in relation to female genital cutting, and the way migration to the United States has changed their views on the practice.

Stephanie Beswick (2001) documented the experiences of Ethiopian, Somali, and Southern Sudanese women in Kakuma's refugee camp. Beswick examined how militarism intensified women's subordination, and how this contributed to an escalation of violence against women. Beswick's (2004) *Sudan's Blood Memory* is based on research among South Sudanese refugees in Kenya, Egypt, and elsewhere.

Edward's (2007) *Sudanese Women Refugees* documents the experiences of Southern Sudanese women in Cairo, Egypt. She highlights challenges that women face and ways they respond to the difficult conditions they encounter in Cairo. Edward uses the experiences of these women to portray a positive image of refugee women.

Similarly, Wanga-Odhiambo (2013) analyzes the experiences and challenges South Sudanese women refugees faced in Kenya and in New York. Wanga-Odhiambo documents the strategies women employed to address challenges, highlighting women's agency and resilience.

Many of the other publications on the Sudanese and South Sudanese in diaspora or exile are mainly biographies, autobiographies, and testimony. This body includes several volumes on the "Lost Boys" or girls of South Sudan (for example, Eggers 2006; Ajak et al. 2006; Makeer 2008).

Authors in Bubenzer and Stern's (2011) edited volume, *Hope, Pain and Patience: The Lives of Women in South Sudan*, discuss the experiences of women in South Sudan in relation to women's leadership (Arabi 2011), motherhood, experiences of female combatants (Stone 2011), HIV/AIDS, sexual violence (D'Awol 2011), diaspora, and exile. Most of the chapters in this book are based on the narratives of South Sudanese women. My own research examined gender and state building in post-independent South Sudan and the activism of women's organizations in the country (N. Ali 2011). Erickson and Faria (2011) discuss the experience of South Sudan Women's Empowerment Network, an organization that South Sudanese women's activists started in the mid-2000s and that played an important role in mobilizing women and communities in the run-up to South Sudan's referendum and beyond. The authors argued that the experience of SSWEN reflected the way diasporic South Sudanese women emerged as "new and increasingly important citizens and activists in the post-CPA-era" (2011, 628).

This book indicates that transnational activism of South Sudanese women preceded the CPA, but that after the signing of the CPA many of the women who were active within the South Sudan women's movement, including in Nairobi, joined the government, which deprived the South Sudanese women's movement of some of the key activists (N. Ali 2011). However, a new generation of activists, including women organized in SSWEN, carried on with the struggle for gender equality and women's rights.

To my knowledge, although in recent years some of the scholars of women's studies in the Sudan started paying attention to diversities and race relations in Sudan, there were no attempts to utilize the rich literature on difference and intersectionality to analyze gender and women's human rights in Sudan, despite the relevance of this body of literature to Sudan.

A few anthropological studies have focused on gendered processes within sections of the Sudanese in Egypt. These include Edward (see above) and Fabos (2010). Fabos's *Brothers or Others* discusses the way Sudanese Muslims who identify as Arabs in Egypt construct their identity vis-à-vis their Egyptian hosts. Fabos argues that Sudanese use the notion of *Adab* or propriety (which implies modesty, hospitality, generosity, reciprocity, dignity, and social equality) (Fabos 2010, 4–5) as a boundary marker of difference.

Literature on the gendered nature of dominant as well as subversive post-1989 opposition discourse (such as the New Sudan discourse) is scant despite the theoretical and political need for such an examination. Until recently, discourses of the New Sudan groups constituted subjugated knowledges, most of which have been "disqualified as inadequate" and excluded from systems of power in Sudan. This is a key reason for the long quotes in this book: it is a way of restoring some of these voices into academia. The Internet and communication technologies and social media revolutionized knowledge and information sharing and activism. Although not widely accessible in marginalized areas of Sudan, it opened up spaces, including for women from marginalized areas, to voice their concerns and share their experiences.

WOMEN IN GENDERED MOVEMENTS AND DISCOURSES

In *Neopatriarchy: A Theory of Distorted Change in Arab Society*, Sharabi (1988) identifies neopatriarchy as the sociopolitical structure that rises when systems of patriarchy and dependency are combined. In the twentieth century, the Arab world has converted the traditional patriarchal structures into modernized patriarchy. This framework of analysis applies to religious and secular forces that dominated the region during the second half of the twentieth century.

Sharabi highlights the development of a distinct and neopatriarchal intellectual social strata that includes traditional Muslim reformers, militant fundamentalists, and socialist and nationalist secularists. Sharabi argues that all these groups share similar (conscious and unconscious) attitudes and practices that often sustain social structures that discriminate against women. Sharabi argues that women's organizations and other social movements can play an important role in dismantling neopatriarchal structures and institutions.

Sharabi's theory of neopatriarchy offers a useful (albeit an incomplete) framework for analyzing the gendered discourses and practices prevalent in dependent, post-colonial Sudan. Sharabi pays attention both to internal and external structures, institutions, and discourses in analyzing various relations of domination, including those based on gender. His analysis allows for recognition of the role of culture and religion in women's subordination, but avoids Orientalist accounts that grant religion and culture explanatory powers, and that construct religion and culture as ahistorical, static categories. A critique that feminist scholars of the Middle East and North Africa have waged (Lazreg 1990, 1988; Badran 1991; Hale 1996; Kandiyoti 1991; Keddie and Beck 1978; Ahmed 1992). Keddie and Beck, for example, have argued that a focus on *Islamic societies* explains the subordination of women in Middle Eastern societies better than a focus on *traditional Islamic culture* (1978, 27). Joseph (1996, 7) and others have argued that understanding the place of women and gender in politics in the Middle East requires an analysis of states, social classes, and ideologies in the region. These and the place of the Middle East in today's globalized world (Moghadam 1993) shape women's lives in the region.

Although Sharabi's theory of neopatriarchy tackles deformed development in countries of the Global South, it focuses on Middle Eastern societies.[5] As such, it is important to emphasize the uniqueness of Sudan. Whether Sudan is part of the Middle East, the Arab world, or Africa has in itself been at the center of the contention in post-colonial Sudan. Dr. John Garang's New Sudan vision questioned binary oppositions in definitions of Sudan's national identity as either Arab or African. Nonetheless, as discussed later in this book, the social groups that dominated Sudan's post-colonial state were not only almost exclusively male, they also defined Sudan's identity as Arab. They tried to impose this identity on a heterogeneous country. In that sense, neopatriarchy provides a plausible (but an incomplete) framework to understand post-colonial politics in Sudan. Below is a discussion of other relevant scholarship on gendered political processes, particularly in African and Middle Eastern societies.

In the African context, a number of studies have criticized the way conventional social sciences stereotyped the experiences of women and the way Western feminism(s) depended on these stereotypes in their analysis of "the situation of African women" (Imam et al. 1997; Win 2007). Oyewùmí (1998, 2003) argues that unlike Western feminism's earlier focus on biology as a rationale for social organizing and power, age functions as a social organizer in Yoruba culture. Scholars have also revealed that in a number of pre-colonial African communities women enjoyed privileged political positions. Colonial expansion in Africa, argue these scholars, which was partly informed by a perception of women as helpmates to men, contributed to the disempowerment of women politically and economically (Tripp et al. 2009; Urdang 1979; O'Barr 1984). A recent important volume (Falola and Amponsah 2013) examines how colonial and post-colonial macro-narratives in Africa could shed light on women's empowerment (or the lack thereof) in Africa. The volume highlights the diversity of the experiences of women in Africa and the way gender and sexualities intersect with race, class, nation, and ethnicity.

Other studies maintain that the policies of the colonial state toward women in African societies were not uniform and affected women of various classes differently (Mbilinyi 1989, 126).

GENDER, NATION, AND CHALLENGES OF DIFFERENCE AND INTERSECTIONALITY

What does change mean for the diverse women of the Sudan? What does it mean for a Darfuri young woman who was raped while trying to fetch wood, whose family and fiancé abandoned her afterward, and who was charged with Zina and imprisoned when she became pregnant as a result of the rape? What does change mean for a woman who lived in one of the unplanned areas of Khartoum, who was forced to move to the outskirts of Khartoum because the government decided to sell the plots in her neighborhood? What does change mean to this woman, who stopped taking HIV treatment because there were no healthcare facilities where she moved? What does change mean to her daughter, who dropped out from school, so she could take care of her siblings and mother, whose health deteriorated? What does change mean to a woman in Juba, whose husband beat her, and whom a policeman asked, upon seeing bruises on her face: have you not cooked tonight? What does change mean to a woman in Hameshkoreib (in Eastern Sudan), who died while giving birth, because her husband refused that the only doctor in the area, who was male, help her? What does change mean for a woman who was arrested because of the way she dressed, charged with "indecent behavior," and flogged; and in whose neighborhood people started whispering: why was she really flogged? (N. Ali 2010. *What Does Change Mean for the Women of Sudan?* Speech by the author at the launch of SPLM's Presidential Campaign in April 2010, Washington, DC.)

How does gender-based domination relate to other forms of domination/ subordination in countries like Sudan, South Sudan, or elsewhere in the Middle East and Africa? How do these relations impact patterns of organizing among and between women's groups and between women's groups and other emancipatory projects? How do exiled communities and movements address issues of difference? How would their construction of difference (or sameness) impact gender-based power relations in these communities and movements? Does an engagement with difference leave any chance for solidarity and coalition building on gender-basis?

As the excerpt from my (2010) lecture above shows, these questions are acutely relevant to contemporary social and political processes in Sudan and South Sudan. The same questions are also relevant to some of the current, most sophisticated, and intellectually productive feminist debates on difference and the intersection of gender on one hand, and race, class, physical ability, age, and other aspects of identity on the other hand. Intersectionality helps us analyze and think critically about the way gender intersects with other aspects or layers of identity (such as race, class, regional position, ability), and how this shapes women's (and men's) unique experiences, including experiences of subordination and domination.

As discussed earlier in this book, in 2013, feminist and women's studies journal *Signs* devoted a special issue to the study of intersectionality in summer 2013. Appropriately titled "Theorizing Power, Empowering Theory," the issue included some of the key writings on difference and intersectionality. Editors of the special issue Kimberlé Crenshaw, Leslie McCall, and Sumi Cho launched intersectionality as a disciplinary field. Cho, Crenshaw, and McCall (2013, 797) rightly argue that "as deployed by many intersectional academics and activists, intersectionality helps reveal how power works in diffuse and differentiated ways through the creation and deployment of overlapping identity categories."

Although Kimberlé Crenshaw coined the word intersectionality in 1989, intersectional analysis has preceded the coinage of the term. Black and Third World feminist scholars have long challenged the tendency among some Western feminists to construct women as a homogeneous group. These scholars also challenged the tendency to define male/female difference and power relationships as the sole determinant of women's subordination. Spelman (1988, ix), for example, has argued that

The notion of the generic "woman" functions in feminist thought much the way the notion of generic "man" [or "person"] has functioned in Western philosophy. It obscures the heterogeneity of women and cuts off examinations of the significance of such heterogeneity from feminist theory and political activity. (Quoted in Yuval-Davis 1997, 25)

Black feminist scholars in the United States have also questioned one-dimensional visions of women's realities that excluded "non-white women and poor white women" (bell hooks 1984, 2). These feminists challenged dominant notions at the time, which considered predominantly white, middle-class movements as capable of addressing all forms of oppression that diverse women faced.

Similarly, post-colonial and Southern feminist and women's studies scholars have argued that many of the mainstream feminist movements in the Global North failed to recognize the specific historical and social experiences of women in the Global South (Mama 1996; Mohanty 1988; Lazreg 1988). This has deprived feminist scholarship from insights that are rooted in the complex, multi-layered struggles of women in many Southern societies against Western domination *and* indigenous power relations and harmful cultural traditions (Roberts 1983). This also alienated Southern and other feminists who found "totalizing and universal definitions of feminism or feminist concepts unresponsive to their sexual, racial, class, age, religious and national specificities" (Moghissi 1994, 5).

In her study of power in Yorùbá society, Okome (2005) argues that using tools "that are designated to study Western societies" (22) conceals the multiple forms of power in African societies. Okome states that to study African societies properly, it is important to recognize the difference within these societies. She argues gender "is not deployed in the same manner in African societies as it is in the West" (22).

Feminists concerned with the gendered nature of ethnicities and nationalisms (cf. Anthias and Yuval-Davis 1992) have also argued that women's subordination intersects with other social relations, such as race and class, and that understanding this intersection is important when discussing the social distribution of power and resources. These scholars argued that women's position in collectivities organized around the nation or ethnicity should be comprehended in terms of "structures of domination" and "as articulated by other social relations" (Yuval-Davis 1997b, 11).

Feminists also criticized the tendency to render gender as secondary to other categories and power relationships such as race, nation, and social class. Political discourses in the Global South have at times subordinated women's issues to those of social class and national liberation or used women as markers of national identity.

Research among refugee communities and communities in the diaspora has examined women's organizing in these communities, and the tendency of some community leaders to label these attempts as counter-productive (Rozario 1996; Gupta 1997; Narayan 1997; Y. Ali 1997; Anthias and Yuval-Davis 1992; Garcia 1989). Yasmin Ali's research among the South Asian Muslim communities living in Northern England, for example, showed that male leaders in these communities ossified the community's culture (Y. Ali 1997, 51). These communities often view women's independent organizing around their concerns of women as divisive. Community leaders in these communities have discouraged the activities of organizations such as Women Against Fundamentalism (WAF) and Southhall Black Sisters (SBS) (Rozario 1996; Yuval-Davis 1997a).

The phrase intersectionality helps scholars, activists, and policy makers avoid some of the shortcomings of using the concept of "difference" to approach questions of race, gender, and other power relationships. Some theorists have argued that focusing distinctly on difference could mask the conditions that give primacy to certain forms of difference (Manyard 1994). As Kandiyoti (1996, 18) has argued, difference is a slippery concept that might either "degenerate into unprincipled forms of relativism" or, alternatively, result in polished conceptions of political alliances and coalition building.

Third World feminists have argued that the preoccupation with sexual difference and with difference between the West and the Global South has sometimes led to the homogenizing of the experiences and problems of women in the Global South (Amadiume 1997; Alvarez 1990; Mohanty 1988; Lazreg 1988). According to Mohanty, "an analysis of 'sexual difference' in the form of cross-culturally singular, monolithic notion of patriarchy or male domination leads to the construction of a similarly reductive and homogeneous notion of . . . 'Third World difference.'" The Third World is constructed as a stable and "ahistorical something that apparently oppresses most if not all of the women in these countries" (1988, 257). Alvarez has argued that North American feminist research at times had generalized the experiences of some Latin American women, although these women did not necessarily represent the interests of Latin American women (Alvarez 1990, 266–67).

Difference can also easily be reduced to cultural difference. This often takes place when this preoccupation is limited to a demonstration of respect for difference without questioning the sociopolitical power relations involved (Manyard 1994). As such, it might degenerate into an uncritical celebration of multiculturalism, reducing feminist theory and politics into a depoliticized pluralism (Zin and Dill 1996). This has sometimes led feminists to tolerate forms of gender-based subordination in other countries that they would not tolerate in their own societies (Manyard 1994). To overcome this problem, Manyard argues that it is not enough to pay attention to difference. It is important to pay attention to the social relations *that convert difference into oppression.*

Another problem that might render a feminist focus on difference between societies in the Global South and the "West" unproductive is that this can conceal internal power relations. As Kandiyoti warns,

> Identifying an "external" site for the production of difference [. . .] namely the West and its internal allies, in contradistinction to the "truly indigenous," conveniently by-passes the need to take on board the equally heterogeneous, ethnically and religiously diverse and ideologically divided nature of such societies and potentially delegitimizes the voices of those politically defined as marginal. (1996, 17)

This is particularly true in countries like Sudan and South Sudan where processes of nation building have involved internal exclusions of cultural, racial, and regional Others.

A key concern is what might happen to feminist concepts and radical theory when they travel in academia and in policy and activist fora. Reflecting on her widely cited essays "Under Western Eyes" and "Under Western Eyes Revisited," Mohanty argued that "Radical theory can in fact become a commodity to be consumed; no longer seen as a product of activist scholarship or connected to emancipatory knowledge, it can circulate as a sign of prestige in an elitist, neoliberal landscape" (2013, 971). Mohanty examined how her work was appropriated into hegemonic feminist knowledge production, after emptying it of its fundamental commitments to decolonization.

Intersectional analysis involves a concern with the question of sexuality, about which there is increasing interest in African studies (Tamale 2011; Roscoe and Murray 2001; Ekrine 2013; Epprecht 2013), but which is still a taboo subject, especially in Sudan. Discourses that seek to undermine a concern with gender in Sudan's politics and society often associate this with support for LGBTQs.

Some scholars have analyzed the relationship with liberation movements and LGBTQ communities. Currier (2012) discusses how sexual and gender dissidents become "contested subjects in nationalist discourses of cultural and racial authenticity." She documents how Namibian gender and sexual dissidents contested homophobic statements by the leaders of the South West African People's Organisation (SWAPO), the ruling party in post-independence Namibia, since 1995. Focusing on Sister Namibia, a feminist organization, and The Rainbow Project, an LGBT organization, Currier considered "Namibian gender and sexual diversity organizing as a decolonization movement contesting SWAPO's grip over the trajectory of decolonization." She argues that organizing around sexuality challenges the dominant nationalist discourses (Currier 2012, 442).

Homosexuality (and advocating on behalf of LGBTQ) communities are prohibited in both Sudan and South Sudan. The same "public order" laws that discriminate against women, discussed later in this book, also discriminate against sexual minorities.

Taking into account the above discussion on difference and intersectionality, one of the main questions I ask in this book is: to what extent can women's groups form strategic alliances and to what extent can they form strategic alliances with movements seeking change and transformation in Sudan and South Sudan? Is it possible for women and women's organizations to build a concern with gender into the agendas of emancipatory movements, such as movements that have New Sudan agendas, for example?

Feminist scholars have engaged related questions on strategies for coalition building in the form of "reflective solidarity" (Dean 1996), where the "we" is not taken for granted and "a discourse ethics that account for difference and a universalism that does not abandon specificities" (Dean 1996, 176). Others suggested "partnerships for change" (Jordan 1985; Scott 1998) or the construction of an "imagined community of Third World oppositional struggles" (Mohanty 1991). Given the critique of the assumptions of a shared oppression by mainstream feminist theorists, a number of theorists explored possibilities for building solidarities on the basis of political programs and not on the basis of shared oppression.

Should the possibility for building solidarities arise, however, solidarity should be based on "transversal" politics (Yuval-Davis 1997a, 1997b): a concept which Italian feminists coined, and which sociologist Nira Yuval-Davis introduced in English-speaking feminist scholarship. Transversal politics is "a mode of coalition politics that recognizes the differential positioning of collectivities involved" (Yuval-Davis 1997a, 120).

Such coalition building should be based on dialogue and on the recognition of the different positions of the collectivities involved in the struggle (Yuval-Davis 1997a). It should constitute a form of "inclusive solidarity" that would minimize the possibility of one movement's monopoly of "defining the issues or identities that matter because multiple forms of oppression exist" (Ferree and Roth 1998, 629). This should be a political decision that leads to coalition building on the basis of the "bridge building labour of participants" (ibid.).

While transformative politics require building alliances between women and men, "unless there is equality within that coalition, there's no guarantee for an egalitarian revolutionary process" (Acklesberg 1985, 80). Whether coalitions are built between women's organizations or between women's organizations and mixed-gender movements, it is important to consider matters such as differential access to material resources, training, and education for each of these groups. These factors define who sets the agenda within the coalition. In that sense, the functions of the marginalized groups in the coalition might sometimes be no more than establishing legitimacy and marking the "inclusiveness" of the coalition. Moreover, given the historical sociopolitical and economic context within which movements in countries like Sudan and South Sudan evolve, and as this book shows, such coalitions might end up in subordinating gender-based subordination to other projects that are considered more "fundamental." As such, it is important to take into consideration the nature of the political parties or movements with which feminist groups attempt to build coalitions, whether these groups are open to gender-based criticism, and whether they tend to dismiss local feminist politics as "irrelevant," "inauthentic," and "Westernized" or not (Narayan 1997, 6; Moghissi 1994; Moghadam 1994; Rozario 1996).

In recent years Southern feminist scholarship has pointed to the importance of forging alliances with the international feminist movement, through a critical engagement with difference, and taking into consideration issues of unequal power relations discussed above.

Writing about Brazil, Alvarez argued that the country's high debt and severe economic crisis "tied it more closely than ever to policies and dictates of central capitalist nations and the regulatory institutions they control, sharply constraining the state's ability to implement the feminist-inspired . . . programmes" (Alvarez 1990, 273). Since women bear the brunt of failed development plans, they could draw upon international feminist solidarity to influence Third World states. These coalitions could address the gender-specific effects of the international debt crisis, structured adjustment policies, trafficking, and other problems that affect women.

This chapter discussed the key concepts that have informed the analysis in this book, and their relevance to Sudan studies and to Sudan's exile politics. It also offered a selective analysis of Sudan studies in general, and women's and gender studies in the Sudan in particular. The next chapter provides a context and a historical analysis of colonialism, nationalism, and Islamism in Sudan.

NOTES

1. The concept and translation of "gender" and "feminism" dominated the discussions in two regional meetings for women activists and researchers in the Middle East and North Africa. One was on "Women, Law and Development," held by the AISHA network of Arab organizations and hosted by the New Woman Research Centre in Cairo, Egypt, June 1995. The other regional workshop, "An Encounter by Arab Women Researchers," was hosted by the Union of Lebanese Women Researchers in Beirut, Lebanon, June 1996. I participated in both meetings. For similar concerns in African studies, see Imam et al. (1997).

2. However, in the dominant "Old Sudan" understanding of race, the category is understood in terms of the binary opposition of Arab versus African (both cultural constructs, especially the former). Jok (2007, 10) also argues that the contemporary anthropological understanding of race "as the product of social circumstances rather than anything natural or essential about people's physical attributes does not make it less real for everyday Sudanese." For a

helpful recent analysis of race in the modern world, see Appiah (2015). For a discussion of race relations and violence in Sudan, see Jok (2007).

3. For excellent resources on gender, globalization, and social movements, see Moghadam's (2013) *Globalization and Social Movements: Islamism, Feminism, and the Global Justice Movement.* See also Mohanty's (2003) *Feminism without Borders*, Mendez and Naples's (2014) *Border Politics*, and Naples and Desai's (2002) *Women's Activism and Globalization.*

4. The first edition of *Five Women of Sennar* was published in 1991.

5. Sharabi's analysis is closest to feminist "dual systems" theories that have interrogated the relationship between capitalism and patriarchy, except that he addresses the relationship between dependent capitalist development and patriarchy in Middle Eastern societies. In the African context, Gordon's (1996) *Transforming Capitalism and Patriarchy*, which examines patriarchal relations in the context of Africa's peripheral and dependent position, uses a similar analysis of subordination. Like Sharabi, she is aware of the heterogeneity of African societies. Taking a different approach in her analysis of "The Nationalist Resolution of the Women's Question" in India, Chatterjee (1990) looks at the way the encounter between Indian nationalists and the West gave rise to "new-patriarchy." Both works, however, are not informed by Sharabi's framework. This is in part due to what some scholars described as the lack, until recently, of conversations between Middle Eastern scholars and studies on one hand and postcolonial scholarly discourses on the other, with the exception of the works of Edward Said. In the context of North Africa, Cheriet (1996) uses neopatriarchy to analyze gender and politics in contemporary Algeria.

Chapter Three

Colonialism, Nationalism, and Islamism

Socioeconomic and Political Exclusion, and Resistance

Understanding Sudan's history is crucial for analyzing contemporary gendered political processes, discourses, and practices, and their impact on diverse women, men, and communities in Sudan and South Sudan. Sudan's incomplete process of nation building, and the process of state-building, have transpired alongside and have resulted in social exclusion on the basis of gender, social class, and regional, cultural, and racial hierarchies. The intersection of these hierarchies shaped the unique experiences of Sudanese (and South Sudanese) women of marginalization, conflict, political oppression, and exile. In addition to exploring these processes, this chapter highlights the development of key political parties in Sudan, which were part of the National Democratic Alliance (NDA) in the 1990s and in the first half of the first decade of the twenty-first century.

The chapter further analyzes the rise of Islamism in Sudan, and its impact on women and on gender relations. The chapter concludes with a discussion of women's organizing and resistance against gender-based discrimination, and against the social and political exclusion of women and girls.

COLONIALISM AND SUDAN'S GENDERED POLITICS

There is extensive literature on how the Anglo-Egyptian rule (1898–1956) created regional disparities in Sudan, but very few studies have focused on the gender-specific impact of colonialism on Sudanese women and men (see Boddy's *Civilizing Women: British Crusades in Colonial Sudan*). British colonialism depended on a system of native administration in ruling colonial territories. In settings like Sudan, this involved empowering traditional leaders and hereditary rulers as mediators with the colonized. In return, these leaders enjoyed facilitation of their trade, and involvement in colonial agricultural schemes (T. Ali 1988, 24–33). Colonial administrators also assured their allies of the implementation of Islamic shari'a law as interpreted by the Council of *u'lama* (T. Ali 1988, 33). This reinforced the rule of shari'a law, including in marriage and family affairs. In areas such as the Nuba Mountains, colonialism undermined the dominant matriarchal system (interview with Azrag Zakaria, representative of the Sudan National Party [SNP] in the NDA Leadership Council, Cairo, June 5, 1998).

In colonized countries, modern education played an important role not only in training government administrators, but also in developing a leadership that would assume power after independence. The reason the colonial administration introduced modern education in Northern Sudan was to develop a cadre of government administrators, as well as a cadre to run the cotton schemes (Holt 1961, 121; Bashir 1969, 90). Yet this educated male middle class spearheaded the nationalist movement in the country (Harir 1997, 35), and dominated the post-colonial state, along with sectarian leaders. These dominant social groups defined Sudan's national identity as Arab and Islamic (Harir and Tvedt 1997; Deng 1989; Kok 1996, 556). The ruling social group was also exclusively male, given that colonial administrators defined the public space as male (Amadiume 1997).

Colonial rulers did not introduce girls' education in Sudan so as not to upset their allies in the religious establishment. In 1906–1907, Shaykh Babiker Badri established a girls' school in his own house in Rufa'a, on the White Nile. He argued that educated women made "better mothers" and "modern wives" for the educated elite (Badri 1999). This remained the only school until 1911, when girls' education expanded into five other towns. Intermediate education for girls started in 1945, and girls' secondary education started in 1949 (Sanderson 1968). Between World War Two and political independence (1946–1956), boys' education expanded so as "to meet future needs" of the country, but girls' education was not encouraged (Bashir 1969, 345).

Women's access to higher education in Northern and Central Sudan started in 1945, when the first Sudanese woman, of Greek origin, joined the School of Arts in Gordon Memorial College (later University of Khartoum). Four other women joined the university in 1946. Although until the end of the 1950s women who joined the university numbered in the tens, women participated in academic, social, and political student life. In 1957, a female student was elected for the first time as a secretary for external affairs in the Khartoum University Students' Union (Saad 1972, 172).

Education in South Sudan was linked to colonialism's Southern policy, which favored the creation of an East African belt that included Southern Sudan, and was thus left to the missionaries (Hall and Amin 1981, 213). This increased the gap between the North and the South, and delayed the development of a national consciousness. It also delayed the politicization of the South Sudanese (Nyaba 1997, 15). Modern girls' education in South Sudan did not start until the 1930s. Unlike Northern Sudan, there was no local resistance to girls' education, and girls in areas where there were no girls' school attended boys' schools (Hall and Amin 1981, 231).

The male, educated middle class in the North established the Graduates' Congress in 1939. This was a forum for the rising Sudanese intelligentsia (Hale 1996, 164). The Congress submitted a memorandum to the Governor General of Sudan, asking for self-determination for Sudan after World War Two.

Sudan's nationalist movement was to a great extent neopatriarchal. This was reflected in poetry, for example. One of the poems named the nation *Azza*, a woman's name, which also means "precious." Composed and sung by Khalil Farah in the 1930s, the lyrics of *Azza fi Hawak* (In your love, Azza) roughly translate as follows.

"Azza, in your love, we are like mountains, and for anyone who dares to *infiltrate* your *purity*, we are like catapults." Another part of the song says "Azza, have you seen how the young men awoke? Have you seen how they renewed the old [heritage]? . . . [You] are a tribe and a daughter of tribes that filled the world with men." In such discourse, the nation is feminized: it is both the site of colonial infiltration *and* the passive site for national male courage and resistance. The male nationalist is constructed as a savior who protects the precious/beloved woman/nation. The woman/nation is seen as passive, although women played key supportive roles in Sudan's anti-colonial struggle.

Azza fi Hawak is dear to the hearts of Northern Sudanese women and men. My mother had told me Khalil Farah used the name *Azza* to symbolize the nation because he did not want the song to seem as nationalist or resistant to colonialism so as not to run into trouble with the colonial administration. Also, upon sharing the above analysis with a group of political activists in the early 2000s, it was clear that some were shocked and traumatized. A fellow activist shared with me the full poem and asked me to read it and to "try to find its true meaning." Transformation requires that we look critically into texts and things dear to our hearts, and this might be painful at times.[1]

Gender was the site of another battle between the nationalist movement and British colonialism. When the British outlawed female genital cutting/ mutilation (FGC/M), opponents led a protest in Rufa'a in 1946. *Ustaz* Mahmoud Mohamed Taha, founder of the Republican Brothers' movement, led the protest. Taha, who offered interpretations of religion that safeguarded women's human rights, argued that the colonial administration used the issue of circumcision to further control the Sudanese, by portraying them as barbarians who were not ready for self-rule.[2]

While women played important supportive roles in Sudan's anti-colonial struggle, the nationalist movement did not need to mobilize women, given that Sudan achieved independence via diplomatic negotiations. As such, there was no pressure on the nationalist movement to lure women through slogans or programs for social change or on improving the status of women. In African countries where anti-colonial and nationalist movements carried arms to oust colonialism, such as Algeria, Eritrea, Mozambique, Guinea Bissau, and Cape Verde, nationalist resistance involved the mobilization of women and communities. Some of the movements in these countries explicitly committed to the emancipation of women. This does not mean that these countries achieved gender equality after independence. As Stephanie Urdang (1979) has argued in *Fighting Two Colonialisms: Women in Guinea Bissau*, women had to wage a new struggle against gender inequality after Guinea Bissau became independent

With a few exceptions, much of the research and writing on Sudan tends to approach the country's post-colonial history in terms of binary oppositions such as Africanism versus Arabism, Islamism versus secularism, and democratic versus military dictatorial governments. A problematic binary opposition is what El-Battahani (1988, 3) calls "the descriptive classification of post-colonial government and politics in the Sudan on the basis of institutional frameworks which classify the governments into democratic (1956–1958), dictatorial (1958–1964), democratic (1965–1969), dictatorial (1969–1985) and so on." El-Battahani argues that the military/democracy binary opposition conceals an extended pattern that determined the nature of each regime that controlled Sudan since independence. He suggests an alternative analysis of power relations in the Sudan (El-Battahani 1988, 6).

El-Battahani argues that despite the change and reconstruction of parliamentary authority in October 1964 and April 1985, the social character of the groups that ruled had persisted. An alliance of traditional agricultural and merchant capitalist forces and state bureaucracy maintained power and hegemony throughout the different eras despite superficial institutional change (El-Battahani 1988, 7). This alliance was also almost predominantly Northern and exclusively male. The pattern of domination changed only superficially as multi-party democracy was only good for the ruling groups in the transition from colonial rule, after which the state apparatus resumed its oppressive character (T. Ali 1989, 60). Sudan's economic policies after independence allowed for the consolidation of the merchant class, which did not require the mobilization of labor. This class was conservative in terms of its stand on gender relations.

Another problem was the unequal power relationships between Sudan's center and its peripheries. In 1947, a conference held in Juba confirmed Sudan's unity in diversity. This conference mandated respect for the cultures and citizenship rights of South Sudanese communities. It also recommended economic and educational development in the South (Malwal 1987, 10). During the debates prior to independence in December 1955, Southern Sudanese representatives demanded respect for commitments in the Juba Conference to federalism. This did not materialize, and war erupted as a result in 1955, when ranks of the army in the South carried out a mutiny, attacked Northerners in the South, and called for separation of South Sudan.

Constitutional development was also problematic. A draft constitution emphasized the Islamic nature of the state and declared Arabic the official language. This undermined the efforts of Southern Sudanese politicians who wanted to solve Sudan's problems by ensuring inclusion at the national level instead of the secession of South Sudan. Armed resistance accelerated in the South, and Khartoum responded violently.

Following the October 1964 revolution, a Round Table Conference held in 1965 reached consensus on the issue of regional autonomy for the South, but the reluctance of the sectarian parties to implement its resolutions further aggravated the war (Bashir 1980, 5).

In 1969, a coup led by Gaafar Numeiry and backed by some of the leaders of the Communist Party of the Sudan (CPS) toppled the parliamentary government. After seizing power, Numeiry dissolved the parliament, froze the constitution, and banned political parties, including the CPS. Numeiry established a Revolutionary Command Council (RCC) where all but one member were military officers (Woodward 1990, 138). The new regime formed a ministry of Southern Affairs and the RCC included a Southern Sudanese who was also a CPS member. The regime recognized the multicultural nature of the country and promised regional autonomy for the South (Rida 1975, 280–281).

By the early 1970s, problems started to arise, both between CPS elements and others within the regime, and within the CPS, especially when the regime attempted to create its own organization, the Sudan Socialist Union (SSU). Tension between the CPS and the regime also intensified because of the regime's friendly relations with Egypt despite oppression of communists by the Egyptian government at the time (Niblock 1987, 138). The CPS carried out a coup that lasted for three days in 1971. The regime launched a successful counter-coup, followed by an attack on the CPS and its supporters (Khalid 1990, 225). A new power arrangement took place, and the regime moved gradually toward privatization (T. Ali 1988, 22).

By 1973, the Numeiry regime consolidated its SSU, intended as a mass revolutionary party (Niblock 1987, 264). The regime negotiated a peace agreement with the Southern Sudanese opposition in Addis Ababa in 1972.

This started as talks between Northern civil servants and Southern tribal chiefs in 1971, and developed into dialogue between the central government and the Anya Nya Southern liberation movement. An agreement on issues of language, religion, nationality, socioeconomic development, security, and military arrangements was reached and subsequently ten thousand Anya Nya combatants returned to Sudan (Malwal 1987, 14).

The Numeiry regime moved gradually into an alliance with Islamists in the second half of the 1970s. In 1983, Numeiry and his new allies in the Muslim Brothers movement violated the Addis Ababa peace agreement, and sought to weaken the Southern autonomy established by the Agreement. The government introduced new security and military arrangements. It also revisited the issue of language so as to retain the prevalence of Arabic language.

Following the discovery of oil in Sudan, the regime decided to build an oil refinery in a Northern city. Shari'a Islamic law replaced the quasi-secular system in the country (Article 16 of the 1973 constitution gave equal recognition to Islam, Christianity, and traditional religions) (Malwal 1987, 14). This had drastic effects on women as discussed later in this chapter.

Until 1971, the Numeiry regime allowed the SWU plenty of space to effect policy changes. The regime promoted women's participation in the area of social services. It retained the gains that women made in the mid-1960s in the areas of personal status laws and equal pay for equal work (Niblock 1987, 262–65, 258). In 1972, however, the regime replaced the SWU with the Union of Sudanese Women (USW). The regime also established a committee responsible for women's affairs within the SSU, and appointed a general secretary on this committee (Hall and Amin 1981, 7). The regime allowed for these changes so as to undermine the traditional establishment (the Umma Party and DUP). It used women as markers of modernization and development in the tradition of other leaders in the Middle East (cf. Moghadam 1994; Kandiyoti 1993).

From 1972 on, however, the regime moved gradually toward incorporating the Umma Party and the Muslim Brothers. The year 1977 saw a reconciliation agreement between the regime, the Umma Party, and the Muslim Brothers (who called themselves the Islamic Charter Front). This era saw deterioration in the status of women, which coincided with rising conservatism due to male migration to the oil-rich Gulf States, among other factors. The regime's shift toward the right reached its peak in September 1983, when the regime officially introduced shari'a laws. This affected the situation of women drastically. Declaring himself an Imam (religious leader), the president imposed a dress code on women, and restricted women's movement.

ISLAMISM IN SUDAN

Gender and Islamism have been the subject of extensive scholarly and policy debates since the late 1970s, but especially following events of September 11, 2001. In Sudan, the impact of the rise of political Islam to power in 1983, and the NIF/NCP's coup in 1989 brought to the forefront key questions about the impact of politicized Islam on women and gender relations. These questions have become prominent following the Arab protests that started at the end of 2010. In North Africa, these protests resulted in the overthrow of autocratic regimes in Libya, Egypt, and Tunisia, but elections brought to power Islamist opposition movements with conservative and oppressive gender ideologies. Later in this chapter I discuss the gendered politics of the National Islamic Front (NIF)/National Congress Party (NCP) within a wider discussion of the rise of politicized Islam in the Middle East and North Africa. I highlight Islamist discourses and practices and the impact on women in Sudan. I also examine Sudanese women's resistance to oppression in the name of religion.

The era following the 1985 uprising witnessed a series of unstable coalitions of the Umma Party, the Democratic Unionist Party (DUP), and the NIF. The economy continued to deteriorate and war escalated despite efforts of the National Alliance for National Salvation (NANS), a coalition of trade unions, political parties, and peace activists, to build peace. Disconcerted with the bickering between the Umma Party and the DUP, and the subsequent alliance between the Umma Party and the NIF to form a majority in parliament, the workers and tenants unions and professional associations organized demonstrations in December 1988. The groups chose the name of the modern forces, in contrast to the traditional parties and the NIF.[3] They insisted on a peaceful solution to the civil war. They also demanded the repeal of the September 1983 shari'a laws. The army also joined forces. One hundred fifty high-ranking officers who joined the modern forces submitted a memorandum to the Prime Minister in February 1988, demanding reform (Jamal 1991, 104; Kaballo 1989, 76).

The army demanded that the government either seek an immediate political solution to the war or provide the army with enough equipment and resources. The Prime Minister responded by joining the peace process, dissolving the partnership between the Umma Party and the NIF, and forming a new coalition that included all the parties and trade unions, forcing the NIF to go to opposition. By mid-June of 1988, the government announced a cabinet meeting—scheduled in early July—that would repeal the September laws formally, pending a review by a legal committee with representation from all political parties. A meeting between the government and the SPLM/A (which continued its armed resistance to the central government after the downfall of Numeiry) was scheduled on July 4, with the aim of reaching a permanent settlement. Less than a week prior to the meeting, a group of mid-ranking officers seized the parliament, the broadcasting station, and the republican palace (Jamal 1991, 104). Even before the clear link between the NIF and the coup was uncovered, most analysts argued that the timing of the coup reflected the NIF's desire to halt peace (cf. Kaballo 1989; Jamal 1991).

The declared reasons for the coup included the democratic regime's failure to address the economic crisis and its failure to stop the war. The new regime declared a state of emergency and banned all demonstrations and public meetings. It suspended the 1985 Transitional Constitution and dissolved the parliament. It also dissolved all political parties and trade unions, and arrested members of the former administration (Kaballo 1989, 76).

The leader of the coup, then Brigadier Al-Bashir, formed a fifteen-member military panel named the Command Council of the Revolution of National Salvation (RCC). He declared himself the head of state, Prime Minister, Defence Minister, and Commander in Chief of the Armed Forces (Khalid 1990, 435). By July 1, the new regime had dismissed twenty-eight army generals, including the Commander in Chief of Sudan Armed Forces, the late Fathi Ahmed Ali, and the chief of staff.[4] The regime formed a civilian cabinet on July 9.

The 1989 Emergency Law vested wide powers in the hands of the army and National Security, including the authority to obtain information from any political opponent and the freedom to investigate and/or confiscate any belongings and the arrest of any person for any period of time without legal procedures. The RCC issued an order threatening ten years' imprisonment for any opposition activity, including peaceful protest, and the death sentence for any use of force against the RCC or the "revolution" (Kaballo 1989, 76; Qau'd 1999, 30). The regime asked the SPLM to return home and declared a unilateral cease-fire for one month.

The regime did not declare its Islamist orientation from the start, nor did it uncover its link with the NIF. The regime imprisoned head of NIF Hassan Turabi, along with other party leaders and trade unionists. The nature of the forces that executed the coup soon became clear, however, given the conflation of their declared objectives with the agenda of the NIF, "a political religious party whose agenda was nothing short of the complete restructuring of society according to a narrow vision of Islamic law and culture" (Leatherbee and Bricker 1994, 4). The regime declared a revolution in education and mass media and established a ministry of social planning to further this project.[5]

The regime imposed a dress code on women, and introduced laws that affected women along class lines (N. Ali 1995; Anis 2001 and 2002). During the first half of 1992 the regime burned the houses of 500,000 of the displaced and poor population living in shanty towns and repatriated them by force to new areas outside the cities, where no infrastructure existed, a practice that continues to the time of writing (2015). Most of those affected were women from Southern and Western Sudan. The government also repatriated people in the Nuba Mountains (in West/Central Sudan), who were mostly women, to so-called peace villages in Northern Kordofan in order to avoid presumed collaboration between the Nuba and the armed opposition. As I explain later in this chapter, women suffered most.

The regime's political repression coupled with the high level of inflation and the deterioration of living conditions led Sudanese into exile in unprecedented numbers. Their number is estimated as more than five million.[6] Many considered themselves political refugees even if the host government did not grant them official refugee status (Sudan Catholic Information Office, October 1999). The regime has been listed as a severe violator of human rights by numerous international human rights bodies. In 1992, the UN Commission for Human Rights issued a resolution in its 48th session, appointing a special Rapporteur to observe the conditions of human rights in Sudan. In April 1998, the UN expressed concern for the conditions of human rights in Sudan and recommended the deployment of human rights field officers to monitor the situation in the country (UN ECOSOC 1998).

To confer legitimacy on its rule, the regime established a system of people's committees and conferences, similar to the Libyan system. The duties of the popular committees included the preparation of lists with the numbers of population in each area and the organization of the sale of basic commodities in addition to information and security. The national conferences addressed issues of politics, the "southern question," and the economy. Neither the popular committees nor the national conferences found any enthusiasm outside the circle of NIF supporters (H. Ali 1996, 311).

After six years of rule, the NIF reviewed its experience of national conferences and found that it was not able to widen its popular base. While denouncing democracy, the regime wanted to establish constitutional legitimacy and to avoid the label of military dictatorship. The regime called for elections and national consensus with the aim of recruiting the parties that had raised Islamist slogans during the 1986 elections (the Umma Party and the DUP). Members of all the (dissolved) political parties, however, had to participate in the elections in their personal capacities. All political parties refused to participate in the elections and argued that this would confer an undeserved legitimacy on the regime (H. Ali 1996, 314). The polls resulted in the election of Omer Al Bashir as president. On the ninth anniversary of the coup, the government circulated a new constitution where the government coined the term *altawaly* (succession) to refer to a system of rule that implies commitment to multiplicity. That followed a referendum that the government claimed to have achieved a crowd of 91.9 percent. Non-government observers reported a low turnout, however. The regime suffered a serious rift that led to the formation of the People's Congress Party, under the leadership of Hassan al-Turabi at the turn of the century. This was the atmosphere against which Sudan's opposition in exile operated until the mid-2000s.

During the period from 2005 to 2006, the regime signed a number of peace agreements with the opposition, the most notable of which was the Comprehensive Peace Agreement (CPA), which it signed with the Sudan People's Liberation Movement/Army. The regime signed another peace agreement with the NDA in the same year. It also signed the Eastern Sudan Peace Agreement with the Beja Congress and the Free Lions Movement in 2006. Women's participation varied, but was limited in all the negotiations (cf. Ali 2005; Itto 2006).

The rise of politicized Islam in Sudan and its claim on state power coincided with the rise of similar movements either as state or anti-state discourses in countries of the Middle East and North Africa during the 1970s and 1980s. In the case of Sudan, however, the "resurgence" did not in reality replace secularist institutions by Islamic ones, given the nature of the forces that controlled the post-colonial state in Sudan. As John Voll has argued,

> Islamic groups had consistently been an important part of the Sudanese political scene. The resurgence does not, then represent a religionizing of a previously secularist political scene. (Voll 1983, 135)

Although in the second parliamentary era (1964–1969) one political party (the National Unionist Party of Ismail al-Azhari) asserted its secularism, the party's secularism was set mainly as an oppositional discourse to sectarianism. Moreover, the leader of the party often emphasized the Arabism and Islamism of Sudan and did not deny the political relevance of religion (Voll 1983, 135). Many leaders in the Sudanese Communist Party did not publicly announce a secularist position even when they were in power during the early years of the Numeiry regime.

When the partnership between the Numeiry regime and the CPS ended in 1971, the latter charged the CPS with "anti-Islamic" sentiments and "atheist affiliation," a charge which many members and leaders of the party denied (Voll 1983, 136). It is important to note, however, that before the late 1970s, the religious nature of politics leaned toward unorthodox popular Islam.

Taking the above into consideration, it is useful to address the causes of the ascendance of politicized Islam in Sudan within the general context of Africa and Middle Eastern societies. Several explanations have been given to the ascendancy of politicized Islamist movements starting in the 1970s (Moghadam 1994; Fluehr-Lobban 1994; Kandiyoti 1991; Tibi 1991; Stowasser 1993; Warburg 1985; Ali 1991; Sharabi 1988; Halliday 1996). Many of these authors agree that the rise of Islamism was more a response to internal crises, and that Islam itself does not constitute a tool for explaining the rise of these movements (Halliday 1996, 114).

The rise of these movements is rooted in the crises that hit the Third World during the 1970s and 1980s. Development plans in the Middle East and North Africa, failed to generate the expected results (Baffoun 1994, 180). In that sense, the rise of Islamist movements was a result of the failure of populist political projects in the Middle East and North Africa, and the contradictions associated with this failure. Sudan was at a certain stage a potential bread basket for the Arab world. This dream became a nightmare of droughts and famines. The debt crisis, austerity measures, and structural adjustment programs increased unemployment, marginalization, and social disparities.

The demographic structures in countries of the Middle East and North Africa, such as Algeria, are such that the young population outnumbered others. Facing unemployment, disappointed in the prevalent nationalist and secular discourses, and exposed to consumerist trends without necessarily having adequate resources to engage in the process, the atmosphere was conducive for the expansion of extremist movements among the youth. Some scholars argue that women's education and employment have increasingly weakened the dominant patriarchal system without leading to its disintegration. As a result, a return to Islam was the option followed to strengthen the threatened dominant structures (Moghadam 1994, 10).

The oil boom/crisis has also been a factor in the rise of these movements, in the sense that petrodollars were channeled from oil-rich countries to the Islamist forces in different parts of the Middle East and North Africa. This included, in the case of Sudan, the introduction and nurturing of Islamic banking. Disparities in the economies of the oil-rich states on one hand, and the increasing indebtedness of resource-poor non-oil-producing countries on the other hand, resulted in migration from poor countries to the rich countries of the Gulf, dominated by strict versions of Islam. This affected the world outlook of many expatriates.

Islamist groups also found common ground with the repressive Middle Eastern neopatriarchal state in the second half of the twentieth century. One of the main characteristics of such a state and social formation is that it is built on a monolithic cultural and social understanding which silences innovation and excludes alternative visions (Sharabi 1988). In that sense, Islamism has been a redemptive ideology and a technique to confront challenges of dependency and underdevelopment in the Middle East (Sharabi 1988 and 1991, 31).

Islamist groups benefited from the weakness of the left wing and national secularist movements (Sharabi 1988, 1991).[7] On their part, dominant regimes at the time used religious discourse to silence left-wing secular opposition to major economic changes, such as Sadat's liberalization policies in

Egypt. Similarly Sudan's al-Nimeiri used religion to enhance a fading legitimacy, including after the introduction of austerity measures. In addition to this, neopatriarchal regimes have sometimes appropriated the discourse of politicized Islam so as not to lose ground to the Islamists who usually establish their legitimacy on the ground of being more Islamic and authentic than the ruling regimes (Sharabi 1988; Moghadam 1994).

The existence of the Israeli State in the Arab territories has always invoked feelings of powerlessness in the region, especially after the 1967 defeat of Arab states by Israel, which Islamists blamed on the secular and nationalist ruling regimes in the region at the time. Several of the Islamist movements that emerged in Egypt and elsewhere after 1967 claimed that a return to Islam was the only way to victory. The corrupt and non-democratic nature of the ruling regimes in the region created a vacuum that the rising politicized Islamist ideologies wanted to fill. Sudan was no exception.

As mentioned above, politicized Islam, be it a state discourse as has been the case in Sudan since 1983 or an anti-state discourse as was the case in Egypt and Tunisia prior to the protests that took place in 2010 and 2011 respectively, has had negative impact on women. Women often experience severe forms of social control at the hands of these movements, given these movements' gender ideology is based on a narrow understanding of Islam as expressed in the shari'a laws which were devised in the seventh year of Islamic Hijri calendar. These are again based on certain views with regard to gender equality, gender roles, the scale and content of women's education and women's capabilities, and where women are situated in the public\private dichotomy.

The dominant understanding of shari'a law, based on the *u'lama* understanding of Qur'an and hadith, include certain regulations that govern gender relations and the family. These are connected to a worldview that is inconsistent with equality as defined by international human rights discourses manifested in conventions such as the Convention on the Elimination of all forms of Discrimination Against Women (CEDAW). The most controversial among them is the permitting of polygamy, the provision of unilateral divorce without grounds for men only, and the assignment of child custody to the father and his family upon divorce (after a certain age or if the wife is to remarry) (Kandiyoti 1991, ix).

Another controversial area relates to the notions of *qiwma* and *wilaya* (guardianship of men over women) and *taa'a* (obedience of women to their husbands).

In the case of the Sudan, the dominant discourse builds upon the gender division of labor prevalent in Northern and Central Sudan's neopatriarchal societies which values women's domesticity, and their roles in reproducing and caring for children. The same discourse constructs the man as responsible for bread winning and for protection of the household and the nation.

This same discourse relegates women to the private sphere. When in public, they should be covered in *Hijab* (veil).

Women's freedom to choose their clothes, profession, and education are limited under claims that women are tender and precious and should be protected and hidden at home—a discourse that clearly objectifies women although it claims that it respects and protects them (N. Ali 1995). The pragmatic nature of this discourse is revealed in its resort to totally contradictory practices when the need arises. One example is the NIF's strategies for mobilizing women to join the Popular Defence forces (as explained below).

THE POLITICS OF THE NATIONAL ISLAMIC FRONT

Like similar movements in the Middle East and North Africa, the Muslim Brothers movement in Sudan started to consolidate its political and economic base utilising various techniques in the 1970s. Supporters of the movement started to send funds from Saudi Arabia and the Gulf States in 1973. After the rise of oil prices in 1973/1974, finance capital from oil-producing countries started to play an important political and economic role in countries like Sudan. This accompanied an expansion of "Islamic style, interest free banking" (Shaaeldin and Brown 1988, 121).

The first bank of this kind, the Faisal Islamic Bank (FIB), opened in Sudan in May 1978. The FIB and subsequent banks catered mainly to social groups that the Muslim Brothers targeted, such as petty traders, entrepreneurs, and Sudanese expatriates in the Gulf countries (Chiriyankandath 1991, 48; Jamal 1991, 105). Taking advantage of tax exemptions and other government facilities, the bank expanded and its performance outstripped other private and nationalized commercial banks in terms of profit generation and in terms of growth by 1982 (Shaaeldin and Brown 1988, 121). This was one of the most effective ways to widen and enhance the economic base of the Muslim Brothers. The Muslim Brothers movement created other similar institutions including the Islamic Insurance Company and the Institution of Islamic Development (Taha 1993, 55).

Flourishing at the peak of the debt crisis, these institutions played a limited role in financing productive sectors of the Sudanese economy such as agriculture and industry. Its activities in the agricultural sector were restricted to financing the activities of the relatively small Agricultural Bank, or lending to merchants involved in large-scale operations who would then extend finance to small farmers through the exploitative system of *shail*. Farmers borrowed money and paid after harvest, to the disadvantage of the farmers (Shaaeldin and Brown 1988, 127).

Islamist banks were also involved in sorghum hoarding and monopoly throughout the 1980s, creating fake crises in order to raise their profits (El-

Makki 1993, 10). Given that these banks dealt in *murabaha* (profitability) and *mudaraba* (speculation), they limited their activity to short-term operations with secure profit, arguing that interest rates on stocks were non-Islamic.

In the political sphere, the Islamist movement utilized the atmosphere of national reconciliation between the Numeiry regime, the Muslim Brotherhood, and the Sectarian parties in 1977. Collaboration with the Numeiry government was a good chance for the Muslim Brothers to develop the strength of the movement when most of the other parties had very limited space to work underground (Chiriyankandath 1991, 48). They were also able to map the dynamics of influential political and social groupings such as the trade unions, political parties, student groups, and the military. The movement also utilized the atmosphere to foster its regional and international relations. Hassan al-Turabi, the leader of the movement, met with international and religious figures and discussed their stands on the major issues facing countries of the Middle East at the time.

In collaboration with the Numeiry regime, the movement established the African Islamic Centre. They also established several charity organizations such as the *Da'awa* Islamic Organisation, so they can reach out to the wider society.

According to Makki, infiltrating the army was one of the most difficult tasks, given that the army was one of the earliest institutions to be secularized in Sudan, and also because of the suspicion of Sudanese Army officers toward indoctrination. Since 1981, a number of committed Muslim Brothers joined the army as specialists in engineering, medicine, computer science, etc. The movement also utilized social relations in the process of Islamizing the military. The movement sent some of its members for military training in Pakistan, Iran, and Lebanon.

The leadership of the Muslim Brothers was also seeking to Islamize the country's legal system. As mentioned earlier, the issue of Islamic law has dominated the political scene in the Sudan since independence, to the extent that, as one researcher puts it "it has become difficult to draw a line between the political and the religious programs of the Northern political leaders" (Wakson 1987, 94). The country gradually moved toward Islamization since the late 1970s, to the extent that the leader of the Muslim Brothers stated in 1981 that "the battle against secularism has been won in the Sudan (Warburg 1983, 17).

Numeiry's regime introduced shari'a law when its alliance the Muslim Brothers reached its peak. Facing severe economic crises, shortages in basic commodities, and debt, Numeiry applied shari'a laws in 1983 and declared himself an *Imam* (Islamic ruler). After the 1985 uprising, the group was renamed the National Islamic Front. Below I consider the effects of Islamism on women in Sudan.

GENDERED DISCOURSES AND PRACTICES OF THE NATIONAL ISLAMIC FRONT

Given the NIF's commitment to an interpretation of shari'a Islamic law that discriminates against women (An-Na'im 1987), its rule has had a destructive impact on women and communities in Sudan. The control of women and women's bodies became a key tool for ensuring social control over society. This has been evident in discriminatory laws, restricted movement, precarity for women in the informal sector, and a compulsory dress codes. As I discuss elsewhere in this book, economic crises, conflict, and resultant displacement have added to the above in shaping the experiences of women directly facing these precarious conditions.

One of the main areas that reflect the NIF's gender ideology was personal status laws. The introduction of "September laws" in 1983 allowed for the hegemony of the NIF's perception of shari'a over customary and civil codes, which had included provisions that supported rectification for women in family matters (Moghadam 1994, 154). Criminal law also sought to limit women's movement in public space given the new crime of "attempted adultery." Although Islam provides strict conditions for proving "adultery," this law made the very presence of any woman with a man who was not from her first kin, in a public space or in a car, "attempted adultery." Female liquor brewers were also attacked and lashed after 1983, on the basis that alcohol consumption was not compatible with Islamic law.

The post-1989 government took various steps regarding gender relations. A conference on the Role of Women in National Salvation took place in January 1990, where the president stated his position with regard to women's questions by presenting his understanding of the ideal woman as one who "cares for her husband and children, who does her household duties, and who is a devout Muslim" (SHRO 1994, 7). A report at the same conference suggested that the government limits women's employment to areas considered suitable for women such as working as teachers and nurses. A third paper, on the school curriculum, confirmed the roles of women as housewives and mothers. All these proposed areas of change built upon already existing neopatriarchal norms but reflected the gender ideology of the NIF.

Another example that reflects the NIF's oppressive gender discourse and its gendered allocation of roles is Article 52 of the Personal Matters Act for Muslims of July 1991. The article confirmed the husband's right to a wife who takes "care of her husband and obey him . . . preserve *his* honour and dispose wisely of *his* money" (Biro 1994, 34, emphasis added). The wife's rights on the other hand, according to Article 51 of the same act, included the right to dowry, maintenance,

> To be treated tenderly and be defended against [aggression] directed to her or her money, the right to visit her parents and relatives whom she is prohibited to marry and to be treated on equal terms with other wives of her husband if he is married to more than one wife. . . . The wife does not deserve maintenance (among other things) if she works outside the home without her husband's approval. (Biro 1994, 34)

As the above article shows, the act sought to normalize practices such as polygamy. It objectified women and reduced them to the status of dependent minors, consolidating the prevalent neopatriarchal relations.

Article 5 of the Personal Matters Act affirms women's unequal status. It requires two witnesses to the marriage contract for marriage validity. The two witnesses, states Article 16 of the same act, should be "two men or one man and two women who are Muslims, adults, worthy of trust and who understand that affirmation and acceptance means marriage" (Biro 1994, 35). This law is not unique to post-NIF/NCP Sudan. It reinforces women's subordination to male members of their families not only in marriage but also in relation to work and mobility in general. In accordance with this legal discourse, there has been systematic dismissal of women from public service. This has not been announced as a formal policy, however, as the government has often concealed this by dismissing women during mass purges, or representing it as part of the country's economic measures. Women have been dismissed from strategic positions such as the Foreign Service. In the attorney general's office, out of sixty employees dismissed almost 60 percent were women, a number of whom had been in senior positions for several years. The justification put forward for that act was that married women were often absent from work.

This exclusion of women occurred alongside mobilization of women to participate in the Popular Defence Forces (PDF). Encouraging the development of women's physical strength is basically seen as a protective measure against rape and killing *in the absence of men*. As one of the female officers in the PDF states, "(we felt that) it was very important for women to join the PDF after what we saw happening to the women and children of Bosnia" (Bukhari 1995).

While in recent years the Ministry of Social Welfare has supported income generation programs in partnership with donors, the government targeted women working in certain activities in the informal economy. Austerity programs, and Sudan's wars in the South, and in Eastern Sudan, Darfur, Southern Kordofa, and the Blue Nile have driven millions to the large cities. As a coping strategy, women increasingly resorted to petty trading as a key source of family income in the 1990s (N. Ali 1998) and beyond.

Women street vendors who had no licences were mostly affected. The government harassed them and confiscated their belongings (SHRO 1994, 7).

Government officials continue to accuse street vendors such as tea sellers of using this trade as a cover for sex work. This prompted an initiative in 2014, where women activists working as lawyers, journalists, and doctors served tea and coffee in solidarity with the women tea sellers.

Liquor brewers and sex workers suffered flogging, fines, or imprisonment. This affected mainly women displaced to Khartoum and the major cities in the North from Southern Sudan, as brewing was one of very few income generating activities that women displaced by war used to support their families and educate their children. *Marisa*, a local beer, is considered a diet for the whole family in various communities in Southern and Western Sudan. This racialized social and economic oppression of women was evident in the number and backgrounds of women in the women's main prison in Omdurman in the early 1990s. Research at the end of 1992 found that the majority of the 825 prisoners in Omdurman women's prison were from the South and the Nuba Mountains. These comprised 35.7 percent and 32.3 percent of women in Omdurman prison respectively. According to the same study, over 60 percent of these women were illiterate, and 58 percent had been arrested for selling liquor (Fund For Peace 1993, quoted in Africa Watch, November 1994, 38–39). Most of these women were also unaware of their legal rights, had to pay bribes, and were abused by officers.

Racialized subordination has also been evident in the experiences of women from marginalized regions and war-affected areas. Numerous reports and studies (cf. de Waal 1997; Jok 1997a, 1997b, and 1998; Beswick 2001) have documented sexual violence against women and other abuses in war-affected areas of Sudan. One influential female NIF leader reportedly suggested that the "solution to the 'Southern problem' was for Muslim men to take [non-Muslim] women as second wives or concubines, assuming their children would be raised as Muslims" (Gruenbaum 1991, 30). If one agrees with Ismail (1999), this could be an extension of "Arabo-Islamic patriarchy, which is based on racial extremism," where men from collectivities that self-define as Arabs in Sudan marry women from "Other" collectivities and expand "the Arab collectivities," while women from the same dominant groups can only marry within the broader "Arabo-Islamic" collectivity.

Victoria, a young South Sudanese woman who has two children and who was active in the New Sudan Youth Union at the time of interview, talked about her experience:

> They burned the whole village and then they started to rape women and imprison children in "peace camps." I do not even know if some of them survived. I had to run and to walk for long weeks. I had to move from one town to the other until I reached Port Sudan. That is where I met my husband. He comes from the same tribe as me. We got married in Port Sudan and then the security started to arrest him for long periods. They said he was a member of the SPLM. I had to take my children and come to Egypt. From the beginning I

thought, I should *Arkiz* (have my feet firm on the ground) and try to find work to get food for the kids. I work in the houses (as a housemaid). It is very difficult. I do not know what happened to my husband nor if I will see him again. (Interview with the author, June, 1998, Cairo, Egypt)

Attacks on women have not been limited to non-Muslim communities of Sudan, however. Women in the Blue Nile areas and Eastern Sudan and recently in Darfur have been equally victimized. Talking about her experience and the experiences of other women in the Northern Blue Nile area, the late Zahra Abdelgadir stated,

> In the past, government representatives used to come to our Kadalwa areas and force us to make donations of sesame, bee honey and other products, saying that they wanted to use this money to build a mosque in the village. The government accused us of feeding the rebel groups. One day they came to the village and arrested all men. We (women) and our children were all rounded up in the mosque. After a few hours they brought the shoes of the men and said to us, look at these shoes, this is the last you are going to see from the men. We never saw them again. Then they started raping women, it was terrible. (Interview with the author, Sudanese/Eritrean borders, January 2, 1998)

Similarly, women from Garora, south of the Red Sea in Eastern Sudan, spoke about the way they and their relatives were harassed and targeted by the government's army and popular defence forces in the late 1990s,

> I never thought that I would survive. It was very early in the morning. They came to the village and arrested some of the men. They would place the thick plastic sheets we use to cover our huts over the (backs of the arrested men) and then fill an iron with burning coal and run it over their backs. The plastic sheets immediately melted and so did the skins! You have seen the photos, haven't you? We were terrorized and had to move to the Eritrean Garora. They caught some of the women and, you know, raped them. One of the women could not live with it. She committed suicide. (Interview with the author, Asmara, August 2003)

Later in this book I analyze how Nuba and Southern groups respond (discursively) to this subjugation.

A Public Appearance Act (1991) also reflected the official position of the government on the question of the behavior of women in public places. Although the law applied to both women and men, its greatest impact has been on women given their subordinate position in society and the family. Article 152 of the criminal act which defined and sanctioned "indecent and immoral acts," reads as follows:

> 1. Whoever commits in a public place an act or conducts himself in an indecent manner or a manner contrary to public morality or wears an indecent or

immoral uniform which causes annoyance to public feelings shall be punished with whipping not exceeding 40 lashes or with fine or with both. 2. The act shall be considered contrary to public morality if it is so considered in the religion of the doer or the custom of the country where such an act has happened. (Khartoum State 1992)

The public order police forces often use this law to harass women in public spaces and impose charges of "public indecency." Definitions of "public morality," religion, and custom are all vague. Women who do not comply with these measures are subject to harassment and prosecution. One of the extreme measures that resulted from this law was the arrest of female students riding university buses from Ahfad University for Women in December 1997. The students were lashed and fined for not abiding by the dress code specified by the government.

In 2009 the case of Lubna Ahmed al-Hussein attracted international media attention to this law as discussed elsewhere in this book.

In many parts of Northern Sudan, women traditionally wore a garment that covered the whole body and parts of the head. In southern parts of the country, women wore another kind of dress that covered part of the body. Women have also increasingly worn Western clothes. The veil was already spreading among Sudanese women, specifically in universities, before the Islamists seized power.[8] After 1989, the pro-NIF student groups launched campaigns within university campuses that all female students should wear the veil. The Islamists later provided veils at a subsidized price. In 1991, a presidential decree, announced by the governor of Khartoum, required that women wear Islamic dress on grounds of modesty. Governors in other states subsequently followed suit. By 1994, the Minister of Education had ordered that all Muslim students in all universities should follow Islamic dress and that non-Muslims should wear "decent" clothes (SHRO 1994, 7). This debate continues, and is manifested in an October 2010 call by President Omar al-Bashir for imposing a uniform on all university students, especially women.

The government linked its compulsory dress code to livelihoods. Increasingly deteriorating economic conditions and the rampant inflation, which affected the lower and middle classes most (Hamza 1993, 45; Gruenbaum 1992, 29), women employed by the government were prompted to follow the dress code to keep their jobs. As Gruenbaum (1992, 30) states,

In the past women objected to Islamist pressure to wear the hijab (veil) claiming that they had no money to purchase such clothes, so [in 1991] loans equivalent to about $30 were paid to women government employees, to be repaid through payroll deductions. [E]mployed women and students were asked to wear "Islamic Dress" . . . by July 1st [1991] or risk being fired or arrested.

These measures continued in North Sudan, including after the signing of the Comprehensive Peace Agreement in 2005. It has also generated important resistance which I discuss elsewhere (Ali 2011).

The discourses and practices of the NIF/NCP have been the subject of resistance. In December 1997, for example, and with the increase in the forced conscription of male students,[9] who were sent by the regime to the war front, the Sudanese Women's Democratic Alliance (SWDA) organized a peaceful demonstration. They submitted a memorandum to the UN representative in Khartoum, referring to themselves as mothers of the students and demanding that the government stop the forced conscription of these students. It was very clear that the group had used this image to make a political statement. The police beat and arrested the women participants in the demonstration. Women had to pay fines to be released.

There are some organizations that were built around issues that do not directly pertain to women's rights, but around which mobilization of women took place in a way that is similar (albeit on a smaller scale) to the Mothers of the Plaza de Mayo of the 1970s in Argentina. The most active of these was the Families of Martyrs Association, established by the female family members of twenty-eight army officers executed by the government after a failed coup attempt. The association organized annual gatherings and demonstrations, and demanded the trial of officials implicated in executing the officers.

Although the core group is exclusively female, its program is limited to the objectives of restoring democracy in Sudan and bringing those responsible for the executions to punishment. The group did not focus on gender-based discrimination or sexism. It drew on the social construction of women as mothers (or wives or sisters) of martyrs. However, many of the activists who started in this group later became active in independent women's organizations or in political parties. Some became human rights activists or lawyers.

Finally, the NIF/NCP has also restricted some forms of traditional women's organization, such as the *zar* (spirit possession) ceremonies. The *zar* constituted an important way of articulating women's needs and grievances in the past, where women were able to surpass the boundaries of neopatriarchal society. The GOS considers *zar* as non-Islamic and has outlawed *zar* *sheikhas* (women who organize spirit possession ceremonies).[10]

Women constituted an important site for marking the Islamist orientation of the regime and important tools in its civilizational project to reconstitute and control the Sudanese person.

This section highlighted the discourses and practices of the NIF/NCP regime toward women in its early years. Much of this discourse is not alien to Sudan's neopatriarchal politics and society. At times, this discourse overlaps with the discourses and practices of some of the opposition groups on women and gender. I discuss this in the next chapter.

Successive post-colonial governments and politics in Sudan did not transform the institutions and structures which colonialism built. The neopatriarchal "relations of domination and subordination on the basis of class, gender, culture and regional location which prevailed prior to 1956 all continued" (Niblock 1987, xix). The dominant social groups, which were predominantly male, constructed a singular understanding of culture and national identity that reflected the interests of predominant male riverain groups, and excluded women, and people in historically marginalized areas (N. Ali 1998).

MAJOR POLITICAL PARTIES IN SUDAN

The Umma Party and the Democratic Unionist Party

The relationship between the educated middle class and the traditional merchants and landlords was key to the development of the two major parties in Sudan, the Umma Party and the DUP, associated with the Ansar and Khatmiya Sufi sects respectively.

The Khatmiya sect was established during Turko-Egyptian rule of Sudan in the nineteenth century. It opposed the Mahdist movement that overthrew the Turko-Egyptian rule. The other sect, the Ansar, is associated with Mahdiyya, a radical Islamic movement built by Mohamed Ahmed al-Mahdi. This movement succeeded in ending sixty-four years of Turko-Egyptian rule in Sudan. The Umma Party reflected the interests of the agricultural sector, mainly involved in cotton cultivation. The British native administration policy empowered both sects.

Although British colonialism overthrew the Mahdist State, the British colonial administration nurtured Abdul Rahman al-Mahdi, the leader of the Ansar and the grandson of Mohamed Ahmed al-Mahdi, and enabled him to cultivate land, through the exploitation of his followers. The reason was the colonial administration wanted to curtail the influence of the Khatmiya sect, which had strong trade relations with Egypt. This conflation of the interests of foreign and local agricultural capital eventually reduced Sudan's economy into a single cash crop producer (Mahmoud 1985; T. Ali 1989, 61–63).

The Ansar and Khatmiya religious sects co-opted the all-male nationalist movement of the twentieth century, organized in the Graduates' Congress under the umbrella of the Umma and Ashiqqa (later Democratic Unionist) Parties. Through this alliance, the two parties controlled much of Sudan's post-colonial politics and society (Harir 1997; T. Ali 1988; Mahmoud 1985).

The participation of women was relatively limited in both parties. In the DUP, until the 1980s, women's activity within the party was limited to voting in the elections. Female members were mostly either active within the Sudanese Women's Union (SWU) or focused on charity activities. As discussed later, the sect and the party generally adopt a conservative stand on women's rights.

Women have historically been more active within the Umma Party. In the 1940s, female party members established the Society for the Prosperity of Women. This was a charity association that was not working to transform gender relations. The Umma Party had a number of female ministers during the third parliamentary period (1986–1989) in Sudan. Women remain active within the Umma Party although the party continues to have conflicting positions regarding gender equality and women's human rights. In 2014, Sadiq al-Mahdi, the head of the Umma Party and the *Imam* of the Ansar sect, appointed his daughter, Mariam al-Mahdi, as his deputy.[11]

The Muslim Brothers, National Islamic Front, National Congress Party, and People's Congress Party

The Muslim Brothers' movement developed in Sudan between the second half of the 1940s and the first half of the 1950s. Informed by the thinking of Egypt's Hassan al-Banna and Pakistan's Abu al-Alaa al-Maududi, the movement has been mostly militant since its inception (Warburg 1985).

Membership of the Muslim Brothers' movement in Sudan expanded among high school and university students as the masses in the country, especially in the rural areas, were committed to popular Islam embodied in the two major Sufi sects, the Ansar and Khatmiya. The Muslim Brothers' movement mainly represents the interests of finance and merchant capital. Its leadership engaged in unproductive economic activities in the 1980s, such as hoarding basic commodities and selling them in the open market. They were also involved in illegal foreign currency exchange operations.

Members who felt that infiltration into society should take place through Islamic education later led a split in the movement, and focused their activities on education. Pragmatists formed the National Islamic Front (NIF) in the mid-1980s. This movement assumed power through a military-backed coup in 1989. It later split into the ruling NCP, led by Omer al-Bashir, and the opposition PCP, led by Hassan al-Turabi.

Women's membership in the Muslim Brothers' movement, writes Hassan Makki (1982), first evolved around al-Manar magazine, and was consolidated with the establishment of *al-Gabha al-Nisaiya* (the Women's Front) in October 1964 by ten women who were either wives or relatives of male members in the movement. These women defected from the SWU when it started calling for women's suffrage. Hassan Makki argues that the magazine was relatively progressive and supported women's social and political rights, including women's rights within marriage. According to Makki, some of the editorials condemned women's seclusion as a non-fundamental part of religion. In practice, however, matters were different. The movement, including its female membership, opposed women's suffrage at the beginning on the grounds of its incompatibility with religion. When women won the right to vote and to be elected, however, members of the Women's Front participated in elections in the second parliamentary period. That was a pragmatic move given the weight of the women's vote.

Communist Party of the Sudan

Established in 1946 under the banner of the Sudanese Movement for National Liberation (SMNL), the Communist Party of the Sudan (CPS) developed its structures and leadership in the ten years that preceded political independence of the country in 1956. A number of colonial administrators introduced communist and socialist ideas in Sudan, and so did the Sudanese who studied in Egypt (key informant interview with the late al-Tigany al-Tayib, representative of the CPS in the NDA Leadership Council, Cairo, February 1998).

Given that Sudan had an underdeveloped market and an economy based on wage labor, the party developed its activities around Sudan's railway network in Atbara (called the worker's city and the city of steel and fire). It also developed among the workers in Sudan's only port in Eastern Sudan. A third center evolved around the Gezira cotton-plantation scheme among the wage laborers. The party expanded mainly among the Gezira tenants, trade unions, students, and professionals (Hale 1996; key informant interview with al-Tigany al-Tayib, CPS representative in the NDA Leadership Council, Cairo, February 1998). Membership perceived women as mothers and wives and hence at the beginning the party did not attempt to organize them (Hale 1996, 163). The CPS started to accept female membership at an early stage, but its female membership consisted mainly of educated women.

When the Sudanese Women's Union (SWU) was established in 1952, the CPS opted for wider involvement of women in its activities. The SWU played an important role in organizing women and by 1965 its president, Fatima Ibrahim, became the first woman parliamentarian in Sudan. Research on the gender politics of the CPS (Hale 1996, 2006) has indicated that the party focused on promoting women's public participation, but did not pay enough attention to discrimination against women in the private sphere, so as not to reinforce the perception among the Sudanese that the CPS was against Islam (Hale 1996, 158).

Moreover, the party imposed strict rules regarding the conduct of its female membership so as not to lose popular support. In the 1990s, female members of the party criticized its concentration on liberating women from class-based discrimination without providing a specifically gender-based approach to the various issues relating to women (cf. Abdel Hafiz 1998, 36). During the same decade, some of the party leaders started to acknowledge the importance of addressing gender-specific discrimination against women (interview with al-Shafie Khider, CPS representative in the NDA's executive office, Cairo, April 14, 1998). As discussed later in this book, the CPS undertook a progressive stand in support of the demands of women's organizations in exile with regard to the NDA and women's human rights.

RESISTING SUDAN'S POST-COLONIAL ORDER

The Politics of the New Sudan

A number of groups carried out organized resistance against the post-colonial order in Sudan and its injustice, intolerance and emphasis on sameness. Armed resistance erupted in the South and later in other marginalized regions such as Darfur and the Nuba Mountains and Eastern Sudan. Other social groups that resisted Sudan's post-colonial politics include urban-based trade unions and professional associations and small left-wing political parties that were particularly active in the 1980s.

Resistance in the South developed against the "self-centred and self-serving vision of the *Jallaba*" (Kok 1996, 556). That vision obstructed possible consensus on issues as important as "the nature of the state, the functions of government, the role of culture in nation building, the criteria for resource and power sharing and the centrality of fundamental human rights" (Kok 1996, 556). The first political party in the South was the Southern Liberal Party, founded upon political independence "in response to the conditions of (the) liberal parliamentary democratic regime" (Nyaba 1997, 17). According to Nyaba, this party did not reflect the interests of the masses in the region, and its members engaged in various alliances with Northern parties and in turn were pawns to these parties' political interests. This situation changed upon the formation of the Sudan People's Liberation Movement/Army (SPLM/A) in 1983 by some of the Southern army officers and intellectuals who gained credence after the 1972 Addis Ababa agreement. The SPLM/A was founded after al-Nimeiry's unilateral violation of the Addis Ababa Agreement.

Membership in the SPLM included people from the Southern regions, the Nuba Mountains, Southern Blue Nile, a number of political activists from the Beja tribe in Eastern Sudan, and a group of young Northern Sudanese, some of whom defected from the CPS. Sympathetic modern forces in the North (middle- and lower-class professionals, trade unionists, and various secular groups) identified with the SPLM's concept of New Sudan and backed the movement. Some saw the SPLM/A as an ally against the forces of sectarianism and radical Islam. Those who opposed the movement saw in it a threat to the nation's "Arab" identity (Kok 1996, 561).

The SPLM's call for the unity of Sudan on new bases alienated some of the Southern Sudanese elites. Others saw the movement's commitment to liberating the whole of Sudan and to establish a just state politically sound in that it spoke to the grievances of other marginalized groups. SPLM's stand on unity also meant that governments in Khartoum were not able to manipulate anti-secessionist sentiments to discredit the movement as they did with earlier movements that originated in the South (Nyaba 1997; Kok 1996). Gradually, a great number of people from the marginalized areas of Sudan joined the SPLM/A. By the mid-1990s, the SPLA reportedly had around 25,000 armed soldiers (New Vision 1997, 1). In 2005, the movement controlled over two-thirds of Southern Sudan, where it had established its own administrative bodies in 1994.

Women started joining the SPLM in 1984. The movement established a girls' battalion, where women received military training. The year 1985 saw the formation of the first of a number of women's groups associated with the SPLM/A. Interviews discussed later in this book highlight the progressive nature of the SPLM/A's program on gender.

One of the parties closely associated with the SPLM/A is the Union of Sudan African Parties (USAP),[12] established after the 1985 uprising. The need for establishing the USAP resulted from a feeling of ineffectiveness on the part of regionally based parties that decided to participate in the 1986 elections, given the pressure from the NIF and the two sectarian parties at the time. The USAP established its organizational structure and chose its chairman by 1988. It had seven member parties and was represented in the NDA.

Although the USAP had a women's secretariat inside Sudan, it decided not to carry out any organizing among women in exile so as to avoid rivalry over recruitment of women with the SPLM/A that might weaken both organizations:

> When the SPLM/A started mobilization and formation of chapters, it issued a decree that women should have their bureau. So when you have two women's organizations working in the same area, hard feelings could develop. That's why we have abstained from organizing a women's chapter in the USAP. . . . In the future, when there are elections, probably women can vote for whatever organization they want to vote for. (Interview with Abdoun Agaw, formerly representative of the USAP in the NDA Executive Office, Cairo, July 27, 1997)

In the North, historically marginalized communities have organized in regional interest groups to achieve justice for their communities through political mobilization. Most prominent among these were the Beja Congress, the Nuba Mountains General Union (NMGU), and the Darfur Development Front (DDF).[13] All these groups became active after the 1964 October revolution in Sudan and later on transformed their agendas in order to address the national question along similar lines to those identified by the SPLM/A.

The DDF was based in Darfur and its membership was limited to inhabitants of this area from Fur origin, cutting across class boundaries. *Suny*, an underground organization, mobilized communities in areas that were historically the preserve of the Umma Party. The DDF originated in "the general disappointment generated by the traditional parties amongst the people of Darfur and their obvious inability to face the difficulties and problems of the country" (DDF Charter, quoted in Bashir 1980, 9). The DDF saw itself as a multi-racial front that would channel the political, ethnic, social, and political aspirations of the people of Darfur to promote the development of the area in the context of general development of Sudan. As such, the DDF wanted to articulate a united position for the Fur to address their needs and interests and not the interests of the Umma Party. The latter saw the DDF as a threat to its interests in the area. The DDF was dissolved after the Numeiry coup in 1969 together with other groups and political parties. It re-emerged, taking a New Sudan stand, with the establishment of the Sudan Federal Democratic Alliance (SFDA).

The SFDA constitutes "a distinct model of political thought and an organization that aims at bringing all the Sudanese together. The product of multiple experiences of the people since independence, the SFDA aims at addressing and overcoming the problems inherited by Sudan by adopting a federal system of rule" (interview with three members of the executive office of SFDA in Egypt, Cairo, April 22, 1998). All members of the SFDA I interviewed insisted on the importance of women becoming equal partners to men. They also argued that women's basic rights should be a part of any future legal reform.

Like the DDF, the Beja Congress, established in 1958, originated in disappointment with the policies of the sectarian parties, specially the Unionist party that drew most of its support from Eastern Sudan. In the past, membership was only open to the Beja. Early programs of the party were expressed in pamphlets issued by its founder and first president, Dr. Belia. The early discourse of the Beja Congress mainly emphasized the deteriorating conditions of the Beja people that placed them on equal footing with the South. The Congress stressed the need for decentralization in order to ensure that the interests of the Beja were fulfilled. The establishment of the Beja Congress angered the Khatmiya and DUP leaders because it recruited from their membership. In the 1990s, the Beja Congress adopted a transformative agenda, in line with the New Sudan principles.

The Beja are mainly nomadic tribes, and although the Beja women undertake heavy activities within the household, the society is governed by strict patriarchal rules that are based on the seclusion of women. As such, although the Beja Congress had a relatively progressive agenda regarding women's issues, it had postponed the turning of this agenda into concrete programs so as not to offend the community or alienate it. The focus is often on fulfilling women's practical interests such as basic literacy and health services. The Union of Beja Women also focused on women's practical interests.

Another similar organization that is based in Central/Western Sudan, the Nuba Mountains General Union (NMGU), emerged in 1964, first among University of Khartoum students from the Nuba Mountains. Membership was first limited to people from Kordofan, including Northerners and Syrians, regardless of religion. One of its most outspoken leaders was veteran politician and Christian clergyman Philip Ghabboush. In the post-1969 era, he tried to form alliances with the Southern opposition exiled in Eastern Africa, and frequently urged soldiers in the Sudan Armed Forces from the Nuba Mountains to rebel against the "Khartoum Arab governments." Ghabboush left the NMGU and established the Sudan National Party (SNP).

In the 1986 elections, the SNP won seven out of eighteen seats and Ghabboush was elected in the constituency of al-Haj Yusuf in Khartoum, after the Nuba and Southerners displaced in the area voted for him. Displaced women working in the informal economy as street vendors and beer brewers constituted an important force that supported Ghabboush in Khartoum. Women have also been active in the NMGU and the SNP, specifically inside the Sudan. Given that the Nuba Mountains communities are rooted in a strong matriarchal tradition, the communities are egalitarian and favorable to women in many respects. The SNP split into three groups and has been manipulated by the Umma Party, DUP, and the NIF/NCP.

The NMGU, the DDF, and the Beja Congress expressed their grievances through political means, opposing the centralization of power and wealth, and the exclusion of their regions from decision-making processes. Although their impact on national politics has been limited, some of the proposals and concepts introduced by these groups (such as regionalism and regional autonomy) influenced policies at the national level (Bashir 1980). This was expressed, for example, in the joint proposal of Northern political parties regarding regionalism and autonomy in the South that was presented to the Round Table Conference, and in the 1979 plans for regionalism in Sudan (Bashir 1980).

Finally, some of the resistance movements focused on specific single issues in the 1980s. These included the 1984 famine, the protests against the application of shari'a laws in 1983, and mobilization for peace by modern forces (trade unions, professional associations, and students) organized in the Trade Unions Alliance. It was the activism of these forces that terminated al-Nimeiry's dictatorship in 1985 (de Waal 1997). After the 1985 uprising, the New Forces formed a number of parties with left leanings which Sadiq al-Madhi named "petty cash parties." These groups also formed coalitions with parties from the disadvantaged regions. These were expressed in the Rural Forces Solidarity (RFS), launched in December 1985 after the Conference of the *Intifada* (uprising) Forces, sponsored by the Trade Unions' Alliance in

Wad Madani. The SNP was the only member in the RFS that won seats in the parliament during the 1986 elections (Chiriyankandath 1991, 88).

In the 1990s, a number of Northern activists with left leanings joined the SPLM/A. Others have formed the Sudan National Alliance/Sudan Alliance Forces (SNA/SAF), together with democratically oriented army officers who collaborated with the trade unions and professional associations during the 1985 uprising. Others who joined included former CPS members, trade unionists, and other civilians who were disenchanted with both the NIF regime and the narrow-based sectarian parties. The SNA/SAF was launched in 1994 and held its first preliminary conference in August 1995, adopting a New Sudan agenda.

Initially, the SNA/SAF saw that the mentality of those who ruled the country since 1956 has contributed to Sudan's crises (Connell 1997, 36). Since its establishment, the SNA/SAF has maintained that the NIF regime cannot be overthrown via civilian uprisings, given its violent nature and the way it changed the composition of the national army. Accordingly, the movement adopted, together with other New Sudan groups, a strategy of "stepping up the military threat in the Northeast, forcing the government to spread its forces between the north and the south while clandestinely organizing [anti-NIF] support in the capital" (Connell 1997, 36).

The SNA/SAF had mass organizations of women and students, and had a "multi-ethnic composition" (Connell 1997, 35). It claimed to be representing the oppressed, silenced forces, specifically in rural, peripheral areas. It had a women's secretariat, which I chaired between 1996 and 2003, and an associated organization, the Sudanese Women Alliance (SWA), established in 1995.

THE SUDANESE "WOMEN'S MOVEMENT"[14]

Women's modern organizing in Sudan started in 1947, when Fatima Talib, one of the first women to receive high education in Sudan, formed the Educated Girls Association in Omdurman. Membership in the association was limited to the educated and as such it did not reach out to the masses, and was dissolved in 1949. The Association of Sudanese Women, chaired by Khalida Zahir (the first Sudanese female medical doctor), was also established in Omdurman to improve the position of women through education. The organization held lectures to discuss social problems and to provide guidance on health matters to housewives. Another organization was formed by women of the Ansar sect in 1948: the Association for the Advancement of Women. Female teachers who protested low wages compared to men formed the Federation of Women Teachers in 1948. Nurses organized in an association in the same year (Ahmed 1997, 2; Mahmoud 1998, 31). This, according to

Ahmed, was a "sign of awareness" that later strengthened the women's movement. Outside Khartoum, women in El Obeid in Western Sudan formed a Charitable Women Society in 1951.

Kumari Jayawardena (1986) has argued that in Third World and colonized countries, feminism (or the women's movement in the case of Sudan) has grown as part of nationalist movements and struggles and this has shaped the priorities of women's movements and their relationships with nationalist movements, and their attitudes toward Western feminisms. Sudan is no exception. Although women were not overtly engaged in politics, educated women supported the growing nationalist movement. A veteran leader in the women's movement wrote that "national liberation movements were at their peak in Africa and the Arab region. They were supported by demonstrations, solidarity, and fundraising campaigns. Women participated in solidarity with revolutions in Congo, Algeria, Kenya, and Ghana" (Zahir 1998, 41).

Women, according to Hall and Amin (1981, 102), blamed colonialism for the "backwardness of their society," including women's lack of access to modern education. Some felt that independence would translate into better opportunities and education for women. That is why, for example, the first article of the constitution of the first modern women's association was "raising women's national consciousness and promoting education" (Zahir 1998, 40).

Established in 1952, the Sudanese Women's Union had a clear anti-colonial stand. It joined students and trade unions in 1954/1955 in demanding reform of the law for subversive activities, which limited freedom of association (Ahmed 1997, 5).

The SWU sought to unite women in one organization so as to address issues of concern to women more effectively (interview with Azza Al Tigany, Secretary General of the SWU, Cairo, May 11, 1998). Although membership of the SWU was open to women with different political leanings, in the years that followed its formation the SWU came under the control of the CPS and gender issues were overshadowed in the process (Hale 1996).

Women established several journals to share their ideas widely. The *Daughters of the Valley* journal focused on women's traditional roles such as motherhood and housekeeping. Members of the SWU established *Sawt al Mara* (women's voice) in 1954. The journal outlined what it saw as the causes of women's social problems, reflecting the stage of social development in Sudanese society in central Sudan at the time (Hall and Amin 1981, 106). The journal, however, emphasized that women's emancipation did not mean abandoning "national traditions" or emulating "Western women" (Ibrahim 1996, 6).

Women participated widely in the October 1964 uprising, which overthrew Sudan's first military government. Subsequently, women won the right to vote at the age of eighteen, and to stand for elections. In 1965, Fatima

Ibrahim was elected as the first female MP in Sudan. Issues on the agenda of women's organizations at the time included equal pay for employed women, maternity leave, and reform of the personal status law in the areas of divorce, polygamy, and forced child marriage (Ibrahim 1996).

Following the 1969 coup, the SWU collaborated and pressed for change. In 1971, however, the regime abandoned the SWU and created its own organization, the USW. Some of the members of the SWU joined the new organization (Khalid 1991, 185).

As discussed earlier, there is limited research on women's organizing and leadership in South Sudan and in marginalized areas of Sudan (cf. Arabi 2012 and Beswick 2000). But several of the women of South Sudan interviewed for this book said they were only involved in national women's activities through the branches of the USW established in the South after the 1972 Addis Ababa Agreement. While I look at the activities of predominantly Southern exiled women's groups in chapter 6, there is a need for more recording and analysis of the history of women's movements in the marginalized areas of Sudan.

It is equally important to investigate the gendered politics of the 1980s, given that the failure of women's groups and individual female activists to play an active role in the coalition politics of the 1980s has affected women's participation in the exiled opposition and the way the opposition addressed "women's issues" in the second half of the 1990s.

As I explained above, political protest that developed in the 1980s involved collaboration between trade unions and professional associations around general issues that were not directly related to the sectorial demands of the trade unions. Those included the famine of 1984, the subsequent events that led to the overthrow of the Numeiry military dictatorship in 1985, and the attempts at peace building in the post-1985 era. Most of the peace-related efforts were coordinated through the National Alliance for National Salvation (NANS), which was formed in 1985, and consisted of fourteen political parties and twenty-two major trade unions. Women were not represented in this body on the premise that they neither constituted a political party nor a separate trade union (El Bakri 1995, 201).

The trade unions and small parties played a key role in the 1985 *Intifada* (uprising), but the traditional parties and the NIF alienated them. As a result, collaboration started to intensify between small urban-based left-wing groups on one hand, and parties representing the aspirations of people in disadvantaged regions on the other hand, developing, as I stated above, into the RFS. Another form was in terms of continuous dialogue between these networks and the SPLM/A, which continued its armed struggle after the 1985 uprising. I believe that the nature of this politics shaped the Asmara 1995 meeting and declaration.

Progressive groups sought to restore the ground they lost to the sectarian parties and the NIF after the *Intifada* by focusing on peace building. These groups organized a meeting with the SPLM/A in Koka Dam, Ethiopia. They later supported the Sudan Peace Initiative between DUP and the SPLM/A. The two sectarian parties, who at the time knew a military victory over the SPLM/A was not possible, took part in these initiatives (interview with Abdel Aziz Daf'allah, former TU leader and chair of the Political Secretariat, SAF, Cairo, April 17, 1998). Following the 1989 coup, the major sectarian parties and the progressive movements started to work toward a common agenda. This agenda included commitments to the separation between the state and religion and the transformation of economic and political power relations between the regions and the center.

Some of the small political parties sought to involve women, especially those parties that were active in areas such as Western Sudan, where women played important roles in agriculture (interview with Abdel Aziz Daf'allah, Cairo, April 17, 1998; Sirag 1999). These groups did not pay attention to gender, however. They focused on racial, cultural, religious, and socioeconomic subordination. Reflecting on women's involvement in the former Socialist Labour Organization, Daf'allah said,

> This movement first started amongst intellectuals who did not differentiate between male and female involvement and roles. To the contrary, there was work that women could perform better. In the Labour Organization, women undertook all the organizational tasks during the dictatorship of Numeiry. I can give you names: Maymuna Kazzam, Alawiya Mohamed Ahmed, Kurashiya Yusuf and others. Those people shouldered huge responsibilities, and were highly regarded. (Interview in Cairo, April 17, 1998)

Despite women's limited involvement, the collective politics of the 1980s was gendered as male. A question that arises is: what was the nature of feminist politics at the time? The Numeiry regime had weakened democratic women's organizations after 1972 (T. Khalid 1995; El Bakri 1995). After the overthrow of Numeiry, argues El Bakri (1995, 197), "many Sudanese women had hoped that a return to the path of democracy would signal the resurgence of a strong and popular women's movement." This did not materialize, however. Progressive women activists had expected the SWU to "act as the rallying point for their many demands and problems, become a vanguard of the women's movement and wipe out all the wrongs inflicted by 16 years of military rule" (El Bakri 1995, 207). Nonetheless, the SWU alienated progressive women who were not members of the CPS, or who were not guaranteed to follow the party line. The activities of the group during the early days of the popular uprising were limited to holding public meetings where the main speaker was Fatima Ibrahim. Discussions covered underdevelopment, the nature of democracy, and critique of the transitional government, with limited references to women's gender-specific interests (El Bakri 1995, 208).[15] The SWU did not cover many of the issues related to family life, marriage, or domestic division of labor between women and men, given that these were considered controversial. The SWU did not reflect critically on what religion meant concerning women's human rights and some members argued that Sudanese women needed "an enlightened interpretation of Islam" (El Bakri 1995, 208–9).[16] The movement avoided any discourse that might potentially offend the masses (Hale 1996).

In the same period, Islamist women's organizations flourished, especially in urban areas. Some of the sectarian parties, such as the Umma Party, called for establishing a national women's organization in 1985 to articulate the interests of women. Differences, including over whether or not to include women who collaborated with the Numeiry regime, hampered attempts to establish this organization (personal communication with an Umma Party woman leader, Cairo, 1998).

In short, during the 1980s, as El Bakri (1995) has argued, the women's movement was in a state of crisis. No individual or collective voice was raising women's issues, except in the interest of some political forces. The majority of women remained outside organized political activity in the women's movement and in political parties. Government policies did not give adequate consideration to gender issues. Rising Islamism appealed to many young urban women, and the existing women's groups were unable to address women's issues or to transform women into a critical political force (El Bakri 1995, 199–200).

This coincided with what the late Suad Ibrahim Ahmed called "politics, God forbids," which prevailed among activists in the women's movement after the 1985 uprising. This was the result of al-Nimeiry regime's denouncement of party politics and activism, and because of the general social tendency to look negatively at women's participation in politics (Ahmed 1997).

Women provided support for male activists and politicians within the family (interview with Mubarak El-Mahdi, Cairo, July 1998) and played organizational roles in some of the urban-based left-wing political organizations (interview with Abdel Aziz Daf'allah, Cairo, April 17, 1999; Sirag 1999).

The peace sponsored a number of meetings and workshops after 1985, either formally, in collaboration between the NANS and the SPLM/SPLA, or informally in academic fora in Ethiopia, the United States, and Norway. The first series of meetings included the Ambo workshop and the meeting of the forces of the uprising, "all party working group" in January of 1988, the February 1987 Wilson Institute meeting in Washington, and the Interactive Peace Meeting in Harare in 1988 (Bagadi 1989, 110). All these efforts aimed at preparing for convening a constitutional conference. However, activists in the women's movement were not part of this process, and the issue of women's participation surfaced only occasionally. Elsewhere I examined the outcomes of these meetings using gender analysis (N. Ali 1999a). The post-1989 opposition politics constituted an extension of the post-*Intifada* coalition politics that addressed peace, democracy, and famine.

This chapter included a brief discussion of nationalism, Islamism, and social movement politics of the 1980s from a gender perspective. It also provided background information on the origins of Sudanese political parties and modern women's organizing. This history and the structures, institutions, and social relations that became dominant in Sudan as a result have contributed to the shaping of exile politics in the 1990s and early 2000s, among other factors. I discuss this in the next chapter.

NOTES

1. In recent decades, artists such as Mohamed A. Bakry, Abbakar A. Ismail, and Khalid Kodi haved used their art to dismantle aspects of Old Sudan artistic and other expressions. A discussion of this work is important but warrants a separate article or book.

2. For an elaborate account of the approach of British colonial officers and later British women to female genital cutting in Sudan and how British colonialism addressed the practice, see Boddy (2007).

3. Like many others, Berridge (2015) cautions against the uncritical use of the binary oppositions of modern versus traditional forces.

4. All those who signed the February 1989 army memorandum to the Prime Minister were dismissed from service following the NIF coups. According to the estimates of General Abdel Rahman Said (head of the Legitimate Command and member of the NDA Leadership Council at the time of research), the NIF government dismissed over 2,500 officers, and more than 20,000 soldier from other ranks (cited in Qa'ud 1998, 31). Similarly, the government reportedly replaced 20,000 civil service employees by NIF members and supporters (Wenger 1991, 6). By 1994, the government had dismissed about 40,000 civil servants, including hundreds of trade unionists, university lecturers, judges, workers, and diplomats (Qau'd 1999, 32).

5. Seventy-five percent of the musical library in the Sudan broadcasting and TV corporations was destroyed, on the premise that these contradicted Islamic principles. According to the director of the National Broadcasting Corporation, "a big change has occurred as to the nature of programmes, where it is easy to realise the Islamic bearing in programmes, specially political and cultural programmes. That is why we removed so called religious programmes" (cited in Qa'ud 1998, 34).

6. Conflicts also caused internal displacement for a vast number of the population. The US Committee for Refugees specified Sudan as having the largest internally displaced population in the world (SCIO 1999).

7. In his book *Azmat al-Islam al-Siyassi* (The Crisis of Political Islam), H. Ali (1991, 274) argues that the ascendance of progressive forces will force the Islamists to develop their programs—like what took place in Latin America with the emergence of liberation theology.

8. For an analysis of why middle- and lower-middle-class women in an urban setting (Cairo) chose to wear the veil in the 1980s, see Macleod (1990).

9. The regime also used non-coercive means of conscription, by convincing young male students (through the mass media) of the rewards of what they considered martyrdom.

10. Some of the women's organizations, such as the SWU, consider *zar* primitive (Hale 1996).

11. Mariam al-Mahdi has been active within the Umma Party and within the wider opposition since the 1990s. She spent several years in NDA-held areas in Eastern Sudan.

12. The material on USAP has been compiled from a KII with Abdoun Agaw, representative of USAP in the NDA executive office at the time of initial research, on July 27, 1997, in-depth interviews and public lectures by USAP leaders.

13. There is limited research on the movements addressed and about the politics of the 1980s. As such, this section draws extensively on interviews with leaders and activists in New Sudan groups. I also draw upon Bashir (1980).

14. I use the term "women's movement" in this book to refer to the collective action of Sudanese women interested in achieving gender equality and women's human rights.

15. El-Bakry (1995) and Hale (1996) provide a thorough analysis of the programs of the Sudan Women's Union, the National Women's Front, and the Umma Party women's secretariat.

16. SWU members, especially Fatima Ibrahim, Chair of SWU, maintained the same position in exile.

Chapter Four

Gendered Discourses and Practices of the Sudanese Opposition in Exile

Whenever I think of Sudan's opposition politics in exile in the 1990s and early 2000s, I remember the opening lines of Charles Dickens's classic *A Tale of Two Cities*:

> It was the best of times, it was the worst of times, it was the age of wisdom, it was the age of foolishness, it was the epoch of belief, it was the epoch of incredulity . . . it was the spring of hope, it was the winter of despair, we had everything before us, we had nothing before us, we were all going direct to Heaven, we were all going direct the other way.[1]

Compared to more recent attempts to unify Sudan's opposition around a transformative agenda, which intensified in 2013, 2014, and 2015, the 1995 Conference of Fundamental Issues was a landmark in the history of the Sudanese opposition in exile and in Sudan's history. As I discuss in the introduction, the Asmara conference resolved, at least discursively, issues that haunted the country since it achieved political independence in 1956. It affirmed the secular nature of the state. It included a commitment to ending political and economic marginalization. It also committed to redefining Sudan's identity and to ending cultural hegemony. The Asmara Resolutions favored a united Sudan but affirmed the right of the people of South Sudan to self-determination.

Similarly, despite splits and conflict within the NDA, in the Alliance's second conference, held in Massawaa, Eritrea, in 2000, under the motto of "stop the war and build a new Sudan," the opposition produced "a historic document," in the words of Mansour Khalid (2003, 396), who was member of the NDA's executive office. *The Massawaa Declaration* affirmed the voluntary unity of Sudan based on the recognition of religious, cultural, and political diversity; prohibition of forming political parties on religious bases; and of the use of religion for political ends. The NDA committed to good governance based on respect for human rights, the rule of law, and separation of powers. The resolutions of the conference favored decentralization with the aim of ending the hegemony of the center of power on Sudan's peripheries. It recognized equality between citizens regardless of religion, race, or gender. It also adopted affirmative action to end the impact of marginalization on women. In his speech at the Massawaa conference, the late Dr. John Garang described the NDA as "the greatest achievement of the Sudanese people in their struggle for a just peace and a qualified unity" (Garang 2000). In that sense, it was, to a great extent, *the best of times.*

Yet, in many ways, it was also *the worst of times.* The NDA excluded women from its leadership structures,[2] and the resolutions of the conference curtailed women's human rights enshrined in international human rights conventions, including the Convention on the Elimination of All Forms of Discrimination Against Women (CEDAW) on religious basis.

Article 5, which contained the only reference to women in the Asmara Resolutions, was in the section on the relationship between religion and politics:

> The NDA undertakes to preserve and promote the *dignity* of the Sudanese woman, and affirms her role in the Sudanese national movement and her rights and duties as enshrined in international instruments and covenants *without prejudice to the tenets of prevailing religious and noble spiritual beliefs.* (Final Communiqué of the Conference of Fundamental Issues, Asmara, June 1995, 1.B.5; emphasis mine)

In the years that followed the Asmara conference, much of the activism of women's organizations, women politicians, and activists in exile (myself included) centered on the need to reword Article 5. Women activists and politicians, however, perceived the NDA as a homogenous entity. These critics did not ask why the collective position of NDA member parties undermined women's human rights. Critics also did not take into account that all fundamental issues were gendered, and as such, focusing on Article 5 or women's participation was not enough.

This chapter examines the discourse expressed in the texts, narratives, and practices of the Sudanese opposition in exile in the 1990s and early 2000s from a gender perspective. I document the development and consolidation of the NDA in exile. I then analyze the discourses of NDA member parties in themes, but I focus specifically on the Umma Party and the Democratic Unionist Party (DUP), given that these two parties objected to a full commitment to women's human rights enshrined in international human rights convention during the time of research. The chapter explores *how* and *why* the entire, diverse opposition *compromised* these rights. I finally examine the place of gender in relation to what the opposition defined as "fundamental issues."

INSTITUTIONALIZING THE NDA IN EXILE: EXCLUDING WOMEN

In order to fully comprehend the gender politics of the Sudanese opposition in exile in the 1990s and early 2000s, it is important to understand the process that culminated in the establishment of the NDA. Following the 1989 coup, representatives of opposition political parties, trade unions, and the "legitimate command" of the Sudanese army established the NDA in Sudan in September of the same year. Party leaders and trade unionists detained in the Kober prison drafted the NDA's charter, which they circulated in prison.[3] The charter identified the NDA's objectives as overthrowing the NIF (later NCP) regime, restoring multi-party democracy, revitalizing the economy, and safeguarding individual and collective freedoms enshrined in international human rights conventions. The charter provided for an interim period after the overthrow of the regime where member parties would work toward these objectives.

The process was exclusively male. Some of the political leaders I interviewed said women did not take part in drafting the NDA's charter because male politicians developed the charter in prison. The charter found its way out of Kober prison and into the hands of trade union leaders and other political activists. At the time, there were limited efforts to involve women in forming the NDA. According to a trade union leader I interviewed, he and another trade union leader secretly contacted veteran politician and head of the Sudanese Women's Union Fatima Ahmed Ibrahim. The first Sudanese female parliamentarian, Ibrahim was a key opponent to the Numeiry regime between 1972 and 1985. She was also active after the overthrow of the Numeiry regime in 1985. The two trade unions leaders asked Ibrahim to sign the charter "on behalf of Sudanese women." They also asked her to share the document with leaders of women's organizations not associated with the NIF/NCP regime, and to gather their feedback. However, Ibrahim asked to sign on behalf of the Sudanese Women's Union (SWU) instead. The two activists promised to consult other opposition leaders on this issue, and to get in touch with her again, but they disappeared, reportedly for security reasons. (One of the two trade union leaders narrated this story in the presence of the author and of Ibrahim; Asmara, Eritrea, March 8, 1998.) Ibrahim argued the reason the two trade union leaders did not follow up with her was due to a "conspiracy" against her and against the SWU.

Political activists and leaders of parties and movements started to leave the country as early as July 1989 to avoid persecution at the hands of the NIF regime. By the early 1990s, it was clear that a transnational political community was evolving outside Sudan, especially in Egypt, Ethiopia, and Western Europe, particularly in the United Kingdom. This corresponded with an exodus of population to neighboring countries as a result of war and because of political oppression and deteriorating economic and social conditions.

SPLM/A leaders and members had been in exile, mainly in Ethiopia, since 1983/1984, but moved to Kenya following the fall of the Mengistu regime in Ethiopia. A large number of South Sudanese were forced out of their areas when the war erupted in 1983. Some were displaced into large Northern cities. Others became refugees in neighboring countries or in Europe and North America.

Once in exile, party leaders started building political structures and institutions. The opposition held several meetings during the first part of the 1990s, which culminated in the Asmara conference. Those included, but were not limited to, meetings in Addis Ababa in July 1990 and March 1991, London in January and February 1991, Cairo in 1992, Nairobi in 1993, and Asmara in 1994. These meetings helped the opposition build consensus on controversial issues such as governance in a democratic Sudan, the relationship between religion and politics, and the right to self-determination for the people of South Sudan. These meetings also helped strengthen the ties between the key opposition movements, including with the SPLM/A. Women were absent from these meetings, and gender equality was not part of the conversations.

Opposition leaders who took part in the Addis Ababa 1991 meeting, for example, did not even recognize the absence of women. The meeting that followed, however, noted women's absence, and the final communiqué of the meeting emphasized the need for women's participation and of a forum for women activists (interview with Nagib al-Khair, head of the NDA's High Coordinating Preparatory Committee for the Asmara Conference, Cairo, July 6, 1998). The meetings defined the leadership and structure of the NDA, and identified the fundamental issues for the opposition and for Sudan.

The form that the NDA in exile had taken by 1995 and up to the signing of the Comprehensive Peace Agreement (CPA) between the GOS and the SPLM/A in 2005, the signing of the Cairo Agreement between the NDA and the GOS in the same year, and the signing of the Eastern Sudan Peace Agreement between the Eastern Front and the GOS a year later, was the result of a prolonged process of negotiation and compromise between heterogeneous political forces. As I argued above, these political parties and movements were formed in different eras and had different ideologies and conflicting interests.

The overall stand of the opposition on women's human rights and gender equality was reminiscent of the position of South Africa's African National Congress in its early years. According to McClintock,

> While the language of the ANC was the *inclusive* language of National Unity, the Congress was in fact *exclusive* and hierarchical, ranked by an upper house of chiefs (which protected traditional patriarchal authority through descent and filiation), a lower house of representatives (all male) and an executive (always male). (1997, 380; emphasis in original)

It is important to note the different histories, context, and nature of the NDA and the NCA. Nonetheless, McClintock's description resonates with the NDA, which constituted "an old boys' club" that was insensitive to women's concerns or gender equality (Hassan 1993, 22).

The structure of the NDA comprised the Leadership Council, an executive office, and the General Congress. Mohamed Osman al-Mirghani, head of the DUP, was Chair of the Leadership Council, and Mubark al-Mahdi, initially the head of the Umma Party in exile, was Secretary General and head of the executive office of the NDA. The executive office had six secretariats. The alliance appended an office for women's affairs to the Secretariat for Organization and Administration. Not all parties had representatives in the Executive Office until July 1997, and until that time—when the Sudan National Alliance/Sudan Alliance Forces (SNA/SAF) put forward a woman representative (myself) in its slot in the executive office—the executive office was exclusively male.

While membership in the NDA's congress was open to "duly authorised representatives of the NDA political entities and trade unions, independent national personalities and women" (NDA, June 1995), the position of women remained vague. Although the congress had specified five seats for women, it did not specify any criteria for women's participation. Women's organizations in exile criticized the NDA for allocating only five seats (on paper) for women in its congress, the Secretary General of the NDA thought five seats were sufficient for women,

> The NDA's position on women has always been very clear. The Asmara declaration has clearly secured the position of women in the future of the Sudan. It has noted the absence of women in the conference and decided that five seats[4] should be allocated to the women in the NDA congress outside the party quotas. It has allocated a secretariat for women to be transitionally under the supervision of the Organization and Administration Secretariat until it is adequately established. (Office of the Secretary General, NDA, statement posted on sudanese@list.msu.edu, August 3, 1997)

Other NDA leaders confirmed that appending the women's bureau to the Secretariat for Organization and Administration was a temporary arrangement, and that the bureau would have the status of a full secretariat once it became functional. The bureau remained inactive, and the structures of the NDA remained male dominated until member parties of the NDA returned to Sudan after signing the Cairo Agreement.

Leaders of the NDA argued that women's lack of representation in NDA structures was because *women* did not agree on a criterion for participation. However, it was the *parties and movements* in the NDA that did not agree on a criterion for women's representation.

As was the case with the ANC during its first thirty years, where women were active at the grassroots levels as women, workers, and as blacks, but excluded from leadership structures (McClintock 1997, 380),[5] women's lack of representation in NDA structures in exile was contrary to the reality of women's activism and resistance in exile and in non-government-held areas as discussed in chapter 6 (also see Abdelaziz 2013). Women were also active in government-controlled areas inside Sudan in the NDA and in independent women's groups (see Anis 2000, 2002, and Al-Hussein and al-Shykh, 1997, 1995).

Unlike the ANC's experience, however, the position of the NDA on women's rights and gender equality did not change substantially even after women's groups became active in exile after the Asmara conference. Although the NDA sought to ensure women's participation in committees such as the committee for humanitarian affairs in Cairo (established in 1996), the committee for human rights in Cairo (established in 1995), and in committees to support the NDA's broadcasting station (established in 1995), this did not constitute a policy of the Alliance.

Instead, advocacy by women and women's groups associated with the opposition resulted in brief references to the importance of women's participation in a number of NDA communiqués after 1998. For example, the communiqué of the March 1998 meeting included a section that acknowledged the "heroic" roles of women in "the national struggle" against oppression in Sudan, and that recommended women's "effective participation" in the NDA at all levels (Communiqué of the NDA Leadership Council Meeting, Asmara, March 18–20, 1998, Article 1.iii).

As in other communiqués, the language of the above communiqué was rhetorical and focused on the non-controversial issue of women's participation in "all NDA units." The text suggested women should participate in NDA leadership structures because of their role in opposing the GOS, and not because this was their right.

In August 1998, the NDA took a further step and devoted one (of eighteen) paragraphs in a communiqué to women:

The NDA commends the struggle of Sudanese woman in and outside [Sudan], and her courageous stand in the face of the unjust policies of the regime in Khartoum. [The NDA] looks forward to the establishment of a national women's organisation . . . [and] to the drafting of a charter that embodies [women's] aspirations. . . . [The NDA] affirms its commitment to the representation of women in the . . . NDA organs. (NDA, Cairo Declaration, Communiqué of the Leadership Council Meeting, Cairo, August 15–17, 1998)

The NDA's discourse on women's representation was less problematic compared to its discourse on women's human rights. Progressive and sectarian parties alike agreed on the importance of women's participation in the structures of the NDA, but disagreed on the criteria for choosing women representatives. The DUP, for example, took a firm stand against changing Article 5, but supported women's participation in NDA structures. Dr. Faruk Ahmad Adam, then representative of the DUP in the NDA's executive office, who later joined the NCP, told me,

Despite women's honourable stand against the oppression of the NIF, the role of women in political decision-making within the NDA almost does not exist. This is a shortcoming and a big weakness that we acknowledge. For us it is a relief that these days there is an extensive debate within political parties around how to solve this problem. Because practically everybody now acknowledges that the role of women in the NDA is still weak. (In-depth interview, Cairo, July 12, 1998)

The secretary for women's affairs in the DUP also said,

We have women lawyers and women who have advanced skills, just like men. So they should participate at all levels. Our [DUP] leadership confirmed there was no problem with promoting women through the party to the NDA leadership levels. We only need to put this into action. (Interview with Magda Khogali, London, April 19, 1999)

The DUP put some of these commitments into action, and so did the Umma Party. During preparations for the NDA second conference, the DUP appointed a woman in the preparatory committee, and the Umma Party included a woman in the NDA secretariat. Al-Sadiq al-Mahdi, Chair of the Umma Party, initiated a discussion on women's representation in the NDA's Leadership Council meeting in July 1997. Al-Mahdi cited the example of the Islamic Republic of Iran, where women participated in big numbers in the elections (interview with Salah Galal, Director of Umma Party office, Cairo, April 19, 1998).

The Umma Party in exile took several steps to ensure women's participation in leadership structures of the party (interview with Salah Galal, Cairo, April 19, 1998). A woman chaired the opening panel of the Umma Party

conference held in Asmara in April 1998. The final declaration of the conference emphasized the need for a national organization for women, and the
need to mobilize women to "enrich" the work of the NDA (Communiqué of
the Umma Party Conference, Asmara, February 1998). Several female members of the Umma Party were active in Egypt and Eritrea. Dr. Mariam al-
Mahdi, who became deputy to the head of the Umma Party in 2014, spent
several years in Eritrea and in non-government-held areas in Eastern Sudan.[6]

When the Umma Party established a center in Egypt in early 1998, wom-
en played key roles in organizing high-profile functions. For example, in
1998 the center hosted an event in memory of more than forty secondary
school boys, forcibly conscripted by the GOS to fight the SPLM/A in South
Sudan. The majority of the students drowned in the Nile while trying to
escape a camp in Eilefoon in April 1998. Women's involvement in organizing this event was strongly connected with ideas of motherhood. In other
events, such as a seminar that focused on the Eritrean-Ethiopian conflict in
summer 1998, very few women were invited.

Interviewees from both the Umma Party and DUP said women's exclusion from NDA structures was the result of culture, traditions, and customs
that impeded women's full participation. As such, some interviewees who
were members of the DUP recommended "positive discrimination" for wom-
en. However, interviewees saw this positive discrimination not as part of a
whole strategy to transform these cultures and traditions, but as an intervention to enhance women's participation *while preserving cultures and traditions.*

Interviewees from the Umma and DUP also argued that the lack of senior
women politicians qualified to assume leadership positions had hampered
women's representation in NDA leadership structures. Eventually, however,
representatives of political parties increasingly accused women of failing to
build consensus on how they should be represented in the NDA. For example, at the Conference for Human Rights in the Transition in Sudan, Kampala, Uganda, 1999 (attended by the author), Faruk Ahmed Adam made the
above argument. The NDA's secretary general made a similar claim in a
statement circulated by his office online in 1999.

As stated earlier, there were a few exceptions. In 1996, for example, the
NDA leadership granted observer status in the NDA Leadership Council to
Fatima Ahmed Ibrahim. Although women's groups did not object to her
appointment, and although one of the groups in Cairo (the Women's Forum)
nominated her as representative for women in the NDA, Ibrahim's membership was viewed suspiciously by the Sectarian parties. A member of the CPS
leadership,[7] Ibrahim's membership was considered a tactic that the CPS
wanted to employ in order to monopolize the NDA. The NDA Secretary
General did not consider Ibrahim's position within the NDA *a right* (although several women's groups supported Ibrahim), but as "an exception, *a*

courtesy, the Sudanese way in order to avoid embarrassment, given that [Ibrahim] had insisted on joining the NDA meeting held in January 1996" (interview with Mubarak al-Mahdi, NDA Secretary General, *al-Khaleej*, September 28, 1998).

As a result, it was easy for the two sectarian parties to suspend Ibrahim's membership when the Sudan TV broadcasted a video in summer 1998, which showed Ibrahim on a visit to the SPLA camps in non-government-held areas. The video, which documented Ibrahim's visit, ended up in the hands of Sudanese National Intelligence and Security Service. It showed Ibrahim criticizing the NDA and making abusive comments against the leaders of the Umma Party and the DUP. As a result, representatives of the Umma Party and DUP in the NDA demanded that the NDA suspend Ibrahim's membership in the NDA. They argued that Ibrahim "violated the minimum consensus" stipulated in the Asmara 95 resolutions within the NDA (interview with the NDA Secretary General, *al-Haya*, September 28, 1998). This incident highlighted the importance of institutionalizing women's participation in political structures as a right.

Later in this chapter I examine why the NDA excluded women from its institutions in the 1990s, despite the existence of an active women's movement in Sudan since the 1940s. It is important at this point, however, to examine another issue that dominated the post-1995 political scene, that is, the curtailment of the human rights of women on religious basis, mainly in Article 5 of the Asmara Resolutions.

COMPETING DISCOURSES ON CEDAW AND ARTICLE 5

As discussed above, the Asmara 1995 declaration was unique compared to previous and subsequent political agreements that addressed the Sudanese crisis in that, among other factors, it included a commitment by all its signatory parties to the separation between religion and politics. The declaration also endorsed all international human rights conventions without reservations, but it restricted the NDA's commitment to women's human rights on religious basis. This lack of full commitment to human rights and women's rights has shaped post-CPA politics in Sudan and added one more reason for Southern Sudanese to vote overwhelmingly for secession in 2011.

The NDA's commitment to separation between the state and religion was a great development, especially in light of Sudan's history, and in light of political attitudes toward secularism in other countries in the neopatriarchal Middle East, where the opposition between the Islamists on one hand, and the secularists (nationalist and left wing) on the other hand, has often been over political, not religious or moral, issues (Sharabi 1988)—although such difference is often constructed as a conflict over moral issues.

Discourses on secularism in Middle Eastern societies were prominent during the era of *al-Yaqza* (the awakening), between 1798 and 1941. Some thinkers argued that a merger between state and religion was contrary to the Islamic traditions. They wanted to replace the Islamic *Khilafa* (succession rule) with secular nationalism that is based on equality regardless of religion or ethnicity. Thinkers like al-Kawakby (1854–1902) considered separation between religion and politics *a return to the real religion*. These reformers also called for reform in the status of women. As a reaction to Western stereotypes of Muslim women, for example, Egyptian reformer Gasim Amin (1863–1908) called for the unveiling and education of women (Barakat 1996, 404–7).

In Sudanese politics, secularism continues to be a taboo subject. The late al-Khatim Adlan (founder of *Haq*, an opposition movement that was not a member in the NDA) wrote that secularism was "the S word in Sudanese politics" in an online discussion. In the context of Sudanese exile politics and opposition discourse, secularism is generally understood as advocating *the separation between religion and politics*.

After the 1964 uprising, the wider left movement was on the rise due to its role in overthrowing the Abbud military regime (1958–1964), and there were debates on establishing a secular constitution for the country. The sectarian leaders succeeded in silencing secularist claims, however, when they excluded the CPS from the parliament, claiming that one of the CPS members uttered abusive discourse against Prophet Mohamed in a public rally. The Numeiry regime further marginalized secularism in politics, especially toward the end of the 1970s, when the regime started to build alliances with the DUP, the Umma Party, and the Muslim Brotherhood. Until it became part of the New Sudan discourse in the 1980s, secular politics was elitist. John Voll (1983, 135) was right to assert that the Islamist "resurgence" did not replace secularist institutions by Islamic ones. In light of the above, the Asmara Resolutions did constitute a turning point, yet this new point was gendered as male and was characterized by a lack of total commitment to women's human rights enshrined in international human rights conventions.

Al-Faqra Khamsa (Article 5)

As in other NDA documents, the Asmara Resolutions *acknowledged* women's roles and interests, but did not *commit* to women's human rights. It emphasized women's *karama* (dignity), not *citizenship, interests*, and *human rights*. The word *karama* is vague and is also open to diverse interpretations, including interpretations that encourage domesticity and discrimination against women to preserve their dignity. It draws parallels between NDA discourse on one hand and nationalist discourses in other parts of the world on the other.

By limiting the NDA's commitment to women's rights on religious basis, Article 5 not only undermined key tenets of the CEDAW and later the African Women's Rights Protocol, it also contradicted preceding NDA commitments to equal citizenship rights of all Sudanese. Opposition parties organized in the NDA agreed on the separation between religion and politics without reservations. As such, Article 5 represented a draw back in the commitments of the opposition to these principles. Article 5 also contradicted the NDA charter, which emphasized equal citizenship rights and equality before the law regardless of gender.

> Laws shall guarantee *full equality of citizens* on the basis of citizenship, respect for religious beliefs and traditions and without discrimination on grounds of religion, race, *gender* or culture. Any law contrary to the foregoing stipulation shall be null and void and unconstitutional. (Article 2.i.a,[8] NDA Charter, version endorsed at the Conference of Fundamental Issues, Asmara, June 1995; emphasis mine)

The charter's reference to respect for religious beliefs, however, was the basis upon which NDA leaders (in the Umma Party and the DUP) who objected the NDA's full commitment to CEDAW claimed that this would *violate their religious rights.*

Many states and parties in Africa and the Middle East share this contradiction between general constitutional arrangements that firmly endorse women's rights on one hand, and lack of ratification of CEDAW (or ratification with reservations) or discrimination within the law on the other hand. Whether in secular (liberal, nationalist, and socialist) or religious theocratic regimes, with the exception of the former Northern Yemen (cf. Molyneux 1991), personal status laws were always derived from Islamic shari'a, Christian law, or discriminatory customary law (Hijab 1988; Kandiyoti 1991). Personal status laws often derive from shari'a and regulate issues of "marriage, divorce, maintenance, child custody and inheritance" (Moghadam 1994, 144). They generally reflect and reinforce male domination. They also often contradict clauses that prohibit discrimination on the basis of gender in constitutions. Post-1983 Sudan is no exception.

In the case of Article 5, while reservations applied to women from different religions, a number of non-Muslim leaders argued that they did not want to violate Muslim (male) NDA leaders' religious freedom by challenging Article 5, especially that those leaders have already made wide concessions in other areas.

The discourses of NDA member parties and movements on women's human rights were diverse and some discourses shifted over time. While I start with the discourses of progressive groups, I will focus on the narratives of the groups that objected to commitment to women's human rights enshrined in CEDAW as these discourses shed light on debates about the relationship between feminism and nationalism. Afterward, I consider how historically marginalized groups discussed women's rights in ways that marked their difference from the *Northern political establishment*.

PROGRESSIVE GROUPS: THE HISTORIC BARGAIN

The positions of diverse movements and parties within the NDA ranged from integrating a critique of Article 5 into the political agenda of the group (the SNA/SAF) and support for the "demands of women's groups who support the NDA" (the CPS), to repudiating any change to Article 5 (the DUP and Umma Party). The SPLM/A emphasized the importance of changing Article 5 and the USAP argued that the party could support *Northern* women's groups if they sought to change the clause. The Beja and the SFDA were silent on the issue, although interviewees from both groups expressed a progressive stand on the issue in the interviews. Generally speaking, and as I elaborate in the next chapter, New Sudan activists emphasized the importance of acknowledging the *specificity of the issues* facing women in various parts of Sudan, while emphasizing the *universality of rights*. All New Sudan forces have either openly or subtly adopted a stand against Article 5.

Al-Sanossi, a former SNA/SAF executive in Cairo, argued committing to CEDAW was essential for ensuring freedom and emancipation for all: "We have no reservations on CEDAW as there is no religious, cultural nor historical contradiction that makes me support Article 5, which denies women their full rights" (interview with Shams E. Al-Sanossy, Cairo, May 4, 1998).

Daniel Kodi, then representative of the SPLM/A in the Middle East, said "a woman is a human being, and all human beings should be treated equally. Religious constraints and traditions that differentiate between women and men should not prevail" (in-depth interview, Cairo, April 8, 1998). Pagan Amom, another SPLM/A leader interviewed for this research, stressed this point too.

The discourse of one CPS leader reveals the dilemma between starting from the perspectives of the masses on one hand, and the need to eliminate worn-out traditions on the other hand:

> We believe that we should start from where the masses stand, and eventually raise the consciousness of those masses. We do not easily surrender to the power of out-dated traditions or that of the sectarian forces, but we are also not anarchists, we are not arrogant toward the masses, nor do we consider liberation a personal issue. We support women's social, economic and political rights without reservation but not in a crude manner. Our position is that we support women in their demands concerning participation in the NDA and changing Article 5. We have no reservations on these issues. (Interview with Salah Abu Gabr, Head of CPS office in Cairo, Egypt, May 6, 1998)

The CPS, SNP, SFDA, USAP, and the Beja favored the change of Article 5. Some of the interviewees argued that marginalization of women resulted from their absence from the Asmara conference. Some of the progressive leaders also argued that the current position of the two major sectarian parties on Article 5 was the result of their desire to maintain an Islamic outlook even though they had agreed to the separation between religion and the state.

Al-Shafie Khider, CPS representative in the NDA's executive office and then Secretary for Organization and Administration, said,

> Women's issues are at the back of everyone's mind in discussions on the relationship between religion and politics. Loud objections to the separation between religion and politics are always related to women: statements like, "people should not gulp down our authenticity, artificial Western civilization . . . etc." all evolve around terms like "girls have gone astray," "girls are wearing trousers," "honour" and the rest of the NIF talk. Even those committed to the separation between religion and politics link these issues to women. Those [who acknowledge women's rights] are a minority. This is manifested in that a conference attended by more than sixty [men] discussed the relationship between the state and religion and did not address woman's issues except at the very end. The issue was raised, from the angle of woman's relationship with the man: that is, "how is marriage going to be handled?" By the way, Article 5 was only discussed [in the Asmara meeting] in relation to marriage. (Interview, Cairo, April 14, 1998)

The positions of some NDA leaders were contradictory. Faruk Abu Eisa, spokesperson of the NDA, who was on the committee that *drafted* the Asmara declaration, wrote a paper in his capacity as Secretary General of the Union of Arab Lawyers in 1994. The paper reviewed different international conventions from the perspective of women's rights, and criticized Arab countries that made reservations on CEDAW on the basis of cultural specificity "to avoid commitment to the universality of human rights" (Abu Eisa 1994, 14). At the end of the article, Abu Eisa recommended that laws in the Arab world be consistent with international conventions, both in text and application, "to advance the status of women" (Abu Eisa 1994, 19).

Abu Eisa was member of the NDA Leadership Council as a representative of "independent national characters" at the time. Toward the end of 1995, he said they worded Article 5 in the way they did so as not to offend the leaders of "the two big parties." He said an alternative text that recognizes women's human rights "except in personal status matters" might have been the only possible alternative to the current format of the article, and that women could work on changing all this when back in Sudan (personal contact, November 1995).

If the stand of the progressive groups was against curtailing women's rights on religious basis, then why has the NDA accepted this position unanimously in June 1995? The above suggests that progressive groups and individuals that supported women's human rights compromised the rights of women in the bargain with sectarian parties over issues considered more "fundamental," such as the relationship between religion and politics, regardless of the leaders' position toward women's human rights and gender equality. Later in this chapter I further analyze this bargain.

Some of the NDA leaders, particularly those representing predominantly non-Muslim constituencies, saw Article 5 as solely relevant to Northern/ Muslim Sudanese. Abdoun Agaw, then representative of the USAP in the NDA Executive Office,[9] for example, stated, "[t]hat clause on the rights of women, [its] formulation took a long time to agree upon. I do not know whether those who objected to [commitment to women's human rights without reservations] would change their views in the future, or become even less willing to make any concessions. That is something that we leave to the next conference of the NDA" (interview in Cairo, May 18, 1997). Agaw further argued that,

> There are people who have been raising the [cultural] rights flag in the face of those who think that human rights should be universally applied without any special provisions. Some people try to attribute their objections to what they describe as religious dictates. As a non-Muslim, I think *it would be considered rude on my part to really try to challenge the stand of those people.* (Ibid.; emphasis mine)

With the exception of SPLM/A's official discourse on Article 5, many of the Southern Sudanese leaders argued that the major parties and communities in the North were better placed to challenge discrimination against women on the basis of religion if they wanted to. Some argued that emancipation of Southern Sudanese women was easier compared to their Northern Sudanese counterparts given that South Sudanese communities were more egalitarian.

Some of these movements compromised women's human rights in observation of the *cultural and religious* rights of *male* sectarian leaders.

SECTARIAN PARTIES: "THE WEST IMAGINED"

In the mid-1990s, both the Umma Party and DUP refused to change Article 5 or to commit to CEDAW without reservations. Both parties threatened to "open-up the Asmara resolutions"—including paragraphs on the relationship between religion and the state and on the right to self-determination for the people of South Sudan—for discussion and revision if the NDA decided to change Article 5. Representatives of the Umma Party in the NDA, for example, said the party had proposed amendments to the Asmara declaration and the NDA charter, and that they were prepared to discuss changing Article 5 once the NDA had incorporated the amendments they suggested in the charter and the declaration (Mubarak al-Mahdi, NDA Leadership Council meeting, March 1998; the late Lamia Habbani, representative of the Umma Party at the meeting of the NDA Women's Committee on Article 5; both meetings attended by the author).

At the second NDA conference in Massawa in 2000, the chair of the NDA and the president of the DUP, Mohamed Osman al-Mirghani, warned conference delegates that if they insisted on discussing Article 5, DUP would want to reconsider NDA's commitment to the right to self-determination for South Sudan. In that sense, as Deniz Kandiyoti (1991, 8) has argued, while discourses on "cultural authenticity" often construct the West as Other, such discourses often serve as mechanisms for social control. They attempt to conceal internal difference, social exclusion, and oppression on the basis of region, culture, ethnicity, or social class. Such discourses, argues Kandiyoti, "obliterate such divisions by demarcating the boundaries of the 'true' community and excluding the 'Other within'" (1991, 8).

The two parties were successful in ensuring other NDA member parties did not advocate for changing Article 5. One opposition leader, who supported a commitment to CEDAW without reservations, said changing Article 5 "will open the door for other, very serious changes. What would the women or men gain if the Umma [Party] insisted on revising commitments to the separation between religion and politics for example?" (personal communication, name withheld). This confirms my argument that gender issues were an integral part of the bargain between the progressive and New Sudan forces and the sectarian forces.

The Umma discourse on Article 5 has changed superficially over time. For example, former Prime Minister al-Sadiq al-Mahdi replied to a question on Article 5 when he gave the keynote speech at the Sudan Studies Association meetings in Cairo (June 11, 1997) by stating that "Islam does not discriminate against women." One year later, al-Mahdi expressed a different but ambiguous position. He argued in August 1998 that the issue of Article 5 is important and complex. While Article 5, in its current form, might contradict the possibility of obtaining full human rights for women, it is also difficult for us to change this clause. The reason is that the human rights conventions also *contain elements that contradict our religion* (addressing the Conference on the State and Higher Education in Sudan, Cairo, August 1998, attended by the author). In later discussions with some of the female participants at the conference, al-Mahdi suggested that women's groups develop a women's national charter because CEDAW encouraged "lesbianism, promiscuity and abortion [*sic*] . . . *things that we would not accept in our communities.*" These are serious charges given the overall conservative and homophobic atmosphere in and outside Sudan.

Members of the Umma Party and DUP interviewed for this research made similar claims to justify their objection to changing Article 5 or committing to women's human rights enshrined in international human rights conventions, including CEDAW. They constructed CEDAW as a "Western" product. They constructed the West as homogeneous and immoral. An important finding was that the majority who objected to NDA's commitment to CEDAW had never read the convention. Instead, they read Egyptian press reporting on the United Nations Fourth Conference on Women (the Beijing conference). A member of the Umma Party told me,

> The Egyptian newspapers and other media channels tackled the documents of the Beijing conference extensively. I personally am not a specialist in women's questions but I read these documents, or to be specific [I read] many writings about them in the newspapers, particularly [Beijing platform of action] which addressed *deviant practices* that people wanted to endorse during the conference. (Interview with the author, Cairo, 1998; name withheld)

Another member of the Umma Party said,

> I do not know the wording of this document [CEDAW], but it was talking about the right of woman to a system that grants the right to abortion and some other forms of conduct that *we name as deviant and immoral*, but that are accepted in *their* [Western] societies. They think that this should apply to all societies. *We have our own heritage as a nation. Muslim, Christian and pagan women* [in Sudan] have *consensus over one social system that Sudanese women never questioned.* Thus our references should not be international human rights conventions. We should take good things from these conventions, in a way that suits us and does not contradict with *our customs and traditions.* (Interview with the author, Cairo, 1998; name withheld)

Other interviewees also repeated distorted ideas about CEDAW, and confessed that they had not read the actual document. When I asked about the source of their information on CEDAW, some answered, "but, I followed what the Egyptian press had written about *mu'tamar bikin* [the Beijing Conference], and the International Conference for Population and Development."

The prevalent discourse in the Egyptian media on the UN conferences on women was hostile (Guenena and Wassef 1999; Abd el-Salam 1995). Islamist and some of the mainstream media condemned the Beijing Platform of Action. Islamists argued that the Beijing and ICPD resolutions were against Islam, and that the purpose of the Beijing Platform of Action was to strengthen Western hegemony.[10] In her critical review of the Islamist discourse on the Beijing conference, Abd el-Salam (1995) wrote that the Islamists had described the Beijing Platform of Action as "promiscuous, and argued that it recommended deviant behaviour and homosexuality. . . . [Islamists] argued this will ruin the family and [expose] Third World countries to foreign intervention" (Abd el-Salam 1995, 9).

Egyptian newspapers were also critical of the International Conference on Population and Development and its outcome document. Although Egypt hosted the conference, a CNN program that showed a barber circumcising a young Egyptian girl created backlash. Islamists argued that the outcome document of the ICPD encouraged promiscuity and sex outside of marriage because it allowed for abortion (Guenena and Wassef 1999, 49). The coverage seldom cited the actual documents. [11] In short, the dominant groups within the NDA refused to endorse CEDAW because of false constructions of the document by the Egyptian media, homophobia, and overall conservatism.

It was interesting that some of the newspapers and NIF members in Sudan made similar comments on the Beijing document.

> For those who read the documents of the [Beijing] conference, it is evident that this is not a women's rights conference as they claim. It is a conference that aims at destroying the family and changing society into one where sexual promiscuity prevails, where adolescents are accorded sexual rights, where abortion is encouraged, and where prostitution is considered a personal issue given that it is practised with women's consent. (*al-Sudan al-Hadith*, September 30, 1995)

Sumaia Abu Kashawa (1995), an NCP member who was the chair of the quasi-governmental Sudan Women's General Union, elaborated further,

> The same issues rose in the International Conference for Population and Development in Cairo are raised again, especially with regard to reproductive health and promiscuity. Western countries will not spare any effort, through their delegates and non-governmental organisations, in inserting their concepts in the [Beijing] document, in order to uniformly impose these [concepts] on every country. In that way, Western culture, and Western perception would form the basis of the New World Order. Third world countries, however, are conscious of this matter and are protesting the articles, which do not reflect their culture. (Abu Kashawa 1995, 8)

As is the case with discourses on authenticity versus "Westoxication" prevalent in other parts of the Third World, this discourse builds on prevalent views of the West, and adds to these views from the Islamist imagination. In this way, the government avoids any commitment to women's human rights that might undermine the prevalent order. Terms such as reproductive health and promiscuity are tactically placed together, as if they were interchangeable terms. Western countries and Western concepts are constructed as homogeneous and as antithetical to the equally homogeneous culture of Third World countries. Needless to say, the documents of the conference are neither circulated, nor directly cited in the text. The position of the Islamists toward the Beijing documents has been similar to that expressed in other countries (c.f. Abd el-Salam 1995; Afkhami and Friedel 1997). There are clear parallels between this discourse and the discourse of some opposition groups, particularly the Umma Party and the DUP.

The article in *al-Sudan al-Hadith* cited above continues as follows:

> The most dangerous issue is that [the Beijing Platform of Action] includes sections that are contradictory to family life. [It] perceives the woman as an individual and considers the family as a basic factor violating her rights. . . . The issue of early marriage is seen as a factor affecting girls' education negatively. [It also] emphasises women's economic independence regardless of any customs or traditions. (September 30, 1995)

This discourse is pointedly clear. It criticizes the focus on women as individuals but then replaces this with a focus on community, custom, and tradition as defined by the dominant gender/race/class.

Given the above, building coalitions with Egyptian feminists and feminist and women's organizations seeking to challenge Islamist and negative media discourses on women's human rights (cf. Guenena and Wassef 1999) would have strengthened the resistance of Sudanese women in exile (discussed in the next chapter). Yet with the exception of attending a few activities organized in solidarity with Sudanese women, there was limited collaboration and networking between the two movements!

In his article "Women of the West Imagined: The *Farangi* Other and the Emergence of the Woman Question in Iran," Tavakoli-Tariki (1994) has argued that the political and cultural encounter with the West in the context of colonialism has shaped the women's question in Iran. This included, for example, the production of the veil as a uniform for women, in order to mark the cultural, religious, and political difference of Iranian society. In the quote above, and in the narratives that will follow, objections to CEDAW were based on the way the women of the West are imagined in contemporary opposition discourse! This discourse is influenced by the dependent relationship with that West. It ossifies both Sudanese and Western culture.

In the various interviews, even when I pointed to the fact that what Moghadam (1994) calls the "three Ps: i.e., prostitution, promiscuity and pornography" were not in CEDAW, interviewees pointed to the "West," where they believed that CEDAW originated. The secretary for women's affairs in the DUP had the following to say on Article 5:

> We have reservations on the statement that "women should be treated according to international human rights conventions." I believe that religion is *a constant*, it does not change, but conventions are the work of human beings. So, *it is these conventions that should be changed.* Thus, we are not to recommend that our religion be replaced with *man-made laws.* Article 5 encom-

passes all religions. It stated that each one should follow what their religion tells them. I think that this is not a bad idea. I don't think that Article 5 limits women's freedom. For example, religion does not limit women's freedom to work. Yes it does limit women's freedom regarding *some things* that I think we agree as a Muslim community that it [should be limited]. Don't forget that the Sudanese are religious. We know what is going on around us. *When I now look at the position of women in the West, I thank God that I was raised up in the community where I grew up in. I can't walk naked in the street and think that this way I become equal to men.* To the contrary, this degrades women. (Interview with Magda Khogali, Secretary for Women Affairs, DUP, London, April 19, 1999)

When I asked Khogali what specific rights she was referring to she stated that

First of all these human rights conventions do not apply to us. These conventions include *many* rights that are open-ended (read loose). Islam granted us our *complete* rights. What more do we want? In my case I am an activist, I travel, work with men who are not first of kin. So I think this is my freedom. Polygamy is sometimes practised for moral reasons. If a woman is infertile, for example, the husband has to remarry *because Islam requires a big family.* This does not mean that this woman should be abandoned. It all depends on what one defines as freedom: is it complete freedom, or is it freedom that is limited to what everyone accepts? Other people could do what they want. As such, we can only reword Article 5 without changing its content. (Ibid.)

Similarly, the former secretary for women's affairs in the Umma Party office in Cairo stated that

Islam has dignified women, and if women were granted the rights accorded to them in Islam, we would not need any more rights, because adopting the international conventions endanger the coming generations. (Consultative meeting between the NDA Executive Office and women's groups in Cairo, May 3, 1998, attended by the author)

When I told Khogali (see above) that I thought CEDAW did not encourage using women in commercials and that it did not encourage a specific dress code she said,

And where do you think this convention came from? This is my own conviction. Islam favours women more than men. Here [in Europe] you can see that women are beaten. In our communities, men cannot beat women. Here the man does not have the right to divorce a woman unilaterally, but she can live with someone else [without marriage]. That is why the families are fragmented in the West. These things that they write (CEDAW . . . etc.) are just empty talk. For us, we conserve our society, and *we are better off than they are.* Hijab is there to protect us. This is my own conviction. In this respect, the position of

the DUP overlaps with mine. Until now, no one in DUP, including Sayed
Mohamed Osman al-Mirghani has told us what to say on Article 5. [12] (Interview with Magda Khogali, London, April 19, 1999)

Justifying the objections to recognizing women's full human rights enshrined
in international conventions, specifically CEDAW on the basis of the specificity of *our society and values*, is common in many narratives, even beyond
the Sudan. As stated above, this stems from an understanding that human
rights conventions constitute a purely Western product. The West is constructed as uniform and immoral, especially women. As Jayawardena has
written about the way Western women were constructed in colonized India,
in this discourse, Western women come across as "immodest in dress and
indulging in drinking and promiscuous behaviour" (1995, 9), a model from
which "our women" should be protected. A member of the committee that
drafted the Asmara Resolutions stated that,

> When we drafted [Article 5], we wanted to *preserve women's rights*. We
> differentiated between *women's public and private rights*. The public rights
> we made clear by emphasising equality, democracy, and citizenship rights. As
> for the private sphere, we in Sudan are a believing society, regardless of our
> religions. For us, personal affairs are based on religion and each group should
> tailor its personal status laws according to its own religious beliefs. In Islam
> we have personal status laws for family matters. The same applies to Chris-
> tianity and other beliefs. . . . The current text [of Article 5] can create some
> confusion. Of course there are some with no interest in religion or even with a
> stand against religion. Those would want to erase this article just because it has
> the word "religions" in it. This view might even go further and adopt civil
> marriage! This turns marriage into a contractual transaction, like any commer-
> cial company or trade. This is against all rights; as such marriage *does not
> protect the child, the family, morals, or fidelity*. Our societies, customs and
> traditions, do not permit certain practices that currently exist in Europe and in
> advanced countries. We do not permit those in our society. (Interview with the
> author, Cairo, 1998; name withheld)

Given the neopatriarchal nature of many Sudanese societies, power relations
within and outside the household often curtail women's freedom of choice,
including in matters of marriage and divorce. The law is usually biased
toward men. When I raised this point, I got the following response:

> There is no consensus on laws for divorce or on guardianship and polygamy,
> even in *fiqh* [Islamic jurisprudence]. . . . As for polygamy, women should have
> the legal right to choose to continue with their husbands or to leave them if
> they remarried. Because otherwise many problems arise, if you read *Roz el-
> Yusuf* magazine, you will see that men who adhere to religions that mandate
> compulsory monogamy for men can [have extramarital relations]. . . . There is
> more wisdom in Islam because the problem is not polygamy unless a man

practices it for selfish purposes or if he fancies a woman other than his wife for example. The wisdom behind polygamy is that if the wife is sick and the husband does not want to leave her but at the same time he has other human needs and rights, polygamy can preserve the existing family. This is better than destroying the existing family unit and building a new family. (Interview with Salah Galal, Cairo, April 19, 1998)

Other interviewees said debates over polygamy hid a desire to legalize polygamy for women. One interviewee said,

In my understanding of law if we argued for men's practice of polygamy we would be *preserving the family unit*. Given that the *mother* is the protector of the family and the of family's future, if women practised polygamy then one might not know the father of each of her children. As for men, even if one were polygamous, he would know whether a child is his. So, I support regulating polygamy, not abolishing it. A Sudanese [women's] charter can [regulate polygamy]. (Name withheld)

This discourse mobilizes the ideology of motherhood to justify the limiting of women's human rights and suggests that attempts to eradicate polygamy aim to legalize polygamy for women. Drawing upon similar constructions in a different era, with regard to another pillar of difference (race), can help illuminate this point.

While there are voices that draw upon claims of cultural specificity to legitimize the subordination of women, not many in the twenty-first century would try to support slavery, for example. However, in the 1920s this was not the case. When the colonial administration banned slavery, leaders of the Umma Party and DUP argued that slavery in Sudan was different from "conventional slavery." Those leaders argued that issuing freedom certificates to slaves had encouraged former female slaves to become prostitutes, and had led to laziness and alcoholism among former male slaves. These views were articulated in a memorandum presented to the Director of Intelligence in March 1925. The memo was signed by Sayed Abdel Rahman al-Mahdi (later the patron of the Umma Party), Sayed Ali al-Mirghani (later the patron of the Unionist Party and father to the current head of the party), and Sayed al-Sharif al-Hindi. Given the analogy between constructions of slaves in the 1920s and of women in the 1990s, I quote the document at length:

We find it our duty to advise you of our opinion on the issue of slavery in Sudan. . . . We have been following the government policy towards this class since the reconquest. [W]e cannot object to something over which the whole modern world has consensus. What concerns us is *that contemporary slavery in Sudan has nothing in common with conventional (slavery)*. The slaves who cultivate the land are in fact sharers with the landowners, and have got rights and privileges that distinguish them as a class of their own. Slave owners treat their slaves as if they were family members because they need their labour. You know . . . that labour is currently the most vital issue in Sudan, and that the government, the companies and the individuals involved in agricultural production need every possible hand if the [agricultural] projects are to succeed.

Government officials must have realised during the past few years that *most of the slaves who were freed have become useless. The women have become prostitutes and the men became addicts to alcohol and laziness.* For those reasons, we pledge the government to reconsider the logic *of issuing freedom certificates to people who consider that these documents free them of any responsibilities or commitments. Since those are not slaves in the way understood by international law, there is no need to issue freedom certificates to them. Unless these are to be handed to the landowners* . . . the policy of encouraging the slaves to quit agricultural labour and become beggars in towns, will only yield evil. We hope that the government will take all this into consideration and stop issuing certificates indiscriminately, unless a slave is able to prove mistreatment at the hands of his owner. (Memo from Sayed Ali al-Mirghani, Sayed al-Sharif al-Hindi, and Sayed Abd al-Rahman al-Mahdi to the Director of Intelligence in the colonial administration, March 6, 1925; reproduced in Nugud 1994, document no. 18: 363–364; emphasis and translation mine)

It is very difficult to conflate the institutions of neopatriarchy and slavery, given the ruthlessness inherent in the latter institution. Nonetheless, the above text shows the resemblance in constructions made to justify slavery in the 1920s, and those made to justify the limiting of women's human rights on religious bases in the 1990s.

Given the diverse positions of NDA parties on women's human rights, why have the NDA movements and parties *collectively* forsaken women's human rights? This was the result of the neopatriarchal nature of Sudanese politics, the nature of the alliance that developed in the 1990s, and the crisis of the Sudanese women's movement.

In line with the analysis furnished by El-Battahani (1997), it is important to revisit the nature and interests of various parties in the NDA in order to comprehend the reason behind taking a negative collective position on women's rights. The Umma Party and the DUP reflected the interests of agricultural capital and of merchant capital subsequently. Both parties relied on religious patriarchal sentiments in maintaining their wide base of supporters in rural areas of the Sudan. As such, they continuously won elections in the democratic eras. Maintaining the prevalent neopatriarchal system corresponds well with maintaining the authority of these groups. Although the CPS promoted women's rights to political participation since the 1950s, it tended to undertake a reformist stand toward the patriarchal gender norms prevalent in Northern and Central Sudan.

The SPLM/A, another transformative movement, expressed commitment to secularism although its stand on local customs affecting women is still unclear. The SNA was formed in the mid-1990s as an alliance between urban, mostly left-wing professionals, trade unionists, and former military cadres on one hand, and marginalized groups in the rural areas, women, and youth on the other hand. The movement has adopted a New Sudan agenda, with an expressed secular stand. In the interviews with members of the SNA and SPLM, however, there were members who thought that it was difficult to introduce radical changes in personal status laws, for example, without preparing the grounds for such change first.

The Beja Congress, the SFDA, and the SNP emerged out of formerly regional interest groups that were formed shortly after independence, but that transformed their agendas in the early 1990s, adopting New Sudan principles. Gradually, former supporters of the Umma Party in Darfur and Kordofan (Western Sudan) came to constitute an expanding base for the SFDA and the SNP. Similarly, the Beja Congress has expanded among the supporters of the DUP in Eastern Sudan. While the three groups have adopted the New Sudan agenda, including its secular component, the Beja Congress considers it risky to announce a program that subverts dominant gender norms at present given the extremely conservative nature of its constituency.

While some of the groups in the NDA shared strategic interests and were concerned with transforming the NDA, it was clear that what brought all these forces together was the desire to get rid of a common enemy, the NIF/NCP. Bringing such diverse forces together obviously involved *a bargain*. In fact, the Asmara conference was called the historic bargain.

This unity was *constructed* on a fragile base, however. Several interviewees said the Umma and DUP would part company with current allies as soon as the NIF was removed.[13] Some said the two parties were not committed to the separation between religion and politics, but that they used this as a tactic, as they were not going to be able to overthrow the NDA without coordination with other opposition parties.

The above suggests that the different positions on gender equality and women's human rights reflected ideological differences that became evident in the contest over women's human rights. Women's human rights (or the lack of commitment to women's human rights) played a role in temporarily preserving the opposition's *imagined* unity. The two sectarian parties argued that the call for endorsing CEDAW reflected CPS' tactics to promote its own vision of society.

When the communists say we do not want polygamy,[14] I believe this does not stem from a concern with women's rights. To the contrary, because the communists themselves, when it comes to commitment, I believe communism itself is *promiscuous* [*sic*], Communism at the end of the day means Marx and his ideas of communalism. Here we are not talking about one or two or three or a hundred women, this is left absolutely *loose*. As such, the issue is basically political because they have a stand against religion itself and not [necessarily against limiting women's rights on the basis of religion]. (Interview with the author, Cairo, 1998; name withheld; emphasis mine)

Hence compromising women's strategic interests was central to the historic bargain.

The tension over Article 5 and women's human rights soared in the second NDA conference. Although in contrast to the Asmara conference, there was wider women's participation in Massawaa, given that each party included at least two women in its delegation, the NDA collectively closed the discussion on women's human rights and on changing Article 5 once the chair of the NDA and leader of the DUP, Mohamed Osman al-Mirghani, threatened to revisit the article on self-determination for South Sudanese in the Asmara conference if the delegates insisted on discussing Article 5 as noted above.

In addition to the above, the opposition wanted to prove its authenticity at the time given that the NIF had consistently propagated an image of the exiled opposition as morally corrupt and has called the NDA "the five stars hotels opposition." It has used this tactic mainly to delegitimize the opposition. When I was conducting fieldwork in Cairo, the NIF obtained a copy of a video showing a party held at the end of the Umma Party's conference, held in Eritrea in February 1998. The tape, which showed al-Mahdi celebrating with other participants and with the participation of an Eritrean band—was aired on Sudan TV. Subtitles read as follows: "This is how the struggle should be like."

The Sudanese president, Omar al-Bashir, inaugurated the new oil pipelines during the second half of 1999 by inviting the opposition to quit its practices of "sipping beer" in international capitals and to return to Sudan. The president further advised opposition leaders to "cleanse themselves (from sin) in the Red Sea" before returning home. In a society that is becoming increasingly conservative, these charges were considered damaging by the opposition.

THE PLACE OF GENDER IN "FUNDAMENTAL ISSUES"

Then when people [in the Asmara 1995 conference] started talking about democratic laws, the issue of women was raised. Of course they [DUP] jumped and said "so women's [issues] have come here as well? Just like that from the start? So what do women have to do with that issue? Why do you want to mess up the story [issue]?" A party representative actually said that! (In-depth interview with delegate to the Asmara conference, 1998, name withheld)

The most salient feature of NDA discourse with regard to women's rights and gender equality was relative *absence*—apart from minimal references to women in general documents. Documents that analyzed the causes of Sudan's wars and crises, and that suggested alternatives lacked a gender perspective. The documents of the Nairobi 1993 conference, for example, which resolved a number of contentious issues such as the secular nature of the state, citizenship as the basis for the relationship between the individual and the state, and which emphasized Sudan's cultural and religious diversity made a general reference to gender in the section addressing the relationship between religion and the state:

> Laws shall guarantee full equality of citizens on the basis of citizenship, respect for religious beliefs and traditions and without discrimination on the grounds of religion, race, gender or culture. (NDA, the Nairobi Declaration 1993)

Similarly, the NDA's charter outlined the objectives of the alliance as: *combating the fundamentalist regime*, to *establish multi-party democracy*, rejecting authoritarian rule, and to respect international human rights norms, individual and collective liberties, and rule of law. The document promised a restored economy. It called for the *respect of cultural and ethnic diversity and religious freedom*, and prohibits all forms of discrimination. The charter called for the convening of a "National Constitutional Conference" which would resolve *fundamental issues* and *establish a framework for a permanent constitution*, the *politico-cultural identity of the country*, and *the relationship between the state and religion*. A gender perspective was absent from this discussion of fundamental issues.

As discussed earlier, the Asmara declaration discussed the arrangements needed for the termination of war. Those included *the right to self-determination, relationship between the state and religion*, preliminary arrangements for *the transitional period*, modalities for the struggle to overthrow NIF, the *foundational basis for future Sudan*, humanitarian issues, and structuring of the NDA. It also approved a number of basic documents including the economic program and the press and trade union charters (Final Communiqué of the NDA Conference, June 1995). The Asmara Resolutions also lacked an analysis of how all these issues affected diverse women and men in distinct ways.

Many thought that discussing women's participation and human rights was a waste of time. In 1998 a member of the NDA secretariat combined all NDA resolutions on women in a three-page document. When I praised this step, the response was that the member of the secretariat had noticed that in recent meetings the NDA Leadership Council spent a long time in discussing women's issues unnecessarily. "I decided to combine these documents together so that they can focus on discussing more important issues" (personal communication, Cairo, September 1998).

Minimal references to women's issues continued even after several campaigns that women's groups organized. In one of the NDA Leadership Council meetings, women's organizations and secretariats in some of the member parties presented three memos, which the meeting discussed. The SWA organized a demonstration at the venue of the meeting, and asked the NDA to commit to CEDAW without reservations (with the understanding that when in government, the NDA or its member parties would ensure that Sudan signs and ratifies CEDAW). Yet the communiqué of the meeting did not incorporate the discussions on women's human rights.

Feminist theorists have emphasized the importance of incorporating gender into "broader discourses about social transformation" (Kandiyoti 1991, 2). The opposition was (and continues to be) concerned with overthrowing the NIF/NCP government, and with setting a vision for a democratic Sudan, but a concern with gender equality continues to be absent. El-Battahani has argued that

> Parties to the on-going conflict in Sudan, including the NIF, reject what they perceive as (old Sudan) and instead cache party an alternative "New Sudan." Currently, the NIF talks about a new Sudan that is Islamic in identity. A diametrically opposite concept to that of the NIF is proposed by the SPLM which until recently has called for a secular, socialist Sudan. Now, the NDA's concept of a new Sudan is essentially of a secular, democratic nature. However, within the NDA . . . there is a plethora of competing versions (Arab-Islamic, Arab-African and African) of what "New Sudan" means. Which direction Sudan (or Sudans) should take is not yet resolved but at present, one thing is certain: the "Old Sudan" is dying and the "New Sudan" is yet to be born. (1997, 22)

Junctures and transitions often pose challenges, including for women and girls, but they also open up opportunities for integrating gender into visions for change. I began most of the in-depth interviews with a question on the desired form of change. Responses reflected desires for reform (mainly the Umma Party and the DUP) and desires for transformation (New Sudan forces and the CPS). In most cases, both discourses of reform and transformation lacked a concern with gender, unless I asked about women's human rights or gender equality. Once asked, some of the NDA leaders, especially those seeking transformation in Sudan, made statements that revealed commitment to women's rights and gender equality. One of the interviewees told me that

> Whether we are close to achieving a New Sudan will depend on our ability to address women's issues. Any party that does not take on the cause of women on equal footing with democracy, self-determination for the South, and the relationship between the state and religion, will have a defective path. I do not

think it is true that the challenges that women face will be resolved once Sudan's other problems had been solved. [Addressing the oppression of women] is *one* of the preconditions for solving Sudan's other problems. (Interview with al-Shafie Khider, NDA Secretary for Organization and Administration and member of the CPS Central Committee, Cairo, April 14, 1998)

Differences in the views of reformist leaders on one hand, and leaders seeking transformation on the other were also evident in those leaders' analysis of the situation of women in Sudan prior to the NIF coup. When asked to comment on the role and position of women in Sudanese society, leaders whose views emphasized transformation argued that they were not satisfied with the state of women's emancipation in Sudan, and that more work needed to be done. Those advocating reform were more satisfied with the way women have fared so far in Sudan.

One interviewee argued that women's achievements were the result of the responsiveness of successive democratic governments in Sudan to the demands of women and women's organizations. The only problem facing Sudanese women, according to proponents of reform, was the way the GOS treated women.

It is important to emphasize that the stand of the two sectarian parties with regard to issues of diversity in Sudan has shifted radically, at least at the discursive level, compared to the 1960s, 1970s, and 1980s. As is clear from the quotes in this chapter, no similar shift has taken place with regard to gender issues. The change in the position of the opposition in exile toward issues of diversity and justice was the result of the armed resistance and intellectual strengths of New Sudan movements. The absence of a gender analysis from the earlier programs of the New Sudan forces, and the weak nature of the women's movement, discussed earlier in this book, hindered a similar shift with regard to gender equality. As such, both progressive and sectarian/conservative discourses remain entrapped within the neopatriarchal net, and are bound to remain as such unless they acknowledge the primacy of gender-based difference, and the relations of domination and subordination attached to it.

This chapter analyzed the discourses and institutional practices of the diverse movements organized in the NDA in the 1990s and early 2000s from a gender perspective. I examined the position of these parties and movements on women's participation in NDA structures, and their positions on women's human rights enshrined in international human rights conventions, including CEDAW.

All political parties and movements organized in the NDA agreed on the importance of women's participation in NDA structures, but they differed on the modalities for participation. Regarding commitments to women's human rights, most of the political parties and movements seeking to transform

Sudan expressed commitment to women's human rights enshrined in international human rights conventions. Sectarian parties, however, insisted on restricting NDA's commitment to women's human rights on religious basis. Committing to women's human rights enshrined in international conventions would have subverted some of the basic tools for social regulation and control available to these groups, such as religion, as well as fixed notions of culture and tradition. Globalization and exile are already challenges to these notions of culture and religion.

Despite their diverse positions on women's human rights within the NDA, however, collectively, the parties organized in the NDA ended up restricting women's human rights on the basis of religion. Groups that were prepared to commit to women's human rights traded women's rights and gender equality for the unity of the opposition.

In the following chapter I analyze the discourses and practices of movements that self-identified as New Sudan forces, using a gender perspective.

NOTES

1. Charles Dickens (2013). *A Tale of Two Cities* (first published 1859). Harper Collins.

2. The NDA also excluded other forces, including smaller splinter parties, from its structures.

3. Different political forces narrate different histories of the NDA. Leaders of the major opposition parties, on one hand, argue that the whole process took place in prison. Trade Union activists, on the other hand, argue that this was not true and that the party leaders wanted to appropriate their efforts.

4. Each political party, the trade unions, and the "national characters" were allowed to have a delegation of up to five members in the NDA general congress.

5. McClintock analyzes black women's activism in South Africa, which developed in response to measures that the Apartheid regime imposed to curtail black women's migration to the cities in 1913 and 1937 (McClintock 1997, 380–85).

6. The GOS detained Mariam al-Mahdi in August 2004 because she participated in meetings with representatives of the Sudan Revolutionary Front in Paris.

7. See chapter 6 for Ibrahim's biography.

8. The text was adopted from the Nairobi (1993) Declaration.

9. Agaw became Secretary General for the Government of South Sudan when the country achieved independence.

10. For an analysis of the applications of the recommendations of the Beijing Conference in the Muslim world, see the articles in Afkhami and Friedel (1997).

11. I am indebted to Magda M. Ahmed for sharing with me her archive of the Egyptian press coverage of the Beijing and the ICPD conferences, and for pointing to the fact that the documents were actually not cited directly in the articles. The articles published in *Roz El Yusuf* magazine (September 1995) by Sherine Abu El Naga constituted an exception.

12. The DUP has changed its representative in the NDA working group on Article 5 because she refused to adopt the party's line on the issue.

13. The Umma Party announced its dissociation with the NDA in exile in early 2000 and many of its key exile figures returned to Sudan in March 2000, on the assumption that the NIF had shown signs of tolerance for its opponents. Another reason was the rift within the NIF (between President al-Bashir and leader of the NIF, Turabi).

14. The CPS's position on personal status laws has been reformist so far. The party has called for restricting polygamy, not abolishing it.

Chapter Five

Gender and New Sudan's Vision and Political Practices

Given that gender intersects with other aspects of identity and power relations in shaping the experiences of women and men, transforming gender relations should involve the transformation of Sudan's (and South Sudan's) economic and political structures, institutions, and social relations. It should also involve challenging the concentration of power in the hands of the dominant social and racial groups. In this chapter, I discuss the New Sudan discourse, a subversive discourse concerned with transforming the structures and institutions of the Old Sudan.

While I try to avoid using the binary opposition of *old* versus *new* Sudan, I believe that the New Sudan, as discourse, and to some extent as political practice, has or perhaps had[1] the potential of transforming Sudan's neo-patriarchal structures and institutions, at least partially. Without a clear gender perspective and a commitment to gender equality and to transforming gender relations, however, New Sudan movements would not be able to transform gender relations. Hence it is important to understand and interrogate the New Sudan, as a vision and as political practice, from a gender perspective.

The New Sudan discourse developed as part of opposition politics during the first part of the 1980s. The term, which the late Dr. John Garang coined in 1983, denotes a philosophy, a framework, a perspective, a program . . . and a vision for a just and equitable society.[2] In the 1990s and early 2000s, the term also referred to SPLM/A-held areas and to several opposition movements organized in the NDA. These included the Beja Congress, the Sudan Federal Democratic Alliance (SFDA), Sudan National Alliance/Sudan Alliance Forces (SNA/SAF), and the Sudan National Party (SNP).[3]

In essence, the New Sudan discourse is a critique of the old, neopatriarchal Sudan. It is also an alternative vision for social, economic, and political reconstruction. As a critique, New Sudan discourse maintains that colonialism gave way to internal colonialism in post-colonial Sudan, and that the rule of the NIF/NCP represents the peak of the crisis of the Old Sudan.

The project of nation building in the Old Sudan has been the result of a process of social, economic, and political exclusions on the bases of race, culture, and regional location. A minority in Khartoum and Central Sudan benefited from the dividends of independence while the historically marginalized regions in the eastern, southern, and western parts of Sudan lacked equal access to the country's political and economic resources.

As a framework for an alternative order, the New Sudan seeks to transform the dominant social, economic, and political structures, institutions, and social relations. It seeks to achieve multi-party democracy, decentralization of governance, secularism, social justice, and equal distribution of political and economic resources. New Sudan discourse seeks to restore *Sudanism* in the place of binary oppositions such as Africanism versus Arabism and Islamism (Garang 1998). This discourse emphasized the unity of Sudan on new bases, confirmed through a referendum through which the people of South Sudan would practice the right to self-determination. This right was enshrined in the 2005 Comprehensive Peace Agreement (CPA) between the NCP and the SPLM/A. South Sudan seceded in 2011 after 98 percent of the population voted for independence in the same year. However, the critique remains pertinent to what is left of Sudan.

DO WE ALL BELONG TO THIS COUNTRY?

New Sudan Discourse as a Critique of the Old Sudan

Most interviewees who self-identified as New Sudanists started their definition of what they saw as a post-NIF/NCP order with an analysis and critique of the Old Sudan. Some of these narratives overlapped with my own analysis of the Old Sudan earlier in this book. Citing NDA resolutions, New Sudan leaders said the post-NIV/NCP order should be a multi-party democracy. With a few exceptions, such as Dr. Peter A. Nyaba, one of the SPLM/A leaders and Minister of Higher Education in the post-CPA Government of National Unity, these leaders said post-NIF/NCP Sudan should be united. Such unity, they affirmed, involved redefining the relationship between Khartoum and Central Sudan on one hand, and Sudan's historically marginalized areas on the other.

Amin Fillen, representative of the SNP in the NDA Executive Office and Member of Parliament for SNP in the post-1986 election era was very blunt:

There is a bunch of thieves, from different parts of Sudan: they speak in the name of the people but guzzle the rights of those people. We want justice and equality between the Sudanese. We want to improve the standards of living for people in the margins, specially the rural areas of Sudan. (Interview with Amin Fillen, Cairo, June 6, 1998)

The mayor of Menza and of al-Kadalwa, a community that originates in the *Funj* Sultanate in the Northern Blue Nile area, under the administration of the SNA/SAF in the late 1990s, responded to a question of what the New Sudan meant to him as follows:

We are simple farmers, and have so many problems in our areas, and other than the first [democratic] government of al-Azhari (1956–1958) no one even noticed us. We have always been subject to injustice, and the most severe injustice inflicted upon us came from those people of the NIF. They confiscated our land, turned it into projects and handed it over to strangers. We became guests in our own home and found no way other than carrying arms with the opposition and the NDA. With them we liberated our area from the people of *Inqaz* [Salvation/NIF]. (Musa Ibrahim, *Umda* [local chief] of Menza, Northern Blue Nile, interviewed by Faisal Mohamed Salih, *al-Khartoum* [1480], April 28, 1997)

New Sudan narratives often do not offer essentialist definitions of the margins, Fillen said:

Today we believe that people of the Gezira [in Central Sudan] are not better off in terms of their living conditions or access to healthcare or education, than those in the [Nuba] Mountains. On our way to Port Sudan [in Eastern Sudan] we saw young boys running alongside the train, begging the passengers to throw food to them. I thank God because [compared to them] we are better off. Injustice afflicts all areas outside major cities in Sudan. Take the Abba Island [on the White Nile] for example. The MP for this area was Mr al-Sadiq al-Mahdi [former Prime Minister], but don't think the Abba Island is better off than Port Sudan for example. . . . Some of us were members of parties other than the SNP, but these parties, which ruled because people in our areas voted for them, offered nothing in return for our areas. We never saw them again until the next round of elections. Some, especially those talking in the name of Islam, establish mosques during election [campaigns]. After elections they don't come back, as if there was no Islam between two elections. Members of Parliament were actually implanted in all these remote areas: what does it mean to get someone who hasn't seen Kadugli [in the Nuba Mountains] to run for elections in this area so he could take up a ministerial position for a party? (Interview with Amin Fillen, Cairo, June 6, 1998)

Although the New Sudan discourse, especially in the 1990s, emphasized the importance of multi-party democracy and national liberation, some warned of the dangers of pseudo-democracy. The Sudan Federal Democratic

Party's (SFDP) representative in the NDA, for example, stated in a lecture in Cairo,

> In the margins of Sudan if you talked to someone from the generation of my father, he would tell you *"ya heleil al ingeliz."*[4] We should [carefully examine] this statement, which is often intended as a joke. . . . Most people in my age would say *"day'nak ya Abbud."*[5] . . . After independence . . . the [ruling elite] argued that [Sudan's identity] was Arabic and Islamic. This meant the exclusion of a big number of citizens who did not relate to these identities. As such, I understand why the Southern opposition emerged in 1955 and why it continued. . . . In the South the war did not stop even after Addis Ababa agreement [which the Anya Nya movement and the Numeiry regime signed in 1972]. In the other margins, there also emerged movements that discovered their communities were excluded and started to demand participation in administrating their own areas. The Darfur Development Front, for example, emerged to demand water, hospitals and health units. But in its essence it was calling for equality. Had the vision of our ruling elite widened enough at the time, they could have been able to grasp what that movement expressed. (Dr. Sharif Harir, Vice President of the SFDA and its representative in the NDA Leadership Council, Lecture at the Sudan Culture and Information Centre, attended and recorded by the author, Cairo, June 1998)

One way to address political and economic exclusion, argued Fillen, was through a decentralized system of rule: "Sudan is a continent and it cannot be ruled centrally from Khartoum. There should be a federal system of rule, composed of the *sons* of the areas: they know the area well and know how to handle issues" (interview with Amin Fillen, Cairo, June 6, 1998; emphasis mine).

Notwithstanding Fillen's reference to "sons of the area," this emphasis on decentralization runs through the narratives of New Sudan leaders and activists. As far back as 1989, Ahmed Ibrahim Direig, founder of SFDA and member of the NDA Leadership Council at the time of initial research, called for a federal, decentralized system of self-governance for the regions of Sudan as a way to prevent war (Direig 1989, 91–107). Direig's proposed constitutional reform was silent on gender issues although SFDA members interviewed for this research emphasized their full commitment to women's rights expressed in CEDAW.

New Sudan discourse also challenged the singular religious and cultural identity, which successive regimes in Khartoum sought to impose on a diverse population. Interviewees narrated stories of community resistance against cultural and religious hegemony. Azrag Zakaria, then representative of the SNP in the NDA's Leadership Council, said,

> Fanaticism is one of the main problems of the Old Sudan. The NIF, *Ansar al-Sunna*, and al-Mahdi came to the Nuba Mountains and forced people to join.

During Mahdiya, this generated beautiful art of resistance that became public after the end of Mahdiya. But there were also people who adapted to the Islamist culture and wanted to change indigenous cultures. They failed to do so and lived as strangers in their own communities. (Interview with Azrag Zakaria, Cairo, June 5, 1998)

Zakaria further recounted how exclusion and cultural assimilation affected the people of the Nuba Mountains:

When [the government built] schools in our villages, teachers used to speak in Arabic. At school, they told us not to talk gibberish: *ma trt'un!* When we spoke in our language! Teachers punished anyone who [spoke in the local language]. So this education was not to teach you Arabic language, but to make you forget your own language. They would tell you "this *rut'ana* is backward and belonged to backward people." That is [how they sow] the seed of hatred of our indigenous culture, when they made the people believe that our cultures were backward. You do not define backwardness by reference to language or culture, but in terms of material development or underdevelopment that result from inequality. Teachers were influenced by nationalist ideas [that emphasized sameness] at the time and did not really know that they were oppressing another group and suppressing this group's culture. The conflict was inside us, and [the teachers] did not know about it. This is going to be my contribution. I know that *your research question is on women but I wanted to talk about culture. This is very important.* (Ibid.; emphasis mine)

Zakaria's discourse echoes Fanon's writing on national culture. Sharif Harir expanded on the issue of cultural exclusion when he argued that post-colonial Sudan produced "a new tribe" which came from "the Khartoum-Kosty-Sinnar triangle." This tribe, argued Harir, sought to omit "differences," and, like colonialism, sought to "condition the minds of all Sudanese so they could see everything through the lenses of a dominant culture, and so they can perceive their cultures as trash." In the immediate post-independence moment, argued Harir, "most of us accepted that [our indigenous cultures were trash]" (Harir 1998).

Like Fillen, Harir linked the banishment of cultures to concrete power relations. He also emphasized that marginalization was not exclusive to the peripheral regions of Sudan:

I do not need to go to Darfur to see *marginalisation*, lack of participation, and the *demeaning of human beings*. Those on the margins of Khartoum or even those of us [in Cairo] have been marginalised by the regime in Khartoum. If we were to return to Sudan we would need to see what is new in the Old Sudan. As a first step, we have to acknowledge and act on the diversity and multiplicity of Sudan. Otherwise we will not achieve peace. We have to acknowledge the Other and not exclude them on the presumption that our culture

is superior. . . . We cannot achieve unity if the [dominant] political structures
and institutions in Sudan made any of us feel inferior to others. (Harir 1998)

The above narratives of opposition leaders from movements representing
parts of Sudan currently in conflict (Darfur, South Kordofan, and the Blue
Nile) echoed concerns of South Sudanese and other opposition leaders. John
Luk, an SPLM leader at the time of initial research and Minister of Justice in
independent South Sudan, argued that sectarianism had dominated Sudan's
politics, and that Sudan, defined as Arab and Islamic, excluded the views of
those who thought Sudan was too diverse "in terms of race, religion and
culture." This created tension, argued Luk, among those who did not "fit into
this category of Arabs and Muslims" and who thought identity should be
inclusive. The New Sudan, argued Luk, was a vision that would "save the
country from the persistence of civil war" because New Sudan gives expression to Sudan's diverse identities "in the social, political and economic
spheres" (interview with John Luk, Nairobi, March 24, 1999). Luk went on
to discuss gender equality without any prompting on my side! He argued that
no social group, be it women, South Sudanese, or marginalized groups in the
North, should be left out of the vision of the New Sudan (ibid.).

Narrators highlighted and analyzed racial, cultural, religious, and regional
difference, and how these turned into oppression in post-colonial Sudan
through political and economic processes. A key issue is that gender rarely
factors in this analysis although several of the New Sudan movements, especially the SPLM/A, made clear commitments to women's participation and
gender equality, expressed in the late Dr. Garang's oft-quoted statement that
women in South Sudan were "the marginalized of the marginalized." It is
important to note that recent statements by the SPLM-North and Sudan's
Revolutionary Front often include references to the impact of conflict, marginalization, and political repression on women and girls in Sudan. Nonetheless, a lack of a clear gender perspective detracts from the vigor of the New
Sudan as a critique to the Old Sudan and as an alternative vision. It suggests
that if realized, the New Sudan may give rise to a new form of neopatriarchy
that is less oppressive than the form that has been prevalent in post-colonial
Sudan, but that still marginalizes women.

NEW SUDAN DISCOURSE AS AN ALTERNATIVE VISION

New Sudan discourse also offers an alternative vision to the order that prevailed since Sudan obtained political independence in 1956, outlined in the
preceding subsection. Narratives of leaders in movements that identified as
New Sudan movements in the 1990s and early 2000s offer important insight
into what the concept means. For SNP leader Amin Fillen, it meant access to
"medicine, shelter, food and education."

I guess I was involved in politics since I developed self-consciousness. That was when I became aware of the simple problems facing me and facing my community in our daily lives: water, subsistence, food, transportation, and the need of our goats and cows for grazing. I was raised in an environment where people were not literate. We joined schools by mere chance. We learned a *few things* and thought that if our people followed them, their lives would improve. Those were things such as health and hygiene. We learned about tools that could make cultivation easier. Women faced many problems in our areas such as health and when giving birth. Education and better rule should improve their and our circumstances. Because successive governments were not able or unwilling to develop our areas, we became politically active. Other people call it politics. We believe [politics] is food, shelter, medicine and education. (Interview with Amin Fillen, SNP representative in the NDA Executive Office, Cairo, June 6, 1998)

Leaders of New Sudan movements argued that a New Sudan entailed political, economic, and cultural transformation. According to Pagan Amom, then member of the NDA's Leadership Council,

Change in Sudan needs to be deep rooted in the political sphere by restructuring apparatuses of authority and allowing space for wider democratic participation [for] all Sudanese. [Change] should also involve restructuring of the economy so wealth is not concentrated in the hands of a minority from one region (central Sudan). This will create access for marginalized groups to production, development and infrastructure.

Change [also] means the democratisation of culture. It [involves] abolishing the hegemony of one culture, and making space for multiple cultures by recognising the Other. On this basis I am personally not in favour of an official or national culture or an official language or official dress or national food. The only official or national thing is Sudan. [Old Sudan leaders, refer to languages other than Arabic as] local languages. Does this mean that [Arabic] language is foreign? . . . *Attempting to impose uniformity in the existence of difference and by force brings tension.* This tension becomes the intellectual, moral and cultural basis for wars. And that is why war [erupted] in Sudan even before it was born as a country. My vision of the New Sudan means a return to the essence of the human being; and the creation of a social, cultural and political system that would [enable] Sudanese people to express themselves. There is also the legal side. . . . I see it as promoting equality between citizens regardless of religion, gender or race. (Interview with Pagan Amom, member of SPLM/A's National Liberation Council and Commander of the NDA Joint Military Command at the time of research, on a flight from Asmara to Cairo, June 1998)

Other leaders made similar points without noting that women's human rights should be part of New Sudan thinking, even though they supported women's rights. The late Eliaba James Surur, leader of the Union of Sudan African Parties (USAP), asked a packed room of eager listeners at a lecture he gave in Cairo, "Where are the women? Why are the women here so few tonight?" He then defined the New Sudan along the lines of citizenship rights, equality, democracy, and justice.

> The New Sudan . . . is one that would bring equality and justice. It is not the unity of the land but of the people that we are after. . . . It is not only a union in words, but a union that brings the people of Sudan together as Africans. . . . Sudan is foremost an African country, [but] there was a misconception of what Sudan is. We believe that we are Sudanese first; then Africans or Arabs. New Sudan is the Sudan that will accommodate us all. A Sudan where . . . we shall be able to say "I am a Sudanese by right and not a second class citizen" in any part of the country. (Lecture organized by the SPLM/A chapter in Cairo, August 1998, attended by the author)

Separation between religion and the state is a key tenet of the New Sudan discourse, although narratives on secularism often ignore what it might mean for women's human rights in Sudan. Dawoud Salih, SNP's Information Secretary in Egypt at the time of research, said the New Sudan meant that "religion is for God but the nation is for everyone . . . religion should be an individual concern." According to Salih, "*Father* Philip Abbas Ghabboush (founder of SNP) advocated on the separation between religion and the state, along with unity, democracy, freedom, justice and federalism since the 1980s" (interview with Dawoud Salih, Information Secretary, SNP, Cairo, May 23, 1998).

Salih narrated in detail the position of SNP on democracy, its vision of the future economic system, and its perception of identity, without reference to gender. Discussions on secularism at the time of initial research seldom included a discussion of how different political forces in Sudan have used religion as a way to control women and restrict their legal rights for example. This is because the critique of the Old Sudan never included a critique of the private sphere or power relationships between women and men. Would a coalition between New Sudan movements and women's organizations and activists interested in transforming gender relations and safeguarding women's human rights enshrined in international human rights conventions broaden the scope of this discourse?

We might have seen a glimpse of how such a potential alliance would look like during the vigils that the network No to Women's Oppression organized in Khartoum in and after 2009 to protest the flogging of journalist Loubna Ahmad al-Hussein. Pagan Amom and Yasir Arman, then members of Sudan's National Assembly, were both arrested for participating in protests demanding legal reform and an end to state violence against women. As discussed earlier in this chapter, recent SPLM-N releases often mention the gender-specific impact of war and repression on women and girls

NEW SUDAN'S GENDERED NARRATIVES

Due to the silence of New Sudan texts and narratives on gender at the time of initial research, I asked interviewees who identified as New Sudan proponents about their views on gender equality and women's human rights. The rich responses to my questions testify to the significance and power of in-depth interviews in shedding light on excluded issues and social groups. Some New Sudanists considered the critique of gender-based discrimination against women as inherent in the vision of the New Sudan in that this vision addressed both sexes as citizens and as human beings. Pagan Amom, who stated that the New Sudan meant achieving full humanity for all, offered a socialist–feminist analysis of gender-based oppression in Old Sudan.

> I perceive change in terms of equality for all Sudanese and their right to express themselves regardless of gender. Discrimination against women is a universal issue since human society changed from matriarchal to patriarchal society. This had to do with changing roles in production and hence women were perceived in terms of their reproductive roles. . . . Real change should reclaim woman's humanity and her right to express herself and in thinking and participating in all social activity. (Interview with Pagan Amom, Asmara/Cairo, June 1998)

Other New Sudan leaders also argued that gender equality was integral to New Sudan thinking. John Luk argued that gender was part of the movement's understanding of all the other issues. He emphasized the importance of reviewing legislation in a way that would ensure respect for women's rights enshrined in international conventions.

> Sudanese women have been at the bottom of the ladder. In terms of political participation, social values, customs and religion, they have suffered neglect and marginalization. If you looked at our laws, whether you look at customary laws, or the shari'a for the Muslims, you would find that there are aspects that reduce the status of women if viewed from the perspective of international human rights laws. People may speak of cultural specificity or distinctiveness but still human rights should be universal. Yes there is room for cultural distinctions but I think when they really militate against or disadvantage certain groups of people you cannot live with that situation. Our laws should give equal recognition, protection and should in fact *cleanse our legal system* of those laws that grossly inflict on the freedoms and rights of women. This is true for both the South and the North. The South also has different cultural traditions that are oppressive. These reduce the status of women to a very appalling one. In the North also Islam has some negative effects regarding women's rights. Laws must cater for women's empowerment so that they would play greater roles in society, because right now women are no longer sitting in their homes. Women are at the forefront of the struggle. They have taken up arms and joined the various political and military movements in the

Sudan. It is only natural that they have already claimed their rightful position through participation in the struggle. They are struggling for democracy, and fighting for democracy in the Sudan is for everybody now. . . . Women are being shot on the frontlines, fighting to remove the dictatorial regime and therefore they would not sit back when it is time to build democracy. So they have to be participating from now on in **defining the kind of New Sudan we want**, they have to *define themselves inside that change*. They will not be invited. They have to play their role. Any laws or traditions that militate against the effective participation of women must be addressed and changed. (Interview with John Luk, Nairobi, March 24, 1999; emphasis mine)

As discussed earlier in this book, the New Sudan movements included groups that did not necessarily originate in one of the marginalized regions of Sudan. These included the Sudan National Alliance/Alliance Forces (SNA/SAF). This movement stated in one of its documents that "A gender perspective is central [to] the transformation of the structures of the old Sudan from patriarchy to equality" (SWA, document adopted by SNA's First Preliminary Congress, August 1995, 1).

As the above indicates when asked about gender, various New Sudan leaders either expressed views that reflected socialist feminist analysis (Amom) or provided an analysis of women's gender interests as integral to their agendas. It is important to integrate gender and better intersectional analysis into New Sudan discourses.

MARKING THE BOUNDARIES BETWEEN THE OLD AND NEW SUDAN?

The New Sudan discourse challenges the way successive governments in Sudan have defined identity as singular and static. Identity, in the original New Sudan vision, is perceived as rooted in power relationships and institutional practices. This discourse speaks to the grievances of the people of historically marginalized regions and socially excluded cultural and racial groups. What does this mean for women in marginalized regions of Sudan, and women who are the subject of racial or cultural or religious discrimination? To what extent can the New Sudan discourse offer local, intersectional analysis that can complement the analysis and agendas of women's organizations active in exile and in urban parts of Sudan?

Feminist scholars (for example, Yuval-Davis 1997a) have highlighted how women are often constructed as boundary markers of group identity. With the exception of some of the SPLM/A leaders, such as Luk and Amom, most interviewees from New Sudan movements emphasized the egalitarianism of authentic African communities and cultures (in contradistinction to the conservatism of the North). Some argued that gender inequality in their areas was the result of the lack of access to education and health services, and that these are easier to change than inequalities and subordination arising from the use of religion and culture to oppress women. One SPLM/A leader from the Nuba Mountains, for example, said,

> After 1989, the NIF worked to destroy women completely. A woman is considered solely as a unit for child production or a tent moving in the street [referring to women who wear *niqab*, Islamic dress that covers a woman's whole body, except her eyes]. Personally this is what I felt upon watching a video from my own area in Kadugli in the Nuba Mountains. When I saw the women and female students . . . *Nuba* [women veiled]! According to our customs in the Nuba Mountains, girls and women should be proud of their naked bodies. Women use tattoos and colours to reveal their femininity and beauty. Historically, the Nuba considered a girl who covered her body as someone who wanted to cover a blemish on her body. Young men would not have interest in her. So, *when I watched the tents moving in the Nuba Mountains I felt that this is no more the Nuba Mountains we used to know.* [This is] cultural destruction! A destruction of traditions and of women's livelihoods in the Nuba Mountains. (Interview with Daniel Kodi, former SPLM/A representative in the Middle East, Cairo, April 8, 1998)

Kodi's narrative clearly indicates that changes in the way women dress were an onslaught on the Nuba culture and community. Groups sought to subvert this cultural destruction by distinguishing themselves from the dominant Arab and Islamic hegemonic discourse, at times by arguing that unlike women from Central Sudan, women in some of the marginalized areas were emancipated. Another leader from the Nuba Mountains, for example, argued that equality between the sexes was a given in the Nuba Mountains.

> In our societies, and in African societies in general, women enjoy a favourable position. *Even equality is not an issue; we do not have women who ask to be equal because they are already equal.* In African administrative systems you can find women who are *Shaykhas* (political leaders), and *Kujur* (spiritual leaders and traditional healers). A woman can be an advisor to the head of the tribe. This heritage has come to us from the past, from the Nile Valley civilisation where *our history* in the Nuba Mountains is *rooted*. A number of queens ruled in these civilisations. This changed after Islamization invaded the Nuba communities. Zahra was *Mak* (queen) in the Wali tribe, and her son was named Abdel Halim Mohamed *Zahra*. So with regard to women's rights, although the society might be underdeveloped materially, spiritually and politically it grants women their rights. Perhaps livelihood practices also enabled women to lead in our societies. For us (the Nuba), the role of women in the family and the division of labour within the family and society is such that women not only share half of these roles with men, but there are areas (specially within the household) where women are in control and a man's role is secondary. The woman has her own farm around the house, called the *Jubraka*, and this farm produces food for the family in August and September. This is specific to women. After that she works in the main farm, and she divides

the revenue with her husband in half. Added to that is her role in collecting firewood, fetching water, and doing other household chores. Women's contribution in the household and family life supersedes that of man. This is reflected in other spheres of society. The woman also has her own *makhzan* (storeroom) for the harvest. She also has shares in the general crop. She has her own wealth of cattle. *The "woman's problem" only became an issue when the Nuba opened up to other communities or moved to towns.* When you come to town you develop a schism. You find a society that is new and find a specific new definition of women; you become segregated from women. As such, even people's interaction with the new reality is different. Many of us experience a conflict between the old (order) to which we were used, where you find social and economic equality between the sexes. You develop a cultural conflict. New concepts are imposed, such as inequality between the sexes, domestication of women, and a redefinition of who decides on women's participation. (Interview with Azrag Zakaria, Cairo, June 5, 1998)

Zakaria's discourse on women, which eloquently describes the status of women and men in some of the areas in Southern Kordofan, is epistemologically linked to forced cultural homogenization.

We are now demanding a lift of compulsory acculturation. We do not mind the language, *but there are customs that we cannot abandon* because we have an opinion that is distinct from the culture imposed upon us. Our own cultures are stronger than cultures that are imposed by law, or by society. Women in our community do not have hair that we could describe as "gold poured from her hair" (famous popular song in Northern Sudan) or silky hair. We have stiff hair that gets dressed in a way that we sing for. For us, being skinny is not a beauty standard. There the woman has to be *a'atya* (huge) and tall, so she can carry her duties out. We do not care about skin colour or hair texture. But once [in town], suddenly you are drowned in contradictions to the extent that you deny your own culture. (Ibid.)

Zakaria's narrative raises important and legitimate questions on affirming cultural and racial identity. However, it also raises questions about the division of labor on the basis of sex in Nuba communities. He articulates his discourse on gender on the basis of the process of cultural domination on his community, and links this to power relations. He also uses distinct features of Nuba women to mark the difference between Nuba communities on one hand, and the dominant North on the other. To what extent can this mobilization of an egalitarian past where women and men were equal help in integrating a concern with gender equality within New Sudan movements? How about gender equality in regions like South Kordofan State and in the Nuba Mountains? What role do customary laws play in terms of promoting or hampering gender equality? Of course, I will not discuss all these questions here, since each deserves a separate text, but I will use the experience of a Nuba woman's development organization to engage some of these questions.

The Nuba Women's Education and Development Association (NUWE-DA) is an organization that addresses both the strategic and practical needs of displaced women in Khartoum, especially women from the Nuba Mountains or Southern Kordofan State. This organization has identified understanding and reforming customary law as a priority area for its advocacy and community education work, given that customary law restricts women's property rights and their ability to participate.

The organization has worked with male community leaders (*Shaykhs, Umdas, Mukuk,* and *Sultans*) to introduce reforms in the area of customary law. Kamilia Ibrahim, one of the founders of NUWEDA, shared the following illustrative story:

> In May 2011, a widow who is the mother of a twelve-year-old son testified at a workshop we organized on women's empowerment and legal aid. She said when her husband died; her in-laws told her she needed their permission to use her matrimonial property. They told her she needed their permission even if she wanted to sell a chicken or a pound of flour. Her in-laws told her she needed their permission even if she wanted to buy clothes for her son.

Ibrahim said hundreds of other women faced similar problems, yet the focus of women's organizations in Sudan had been on reforming discriminatory statutory and shari'a laws.

It is thus important to avoid an uncritical acceptance of prevalent norm, even among communities known for egalitarianism. It is important to avoid homogenizing and romanticizing egalitarian African cultures. It is important to interrogate internal power relations that might compound women's oppression. Polygamy, for example, is practiced among many egalitarian tribes in Sudan.

Fillen, from the SNP, who stated at the beginning of the interview that he only started wearing clothes when he joined primary school, criticized Nuba women who chose to transgress the traditional codes of dress or who challenged the traditional division of labor within Nuba communities.

> The few educated women in our areas sometimes wear *tobe* (traditional dress in central and Northern Sudan) and become arrogant. When an educated woman refuses to fetch water or collect wood for fuel, this means we have lost her. Educated women who are connected to the grassroots are seen as the exception. . . . There are other women who became conservative [adopted Islamist ideology]. Society does not accept nor benefit from all these types of educated women. That is why it is often the half-educated or ignorant women who lead the struggle, which is not a problem for us. (Interview with Amin Fillen, Cairo, June 6, 1998)

The problem that New Sudan groups face in that respect is related to the nature of *local alliances* that they may enter into, for example, with local chiefs, the diverse constituencies of respective movements, and the priorities that these constituencies may have. Many of the New Sudan narratives reflect conscious understanding of these realities. Because the project of the Old Sudan was based on the marginalization and deprivation of people now considered key constituencies for New Sudan forces and movements, the discourse of New Sudan movements has been associated with attending to the needs of the masses at the grassroots level.

This can only be a problem if used to undermine equality between the sexes. A recurrent answer to my question on what women's liberation meant was that "women in these areas do not have even the right to live."

During the Article 5 NDA debates, representatives of the Beja Congress, and the Sudan National Party (predominantly Nuba) invited "sisters in urban women's organizations" to remember the problems their sisters in the liberated areas face as a result of poverty and war.

One interviewee has argued that "women in the Nuba Mountains are directly affected by war, they die while giving birth, so their first priority is war and peace. If you asked them to list their priorities from one to ten, equality between women and men can be listed as priority number ten" (interview with Walid Hamid, Nairobi, March 24, 1999).

> In the Nuba Mountains, the government army kidnaps women, men and children. Women and children are kept in the so called peace villages. Young women are then used for the nights. Each soldier takes the girl that he fancies and goes away with her. Elderly women are sent to fetch water and fire wood. These are daily violations, and you know that in our cultures in Sudan if a young girl loses her honour then she thinks that her future is ruined. These are the kinds of problems that women in the Nuba Mountains emphasise. (Interview with Walid Hamid, director of the office of the commissioner of Southern Kordofan [SPLM/A] at the time of research, Nairobi, March 24, 1999)

Hamid listed violations of women's human rights as key problems that affect women living in war zones, to make the point that this determines the priorities of women in those areas, which excluded abstract notions of women's human rights, although these issues are often central to agendas of groups working toward women's rights.

In the Beja areas, the main issues facing women according to the General Union of Beja Women (GUBW) mainly constituted of basic health needs, literacy, and child care (informal conversation with Samira Idris, activist in the Beja Congress and responsible for the Garora Social Services Centre, Asmara, March 1998).

The Beja Congress and the Rashaida Free Lions reflected the interests of non-egalitarian communities. A former representative of the Beja Congress in the NDA said it was impossible to achieve gender equality before meeting women's immediate needs.

In our societies, the life expectancy of women is low, a medium of thirty-five years. . . . There is a high rate of maternal mortality. We have the problem of early marriage. A woman also lives as a suspect who has to prove she is innocent in many ways. Of course this is most prevalent in the villages and among the Beja nomads, but as you approach the cities, things start to change. Even though communities are different, as leadership. . . . *We are maintaining very low profile with regard to the methods of changing this situation* because if we addressed these issues in a violent way then *it can explode in our face and hamper our political mobilization of communities.*

For us as Beja, the issue of women is *thorny,* that is why we are always cautious to address it with a big deal of sensitivity. Not that this big talking about women's rights and feminism is not a concern for us, but in our areas there are real problems facing us right now. There are women who are married off at an early age, and they *die at an early age. These are real problems, and not theoretical talk on the rights of women in the NDA or in a state that we might and might not achieve.* We are concerned with the existence of women in the area: their life and death. Not their culture or identity but their existence. We always lean towards practicality: I bring copybooks, pencils and a black-board, I make a conducive atmosphere for women so they can understand, and then [the woman] can decide for herself whether or not to "contradict with religions." My responsibility is to put her on track. (Interview with al-Amin Shingirai Cairo, June 6, 1998; italics mine)

These are legitimate concerns that women's organizations from across Sudan, South Sudan, and elsewhere should take seriously. They point to the often *unfinished* agendas of mainstream groups. Similarly, New Sudan groups should challenge the Old Sudan in its different manifestation, including its neopatriarchal nature. These groups should look critically at the societies within which they operate.

WOMEN, MILITARIZATION, AND ARMED RESISTANCE

We tell our fighters that we are interested in liberating the human being before we liberate the land, because if we liberated a land where humans were colonised and underdeveloped, of what value would the land be? In some areas in Eastern Sudan, even the name of a woman, especially one's mother, is a taboo. So when new fighters join the Beja Congress we ask them to pronounce the names of their mothers. His mother's name is not going to solve the problems of women, of course but it is a prelude so we can discuss these issues freely. (Interview with al-Amin Shingirai, Cairo, June 6, 1998)

On the back cover of one of the editions (1990) of Franz Fanon's *Wretched of the Earth,* the publisher writes that "many of the great calls to arms from the era of decolonization are now of purely historical interest." Sudan's contemporary histories of resistance suggest otherwise. As discussed earlier, communities in marginalized areas of Sudan have organized in movements that resorted to armed resistance to bring about change. At this writing, conflicts are ongoing in Darfur, Blue Nile, and Southern Kordofan areas of Sudan. Conflict has also erupted in South Sudan at the end of 2013, although violence, including violence in communities and within households, had never stopped, even after the end of the second war (N. Ali 2011). While armed groups currently organized under the Sudan Revolutionary Front/Forces (SRF) are seeking regime change, as were armed movements organized under the NDA, some of the New Sudan leaders argued that the impact of armed resistance (in terms of transformation) were larger than simply overthrowing a regime in Khartoum. Zakaria, for example, stated that,

> We had to tell the [oppressors] that [we were there and we were different] and that we were neglected, that we as "Other" were forced to define ourselves via the Northern Arabo-Islamist ruling groups. . . . We only carried arms to say who we were, right? And what we wanted, right? And to be able to determine how we were going to get there. (Interview with Azrag Zakaria, Cairo, June 5, 1998)

Sharif Harir links armed resistance to the ability to expose relations of oppression.

> I believe that regardless of our political differences, we cannot disagree over the fact that we did not discover Sudan *until we carried arms*. Even those who used to *rule* the country did not discover it until all of us took up arms: we are carrying arms and Turabi [the GOS] is carrying arms. That is how we started to discover Sudan. Sudan was there all the time, but we used to refuse to acknowledge its heterogeneity and cultural multiplicity. (Sharif Harir, Lecture at the Sudan Culture and Information Centre, 1998)

Despite its devastating and far-reaching impact on communities, some believed that armed resistance created a sense of empowerment for people in the marginalized areas. Talking about the Blue Nile area, Musa Abdel Rahman said,

> We will carry the arms until the whole country is liberated and the *Inqaz* is replaced with a government that people desire. Only then would we put down the gun, build our country/area, and talk to the (new) government about our grievances, but if we sensed that [the post-NIF/NCP government] was unjust to us again . . . we will resume our armed struggle. From now on we won't keep silent in the face of oppression. I was trained to carry arms as an elderly man, together with forty other *Shaykhs* (chiefs) from the area, and there are also the young. From now on no one will be able to inflict injustice on us. This is what the New Sudan means to me. (*al-'Umda*, Musa Ibrahim, 1997)

Some of the interviewees felt armed resistance empowered women as well. Some of the Southern Sudanese women interviewed for this research highlighted the important roles of women combatants. They said women's traditional roles and motherhood did not contradict with being combatants (see N. Ali 2000 and Stone 2011). Pagan Amom said his wife's role as a mother did not contradict with her being a combatant, same as his being a father did not contradict with his role as a combatant.

The impact of dominant beliefs on women's roles have, however, imposed limitations to participation of women in armed resistance. Luke recounted the experience of the girls' battalion in the SPLM/A.

> Women were trained as fighters in 1984. I believe later on because of some cultural issues, unlike in the case of Eritrea and other parts of the world where we saw women fighting, I didn't see the women in SPLA really fighting like men in the front line, although that was their wish. As you know from our own traditions women go to the front *when men are finished*, especially in the South. Women are not the fighting category. But of course they have been participating indirectly behind the line, tending to the sick and providing food—supportive roles. That's also participation that cannot be neglected. But I wouldn't say that in the front lines the role of women is as it should be. There have been exceptional cases, but they were very few. (Interview with John Luk, Nairobi, March 24, 1999)

Deng Alor, who was in charge of the battalion, reflected on the experience of the girls' battalion at the Conference on Human Rights in Transition in Sudan. Like Luk, Alor said the battalion disintegrated due to the dominant cultural norms among various tribes in South Sudan. Alor said families were reluctant to allow their daughters to join the battalion so as not to lose potential wealth (in the form of dowry) "to the armed struggle" (panel on women in the Conference on Human Rights in Transition in Sudan, Kampala, February 1999, attended by the author).

Daniel Kodi, however, shared a perspective that challenged prevalent views of femininity in Sudan, including on women's alleged inability to join armed resistance.

> Women soldiers have surpassed male soldiers in many ways. Women are more determined. This is a reality that I know as a commander. Women soldiers also have more endurance than male soldiers do. Women walk for long distances, carrying their belongings and tools without getting tired. When people settle down to rest, women collect wood and cook. They do not rest. Women are good in detecting explosives, providing medical assistance, and in intelligence work. Naturally women have more access compared to men. Men can become a little nervous if they entered a city whereas women know very well how to go unnoticed in enemy-controlled areas. (Interview with Daniel Kodi, SPLM/A representative in the Middle East, Cairo, April 8, 1998)

As I explain elsewhere (Ali 2000), women's participation in armed struggle (in the context of the South) had contributed to challenging social perceptions about femininity. It is important, however, to take into consideration the gender-specific impact of war on women. As discussed earlier in this book, women experienced rape, displacement, and other traumas in Sudan's war. Numerous books and reports have documented gender-based sexual violence during the war in Darfur. The experiences of female ex-combatants in South Sudan, the Nuba Mountains, and Southern Blue Nile areas have been mostly devastating, and communities in war-affected areas continue to face gender-based violence even after the signing of the CPA (N. Ali 2011).

Women (and children) are often the majority of those who are displaced as a result of the war and harassment by all sides of the conflict (focus group discussion, Juba, October 2014; Abdel Halim 1998; de Waal 1997). The gender-specific impact of conflict has been devastating on South Sudanese women, for example (Jok 1997a, 1997b, and 1998). The experience of South Sudan, but also of South Africa and Liberia, show the difficulty of overturning the impact of militarization and violence.

To conclude, the New Sudan discourse is distinct in that it is concerned with difference and the way it is turned into oppression. It can add complexity to the visions and programs of organizations and movements working toward gender equality in exile and in Sudan. Much of this discourse lacks a gender perspective, however. While in recent years this discourse has included references to the impact of Islamism and war on women, the New Sudan vision still lacks an analysis of the impact of the Old Sudan on diverse Sudanese women. The alternative order that New Sudan movements offer should also have a clear gender perspective. While some of the narratives above reflect a political will to achieve gender equality, experiences elsewhere suggest this is not enough unless supported by the constituencies of these movements (Molyneux 1985; Connell 1998).

With this in mind, it is important to ask: To what extent is it desirable and possible to build alliances between women's groups, on one hand, and New Sudan movements on the other? Collaborating with New Sudan groups can link predominantly urban, middle-class women's organizations, including those active in exile, to women at the grassroots levels in marginalized areas of Sudan. New Sudan movements and women's organizations can draw lessons from other parts of the Global South, such as Brazil. Writing about Brazil, Alvarez (1990) has shown how alliances between feminist women's organizations on one hand, and left-wing political organizations and a church committed to liberation theology on the other, linked feminists to women's groups addressing women's immediate needs. This led to the politicization of these feminine interests in the long run, adding to the strength of the women's movement. Would this work in Sudan?

As discussed earlier in this book, the alliance that New Sudan movements built with sectarian parties undermined their expressed commitments to women's human rights in the period following the Asmara 1995 conference.

New Sudan movements emphasize the urgent needs of women and men at the grassroots level. While this emphasis is important, including in terms of widening the agendas of women's groups in urban centers and in exile, it can be a tool to delegitimize the concerns of women's organizations seeking gender equality. Sectarian parties, the government, and other social forces not interested in transforming gender relations can appropriate what New Sudan leaders define as "priorities of women at the grassroots level" and use it to render the concerns with women's rights and gender equality irrelevant.

References to egalitarianism and commitment to empowering women in some of the marginalized areas in Sudan, as a means to mark the sociocultural boundaries between communities in these areas on one hand, and the dominant social, political, economic, and cultural elites in the North on the other, can inform advocacy strategies by women's groups (especially groups representing women from marginalized areas) committed to gender equality and seeking to ensure commitment to women's rights. These groups can appeal to and reshape these "cultural meanings" (Mendez and Naples 2014, 2) expressed in notions of egalitarianism and women's empowerment to challenge "pre-existing structures of inequality" (Mendez and Naples 2014, 2) and push for true political and social commitment to gender equality and women's human rights.

NOTES

1. One challenge to the discourse of the New Sudan is the unfortunate turn of events in independent South Sudan. Although the government of South Sudan never claimed to be implementing the vision of the New Sudan, conflict, corruption, and other developments shed doubt on the New Sudan as an alternative order. For an analysis of the factors that led to conflict in post-independence South Sudan, see de Waal (2014).

2. During its early years the SPLM/A expressed a commitment to creating a Socialist Sudan, but later the reference to Socialism disappeared from the literature of the movement.

3. Connell (n.d.) argued that these groups constituted a caucus that the Eritrean government created within the NDA as a counterforce to the two sectarian parties and the SPLM. Connell argued that the Eritrean government was not successful in "managing" the SPLM.

4. A local expression of nostalgia for colonial times.

5. Expressing nostalgia for the second military dictatorship in Sudan (1958–1964) by those who participated in or witnessed the 1964 October revolution.

Chapter Six

Gender, Intersectionality, and Transnational Activism

Women Resisting Marginalization and Exclusion

In the previous chapters I examined and analyzed the discourses and exclusionary practices of the National Democratic Alliance (NDA), including political groups that identified as New Sudan movements. I argued that while the New Sudan discourse represents a subversive force to the old, neopatriarchal Sudan in many ways, it lacks a gender perspective. In the absence of a clear gender perspective that takes into account other intersecting aspects of identity, democratic transformation, peace building, and post-conflict reconstruction efforts may end up reinforcing gender inequality and deepening other forms of exclusion, rather than transforming gender relations and ensuring equal redistribution of wealth and political power in Sudan (and South Sudan). Women's organizations and activists can play important roles in engendering such processes. As Hisham Sharabi has suggested,

> Of all these groups,[1] potentially the most revolutionary is the women's movement. If this phase of struggle were to open up to radical democratic change, women's liberation would necessarily be its spearhead. . . . If allowed to grow and come into its own, it will become the permanent shield against patriarchal regression. (1988, 154)

In this chapter I discuss how women's organizations and activists engaged issues of women's political participation and the lack of commitment to women's human rights by the NDA. I focus on the Sudan Women's Union, the Sudan Women's Alliance, *Ma'an*, and the Women's Bureaus in the Umma Party, the Democratic Unionist Party, the Sudan National Party,

Figure 6.1.   Part of the women participants in the conference on Human Rights in the Transition in Sudan, Kampala, 1999, with the late Dr. John Garang. Participants in the photo include representatives of New Sudan Women Federation (NSWF), New Sudan Women's Association (NESWA), Widows, Orphans, and Disabled Rehabilitation Association of the New Sudan (WODRANS), Sudanese Women's Organization in Nairobi (SWAN), Sudan Women's Alliance (SWA), and Nuba Mountains Organization Abroad (NOB). It includes the gender officer of UNICEF's Operation Lifeline Sudan at the time, the 28 Ramadan Martyrs Association, the Women's desk officer at Sudan Human Rights Organization (SHRO), and the Secretary for Women's Affairs in the Democratic Unionist Party (DUP) at the time. From the collection of Nada M. Ali, taken by His Excellency Deng Alor.

and other political parties and movements. Documenting the accommodation as well as resistance that women's organizations and activists waged against exclusion in exile is not only important in its own right, it demonstrates that the NDA's exclusionary practices did not go uncontested.

Given the diversity of women and women's groups active in Egypt and Kenya at the time of initial research, and given the role of collective transnational struggles in helping women's movements achieve their goals, I use the lens of intersectionality to explore possibilities of collective action despite the contradictions among diverse women and women's groups.

Molyneux's typology of women's organizations discussed earlier can help illuminate the institutional relationship between different women's organization with exiled opposition parties and movements. Women's organ-

Figure 6.2.   The author with members of the Sudan Women's Alliance in Garora village on the Sudanese/Eritrean borders, and with students in a school run by Sudan Future Care Amal Trust. 2003.

izations in exile were independent (autonomous), associated with one or more of the political parties or movements, or dependent on a political party or movement. The Sudanese Women's Union (SWU) started as an autonomous group and has always identified as independent. Nonetheless, as Hale (1996) argued, the SWU had fallen under the control of the CPS. Despite the CPS's progressive stand toward women, compared to the other parties in Sudan, the SWU's agenda became subordinate to that of the party at times. The relationship between the two organizations had a negative impact on the SWU. On one hand, the SWU could not push toward the creation of a strong and independent women's movement (in the North). The second problem was that maintaining a fictional dissociation with the CPS deprived the SWU of the chance to work within the structures of the party itself to widen the space available for addressing issues of gender equality and women's human rights

Although the SWU membership has been open to any Sudanese woman (interview with Azza al-Tigany, Member of the Executive Office of the SWU in Cairo, May 11, 1998), authority often rests in the hands of members clearly committed in the CPS. This was reflected in that when the first women's network in exile *Lagnat al-Mar'a* (women's committee) was created in Cairo in 1991, two active women[2] identified themselves as representatives of the SWU and participated actively in early exile politics. When women who were SWU members in Sudan who were also members of the CPS started to arrive in Cairo, they decided to form a branch of the SWU, and to replace the existing network with another one in which the SWU would have a larger say. The founding members of the new branch declared the two SWU women members in *Lagnat al-Mar'a* as non-members of the SWU (interview with anonymous, Cairo, 1998; personal communication with anonymous, Cairo, 1998).

An organization that could be described as autonomous and clearly committed to transforming gender relations and other forms of inequality in Sudan is the Cairo-based *Ma'an* (which literally means together but is also an abbreviation for *Magmu'at al-A'mal al-Niswy*—Women's Work Group). A small group of women who were friends started *Ma'an* with the aim of organizing women so women can challenge their subordination, including in political institutions in exile, despite the group's commitment to the general agenda of the NDA at the time (which included separation between politics and religion, democracy, and social justice).

The group's programs and activities addressed the immediate needs of women and communities affected by the precariousness of conflict, oppression, and exile, while also clearly addressing women's strategic gender interests. For example, *Ma'an* fundraised to support the communities affected by the 1998 famine in Northern Bahr al-Ghazal in Southern Sudan. *Ma'an* also collected and donated clothes, copybooks, and pencils to support schools in areas held by the NDA in Eastern Sudan in the late 1990s and early 2000s. Yet the group also held discussions on issues such as feminism, personal status laws, reproductive health and rights, and secularism. The group also organized literacy and other training courses for Sudanese and South Sudanese women in Egypt. As discussed later, in the focus group discussion I conducted with members of *Ma'an*, some articulated views that challenged unequal gender relations and discrimination against women in Sudan. Many members in the group also reflected critically on other unequal relations in Sudan and in exile, including those based on social class, race, ethnicity, and region.

In Nairobi, an autonomous organization that had succeeded in reaching out to diverse women is the Sudan Women's Association in Nairobi (SWAN). Established in 1992 by a group of refugee Sudanese women, the group, which relocated to South Sudan after the signing of the CPA (interview with Mama Lulu, Juba, 2010), offered a platform for women from Southern Sudan and the Nuba Mountains across tribal, cultural, and political affiliation. Associated with UNIFEM (now UN Women's) African Women in Crisis program, SWAN organized high-profile activities in Nairobi and in the areas under the control of the SPLM/A. Like *Ma'an*, the activities of the SWAN addressed both the practical needs of women and communities, and the strategic gender interests of women. Unlike *Ma'an*, whose membership was until 1999 limited and predominantly middle class, the SWAN had a wide membership of 467 (in March 1999). Membership included educated middle-class Southern Sudanese women as well as low-income women who had no access to formal education prior to their exile. SWAN reached these women through its service programs, providing a space for women to meet and talk, extending loans to those in need, and supporting income-generating activities in the form of tie-dye and small-scale food processing as well as providing marketing facilities for women.

Another Nairobi-based independent organization (the leadership of which closely associated with one of the split SPLM groups at the time of research—South Sudan Independence Movement) is the Sudanese Women's Voice for Peace (SWVP), established in March 1994. A non-partisan, non-sectarian, non-profit organization, the SWVP was established to address the challenges that arose because of the SPLM/A split in the early 1990s.

In addition to publicizing the impact of war on women (and children) in Southern Sudan at a time when the crises and war in Sudan lacked international attention, the SWVP focused on ensuring women's participation in peace negotiations between the Government of Sudan (GOS) and the SPLM/A. To prepare women for effective participation in negotiations, SWVP organized training on conflict resolution and leadership skills for Southern Sudanese women. The group utilized the run-up to the Beijing conference, and the conference itself, to highlight the impact of war and oppression on South Sudanese women, and to reach out to regional and international women's and peace organizations.

A number of women's organizations active in Cairo, Kenya, and beyond had associational linkages with some of the New Sudan movements. These included the Union of Beja Women, which had an associational relationship with the Beja Congress and which was mainly active in the non-government-held areas of Eastern Sudan. The Sudanese Women's Alliance (SWA) had an associational relationship with the SNA/SAF. A plethora of women's organizations had established associational linkages with the SPLM/A. These included the NSWF, the NESWA, and the WODRANS. These organizations mainly operated in Kenya and in the non-government-held areas in South Sudan. Below I discuss SWA, NSWF, and WODRANS.

Established in August 1995, the SWA became part of the SNA/SAF when the latter adopted a position paper (which I authored) at SNA/SAF's first conference in 1995. The SWA shared with the SNA/SAF the recognition that women's subordination was the result, among other factors, of the nature of the social, economic, and political structures, institutions, and power relations that prevailed in the Old Sudan. The SWA also shared a commitment to achieving a "new, secular and just" Sudan. At least on paper, the SNA/SAF shared with SWA an understanding that concerns with women's human rights and gender equality should not wait until the change of the NIF/NCP regime. In its official documents, the SNA also shared a commitment to transforming patriarchal structures, and to women's empowerment on political, economic, and social levels. The movement also endorsed CEDAW without reservations.

Authority within SWA rested in the general congresses of SWA and SNA/SAF, but final decisions concerning issues related to women's human rights and gender equality rested in the hands of SWA. SNA/SAF's Women's Secretariat, over which I presided between 1995 and 2002, coordinated the relationship between SNA and SWA. SWA members used their links with the SNA/SAF to *influence the agenda* of the movement, and to build wider support for a feminist agenda "early on in the struggle."

SWA worked in a decentralized manner and its membership came from diverse ethnic groups and socioeconomic backgrounds. The organization used a clear intersectional approach. Its documents emphasized the importance of "including the visions and [reflecting] the practical needs of women who experienced multiple forms of subordination, including women who are affected by war, those subjected to ethnic cleansing in the Nuba Mountains, as well as displaced and refugee women (SWA 1995). The chapters of SWA in and outside Sudan organized their activities according to the priorities of the local membership. While in the non-government-held areas almost the entire membership was from rural areas and had low income, in other settings, including in Egypt, England, and in urban areas of Sudan such as Khartoum, the membership was largely urban and educated. The latter were more visible within the organization, a shortcoming which the organization acknowledged in a report to SWA's first organizational conference, which took place in Eritrea in December 1997.

> We also realize that the majority of SWA membership—with the exception of the liberated areas—consists of women who belong to the urban, middle and upper middle classes. Most of these are educated and belong to the Northern and Central parts of Sudan. This entails better creativity in order to reach out to wider sectors. (SWA 1997)

In the same meeting, Sarah Cleto Rial, a Southern Sudanese activist who was the chair of the Cairo branch of SWA, was elected as the new president of SWA.

A number of women's groups, organized under the New Sudan Women Federation (NSWF), were associated with the SPLM/A. NSWF, an umbrella organization, was established in 1995, following a training workshop on leadership in Loki, Kenya. NSWF coordinated the activities of women's associations in New Sudan (non-government-held areas of Southern Sudan), and supported women economically, politically, and socially. NSWF collaborated with SPLM/A. Its chair was former secretary of women and children's affairs in SPLM/A. However, NSWF advocated for better participation for women within SPLM/A.

The New Sudan Women's Association, established in 1996, was also associated with the SPLM/A. NESWA supported women's political participation and built the capacities of women so they could participate effectively. A third group, WODRANS, which Madame Rebecca de Mabior established and presided over, catered to the needs of widows, orphans, and the disabled in the non-government-held areas in Southern Sudan. The discourse of WODRANS reflected an understanding of gender equality and a commitment to transforming gender relations through the SPLM/A. The authority of both NESWA and WODRANS rested in their general congresses.

A number of women's and gender secretariats constituted directed mobilizations. The women's desks within the DUP and Umma Party both constituted forms of (conservative) directed mobilizations. These parties controlled the direction of the women's desks, including on women's human rights and political participation. While in recent years women members and leaders of the Umma Party enjoyed better visibility, during the 1990s women's active leadership in exile was limited in both parties. Party leaders set the agenda and allocated roles for women most of the time. This is not to argue that women in these parties did not have quasi-autonomous spaces. The women's secretariat in DUP's London chapter, for example, was active in exile politics. DUP's women's secretariat was also active in Cairo, within the Sudanese Women's Forum in Cairo. However, this autonomy was limited. The following case illustrates some of the limitations.

The former secretary for women's affairs in DUP-Cairo, who was appointed in March 1995 "on the basis of a decision by the Political Bureau, and with the blessings of the leader al-Mirghani" (Al-Hussein and al-Shykh 1997, 168), was removed from her post in 1998, when she refused to take the party's line on the issue of Article 5 (interview with Zainab Osman al-Hussein, secretary for women's affairs, DUP branch, Cairo, August 1998). As president of the Sudanese Women's Forum, al-Hussein was able to take an independent stand that affirmed women's strategic gender interests and a commitment to women's human rights. As a member of the DUP, however, she was not able to take the same stand. This shows the importance of autonomous collective action—especially in the case of parties that do not fully support the agendas of women's organizations and in institutions with limited democratic space.

During the 1990s and early 2000s, the Umma Party had a women's secretariat that had become functional. In Cairo, the party established a women's secretariat but many of the experienced female cadre were not part of it. The secretary for women's affairs in the party was in Sudan, and its chair was active in the NDA leadership inside Sudan. The majority of women members of the party who were in Cairo preferred to participate in party activities and did not want to limit their activities to women's affairs. Authority was vested in the party, and in the hands of the leader of the party, Imam al-Sadiq al-Mahdi. Umma Party members interviewed for this research said the party had been advocating for a national women's organization that represented the interests of women since the mid-1980s. According to El Bakri (1995), that was a tactic to win the support of women during the elections of 1986, and to undermine the SWU.

RESISTING THE NDA'S GENDERED POLITICS: WOMEN'S "REPRESENTATION" IN THE NDA

Like the opposition discourse, the discourses and practices of the exiled women's groups were diverse. Most of the women's organizations and the branches of political parties in Cairo were either formed/re-established with a clear political aim of resisting the NIF/NCP regime, or with the aim of addressing the daily challenges that refugee women, especially from South Sudan, faced. My focus here is on the former category, interested in wider questions of transformation and gender equality as integral to democratization in Sudan.

In Cairo, women, particularly Northern Sudanese women who were active in Sudan, organized first in *Lagnat al-Mar'a* (the Women's Committee). Established in 1991, this committee aimed at bringing exiled women who identified as opposition together. As one of the founders of the group recounted,

> I thought of establishing a body so women could articulate a collective and a strong voice. I wrote an article in a newspaper that the former Coordinating Committee of the opposition issued at the time. We organized a meeting at the Umma party's office. Fifty women turned up. That was a big number at the time [1991], and included women from different political backgrounds as well as women with no party background. It included women from the SWU and wives of the officers active in the Legitimate Command as well as members of the Families of [28 Ramadan] Martyrs Association. (Interview with anonymous, Cairo, 1998)

Participants in the meeting established an acting executive office of five, with diverse political leanings, but who were generally progressive. The committee's activities included advocacy, fundraising, and organizing cultural activities.

The committee disintegrated two years later in 1993. While some of the former members argued administrative and financial problems, and the expansion of membership caused the folding of the committee, others argued this was planned, and with the aim of replacing the committee with another body where membership was exclusive for women members of opposition parties (the Sudanese Women's Forum [SWF]). This alienated some of the founders of the committee (including some who were members of opposition parties) from organized women's activism.

Following the disintegration of *Lagnat al-Mar'a*, the SWF was established in July 1993 in Cairo as a forum for opposition women's groups and women's secretariats in political parties. It included representatives from the women's secretariats and desks in the Umma and DUP, the SWU, and the women's office in the Nuba Organization (NOB). It also included women who were members in the SPLM/A, given that the movement launched a branch of NSWF in Cairo only in 1998.

While both *Lagnat Al-Mara'a* and the SWF prioritized women's formal representation in NDA activities in Cairo, the Women's Forum sought to derive the legitimacy of its existence primarily from the NDA. It considered itself as the "only legitimate organization representing Sudanese women abroad (in Cairo) and the only organization that has the right to contact foreign bodies and governments on behalf of Sudanese women" (Basic Rules of the Women's Forum, Cairo, 1993). In this way, the organization presented itself as another legitimate body and modelled its structure after the NDA.

The structure of the organization was similar to the NDA even in terms of the allocation of positions to different political parties (the president was a DUP, the Umma Party had two representatives, and other groups had one representative each in the executive office). The structure of the SWF created problems within the organization that played a key role in its disintegration in June 1998. Umma/DUP competition over offices, which has plagued the NDA performance since 1995, was transferred to the Women's Forum.

The NDA, however, did not recognize the Women's Forum and did not endorse their choice of the representative of women in the NDA Leadership Council. Moreover, although the Women's Forum was still active in 1997, in July of the same year the NDA officially recommended the establishment of "a national women's organization."

The Women's Forum and individual activists in and outside Cairo protested women's exclusion from NDA's political structures. Women's groups severely criticized the High Coordinating Committee (HCC), which the NDA formed to prepare for the Asmara conference. Ihsan Abdallah, an Umma Party activist and a former Minister of State in the post-1986 democratic era, urged the women's groups and individual activists to pressure the NDA and the HCC to become more inclusive of women.

> The HCC is waging a battle to suppress Sudanese women, in a diversion from the principles of civilisation and progress and from UN conventions. The international community has come to focus on marginalised areas and social

group, including women. I call upon women leaders outside Sudan (in exile) to denounce this stand and to open communication channels to correct this situation or to take any other action, *even if this meant boycotting the NDA*. (Abdallah 1995, 3; emphasis mine)

Abdallah, who was advocating mainly for women's participation, did not subordinate women's participation and human rights to wider issues of the unity of the NDA. She hinted at how the NDA had used international human rights conventions selectively to isolate the NIF/NCP regime internationally, while denying women their rights enshrined in international conventions.

As the date of the Conference for Fundamental Issues drew closer, Abdallah wrote an article in *al-Khartoum* daily newspaper in which she asked: Why has the NDA ignored women in its deliberation over the future of Sudan? (Abdallah 1995, 3). Abdallah asked whether this was a glimpse into "what might happen if today's opposition leaders became future rulers of Sudan" (Abdallah 1995, 3).

When I interviewed Abdallah in 1998, she was still critical of the NDA's stand on women.

I am not competing with [men in the NDA] over responsibilities. This work is huge, but those men of [the opposition] outside [Sudan] appended a women's bureau to the NDA. I do not understand why we need this kitchen! . . . Students can have an office because they have distinct problems! But to cram women in a bureau for women's affairs! Does this mean all the other offices are men's offices? . . . None of us has rights in Sudan now, so why should women have a separate office? . . . Why do they want to restrict [women] only to voluntary work? Don't women know how to plan or strategize? (Interview with Ihsan Abdallah, Cairo, July 18, 1998)

Other women leaders also criticized the NDA for excluding women from its structures. Magda Khogali, then secretary for women's affairs in DUP's branch in London, UK, criticized the NDA for failing to ensure women's participation in its structures, despite women's roles in opposing the NIF/NCP (interview with Magda Khogali, London, UK, 1999).

Fatima Ahmed Ibrahim, too, scolded the NDA for excluding women from its leadership structures. A key opposition figure who is also a member of the CPS's Central Committee, Ibrahim had been president of the Sudanese Women's Union since the 1960s. In response to women's criticism after the Asmara conference in 1995, the NDA invited Ibrahim to attend its Leadership Council meeting in January 1996. In this meeting, she advocated for and was granted an observer status in the NDA's Leadership Council. This did not resolve the issue of women's representation in the NDA, however, as Ibrahim joined it in her personal capacity and as a representative of the SWU. The Women's Forum in Cairo sent a memo to the NDA demanding that she become the representative of women in the NDA, but the NDA disregarded the memo. The reason, according to the Secretary General of the NDA at the time, was that the NDA did not recognize the SWF as a *national* women's organization (NDA SG 1997, 1998).

Much of the discourse on women and the NDA in the post-Asmara 1995 era focused on Fatima Ibrahim's participation in the NDA LC. An exception was a statement and campaign (to change Article 5), which the Feminist Group for Reconstructing Sudan (FGR Sudan) organized in the run-up to the NDA's first meeting after the Asmara conference. The group addressed the NDA LC as well as Fatima Ibrahim.

Sudanese women's organizations in Cairo continued their campaigns to ensure women's participation in the NDA in the period that followed the Asmara conference. The SWU devoted its celebration of International Women's Day (IWD) in March 1996 to a discussion on women's political participation, especially in the NDA. Speakers included NDA's Secretary of Organization, Dr. al-Shafie Khider. Khider argued that while safeguarding women's rights was the responsibility of both men and women, "Ideological and political predicaments, including women's negative attitudes toward their rights," and men's perceptions of women's roles as mainly reproduction, curtailed political participation (SHRO Quarterly 1996, 56). Khider's narrative, which challenged dominant perceptions of femininity as causes of the exclusion of women by male opposition leaders, can count as a discourse of resistance.

SWA organized several activities in and outside Egypt to advocate for women's participation, including in the NDA. In December 1996, the organization held a seminar on Sudanese women's history and future prospects. Speakers discussed women's political participation, including in constitution building in future Sudan.

Women activists (including the author) also advocated on women's participation in the NDA whenever NDA leaders were present in or outside Egypt. Women and men in exile also advocated on the Internet. The office of the NDA's Secretary General (SG office) argued the criticism was because people did not have a clear idea on the position of the NDA on women's participation:

> The discussion of the issue . . . came as clarification to some distorted information about the NDA position on women that was circulated by Fatima Ahmad Ibrahim who tried to [impose] herself as the representative of women at the Leadership Council last year [1996], without having necessary credentials. When [the NDA rejected Ibrahim's proposal she retaliated . . . by shedding doubts on the NDA [*sic*] position on women. (NDA SG Office, August 3, 1997)

During the second part of the 1990s, Sudanese women's organizations in Cairo and political parties agreed on the need for women's participation in NDA's leadership structures. The difference always concerned *how* women should participate in these structures, and who *was representative* of women. The DUP suggested in the NDA's LC meeting in March 1998 that each party should nominate a female representative to participate in the NDA General Congress, so that only women members in NDA member parties could participate. The Umma Party also suggested that NDA member parties allocate some of their seats in NDA leadership structures to women. In addition, the Umma Party suggested that women form a "credible national association" that would facilitate their participation in the NDA (NDA SG Office, August 1997). The SWU in Cairo argued that the SWF was a suitable body to represent exiled women.

The SWA argued that although the ideal way to represent women in the NDA should be in their capacity as citizens, Sudanese politics was defective and exclusive, which necessitated other measures to ensure participation. The group suggested that the NDA establish a taskforce to debate women's participation and to come up with recommendations to increase participation. SWA suggested that the taskforce include selected activists from political parties and women's organizations, as well as independent women activists. The group suggested that the recommendations of the taskforce be the basis of a wide discussion in and outside the NDA. *Ma'an* endorsed SWA's suggestion.

The issue of women's representation was only partially resolved during the NDA's second congress, which took place in Massawa, Eritrea. Some of the NDA leaders, especially DUP leaders, started to argue that the lack of women's participation in NDA's leadership structures was the result of women's lack of consensus on the modality for participation. As I argued earlier, this was an extension of the politics of the 1980s.

Next, I examine the way predominantly Southern Sudanese women's groups in Nairobi addressed issues of political participation, after a background on active groups at the time of research.

SPLM AND WOMEN'S PARTICIPATION: "THE SOUTH DOES NOT BELONG TO MEN ALONE"

Compared to women's groups active in Cairo, there was an emerging South Sudanese women's movement in Nairobi. For many of the Southern activists as well as non-Southern members in the SPLM/A, exile did not start in 1989. The movement continued to be in opposition to the government after the overthrow of Numeiry's regime in 1985. Women's participation started at an early stage. Many of the women had already learned much from their experience in the first war. As Madame Rebecca de Mabior, then chair of Widows, Orphans, and Disabled Rehabilitation Association for the New Sudan (WO-DRANS), and who became a gender and human rights advisor to President Salva Kiir following the independence of South Sudan, said,

> We learned a lot from the first war [1955–1972]. When this war started [in 1983], we (women) were able to organize ourselves, to identify what is the role of women in the struggle, and to raise the awareness of women and to [appreciate] the way the grassroots are suffering most. They know what we struggle for; they shall inform those in exile on what the problem is. We [are also] close, to them. That is why we can appreciate and try to help them. (Chair, WODRANS, Nairobi, March 17, 1999)

While women have joined the SPLA since 1984, it was not until 1985 that women started to organize as women. That year, six of the women combatants whose husbands were in the leadership of the SPLM/A met in Addis Ababa to discuss what they could do as women of the movement. The women decided to form a women's organization. As one of those who participated at that early stage recounts,

> Primarily we asked ourselves, as women whose husbands were at the war front, what are our responsibilities, our role towards the movement and what can we contribute towards this struggle? This meeting gave us the inspiration to start a women's association. Madame Rebecca [SPLM/A member and wife of Dr. Garang, leader of the movement] then took this resolution and then met with the women in Itang Refugee Camp to introduce them to this new initiative. The women then decided to hold a meeting where they held an election in which eleven executive committee members were elected. (Osman 1998, 10)

At that early stage, the organization was concerned merely with organizing the women to support the armed struggle, and in meeting some of the practical needs of refugee women. It assisted wounded soldiers and provided food for the army. The organization also supported women and children in the refugee camps, and ran literacy classes for women.

By 1986, two other organizations had been founded. In the same year, the SPLM/A enrolled three of its active women members in the "political school" for two years, to prepare them to join the leadership of the movement. By 1989, the movement had established the position of director of women's affairs and appointed Sittona Osman (who was the chair of NSWF at the time of initial research, and who became South Sudan's ambassador to Italy after South Sudan's independence) as head.

Women participated in the process of preparation for the SPLM/A's first convention, which took place in 1994. Forty-five women attended the meeting, as representatives of associations in different geographic locations. In that convention, twenty-three women were admitted to the SPLM's National

Liberation Council: those included fifteen representatives of women's associations and seven women representatives of geographic constituencies and
refugee camps. Five of these women were elected to the National Executive
Council (Osman 1998, 10).

In the 1990s, other forms of both associative and autonomous women's
organizing emerged, and had developed into a full-fledged movement when I
started the interviews for this research in Nairobi in early 1999. Many of
these groups worked in collaboration with UN agencies such as UNIFEM
(now UN Women) and UNICEF. They coordinated their activities so as not
to duplicate each other's activities and so as to organize their relationship
with the donors (key informant interview with Laketch Dirasse, Regional
Director of UNIFEM, Nairobi, March 23, 1999; key informant interview
with Nadi Albino, Gender Officer in OLS, Nairobi, March 17, 1999; interview with Pauline Riak, Executive Director of SWAN, Nairobi, March 18,
1999). Like the organizations based in Cairo, these groups constantly advocated for women's participation within the structures of the SPLM and its
split factions, and in peace negotiations between the SPLM/A and the GOS.
But compared to the groups in Cairo, the women's movement in Southern
Sudan was gaining momentum given its social, economic, and political impact at the macro level and at the grassroots level (interview with Nadi
Albino, Nairobi, March 17, 1999).

Activists in the Nairobi-based organizations were persistent in pushing
for women's participation at the highest levels. At a workshop on Women
and Political Participation in the New Sudan, held at Silver Spring Hotel in
Nairobi, one of the participants said,

> My sisters: it is our turn now. From now on, [we will not wait for] instructions!
> If we hear that something is taking place, we should just go. . . . It has become
> known that women have a voice, they can speak, [and] they can participate in
> IGAD [talks]. This South does not belong to men alone. It belongs to all the
> people living in it. (Saida Peter [Pagan], March 13, 1999, workshop attended
> and recorded by the author)

Another activist said in the same workshop: "just as there are male politicians, there are also women politicians. In this Movement, there should be a
woman politician in a position that is equal to Garang [chair of SPLM/A]"
(Nairobi, Silver Spring Hotel, March 13, 1999).

Similarly, a pamphlet which NESWA issued in March 1999 challenges
definitions of masculinity and femininity that relegate women to the private
sphere and excludes them from leadership positions:

> We want our New Sudan women to be well informed about politics. They are
> the majority of the [Sudanese] population. The political [and] socio-economic
> power is in their hands . . . but because of ignorance, they are trodden upon,

kept in the kitchen and made to procreate generation [after] generation. *But time has come for us, the women of the New Sudan, to equally dance with our men in the political arena. No man is born a politician and no woman is born a cook! It is our society that shapes us to be what we are.* (emphasis mine)

This quote unsettles dominant constructions of gender roles in Southern Sudanese communities, and within the SPLM. It challenges these constructions. No more could women's role be confined to what Nira Yuval Davis described as the biological reproduction of the nation.

The various women's groups were aware of their precarity, yet they approached this precarity collectively, including by supporting women affected by war and displacement. This support took many forms. NSWF, for example, established para-legal clinics to address conflict-related crises affecting women. These clinics also addressed domestic violence and women's marginalization within the household. Changing the position of women, argued the chair of NSWF, did not need to wait until the war ended.

In New Sudan (SPLM held areas) we are advantaged because we are establishing a new civil society, civil administration and judiciary system that are based on democracy, peace, self-determination and human rights principles. This is the right time for Sudanese people to put their house in good order. We should not wait until the end of the war. (Osman 1998, 3)

Although the women have gone a long way in their involvement in the SPLM, there were still challenges in terms of coordination between the movement and women's groups, especially at the grassroots levels. For example, at county level, women's associations worked with (and often under the rule of) commissioners, for whom women's participation and gender equality were not always a priority (Osman 1998, 10).

In Nairobi, the South Sudanese women's peace movement played a key role in organizing women and in campaigning for women's participation in peace negotiations. A key player was the Sudanese Women's Voice for Peace (SWVP). The group initially started to build peace among warring SPLM/A factions after the split of SPLM/A in 1992. It also advocated for women's participation in the IGAD peace negotiations. With its headquarters in Nairobi and with branches in various SPLM held areas, the SWVP organized training on conflict resolution, peace monitoring, and leadership skills, in collaboration with international and UN agencies. Anisia Achieng, cofounder of the Sudanese Women's Voice for Peace, recounts the story of the organization.

When the war [escalated] in 1983, we had to move to Torit, Juba and Khartoum to save our lives. When this government (NIF) came to power, my colleague Regina and I said at once: what will happen to the displaced and what will happen to women given that all the parties and associations are banned? We organized the displaced and even approached the government within one week of the coup. The government security was very tight and I remained [in Sudan] until I came out on a [health] condition. So when I came here in Kenya I started looking at what we can do. *One institution that was lacking in women's participation—as women's participation is one of my concerns, was [the institution of peace building].* So I sat with other women and we started asking why women were not part and parcel of peace talks in the Sudan? When Regina came we said could we find a way so that women can participate in the peace talks? Women's groups needed a structure. We contacted women here [in Nairobi] and said that we could not achieve anything if we were not part of the talks. Also we needed to create a non-violence mechanism in civil society. (Interview with Anisia Achieng, Nairobi, March 27, 1999)

The founders of SWVP had strong leadership, peace-building, and communication skills, which they used in their advocacy for inclusive peace negotiations. Founders of the groups also worked to transfer these skills to other South Sudanese women in exile through training and coaching (interview with Anisia Achieng, Nairobi, March 27, 1999).

The SWVP invited several political groups to workshops it organized, as well as senior IGAD officials. The group reviewed the participation of women in peace talks and found that women were mostly excluded from peace negotiations, and that women who took part did not have specific roles (interview with Anisia Achieng, March 27, 1999). The SWVP started working with women's groups. It trained women and community leaders, including traditional healers so they can assure women's participation becomes policy. The SWVP was one of the key organizations that advocated for Security Council Resolution 1325. In 2010, 2011, and 2013, I met several of the founders of the SWVP, who assumed high government offices in South Sudan.

Although a complete assessment of the women's peace movement is beyond this book (remember, we are discussing women's resistance to the exclusionary politics of the exiled opposition in the 1990s and early 2000s, and possibilities for coalition building), I want to emphasize two important points. First, the women's peace movement constituted a meeting point for women from Northern and Southern Sudan. They met as Northern versus Southern women, however. Participants in these meetings included women organized in the opposition inside Sudan (but not predominantly Northern women's organizations active in Egypt, Eritrea, or the United Kingdom), and NIF/NCP supporters. Participation of women supporters of the NIF/NCP confirmed the conviction among many Southern women activists that *it was actually women in the North who subordinated their gender-specific interests to the dominant culture and political ideology.*

Second, women associated with the NIF/NCP most of the time did not address the challenges facing women in war-affected areas, according to interviewees for this research. Carla Tongun, coordinator of the SWAN and an activist in the SWVP told me,

> Under democratic governments we had women participants, but they were not effective in the community. We can [address] some of these issues by promoting women's participation, but how much impact does it give for the lives of women? How does this change their lives? Now women [supporters of the NIF/NCP] talk about Islamic culture and religion. (Interview with Carla Tongun, Nairobi, March 24, 1999)

As discussed later in this chapter, racism and racial discrimination, particularly against Southern Sudanese women in Khartoum, also played a role in alienating Southern Sudanese women as citizens, and this added to the skepticism regarding collective action to ensure peace—even though the SWVP drew upon essentialist notions of women as mothers to demonstrate women's effectiveness as peacemakers. According to Tongun,

> There is also racism towards Southern women displaced in the North. Even those who can speak good Arabic and English are not given equal opportunities in the civil service for example. The question is, then, how credible is the women's movement within the NIF[/NCP] government? They are not fighting for the rights of *every* woman! (Interview with Carla Tongun, Nairobi, March 24, 1999)

In the SPLM-held areas, pressure by women's groups and activists started to show results in a number of ways: for example, the SPLM had already appointed a female county commissioner in the areas under its administration at the time of initial research. Earlier I discussed women's participation in the National Convention. Women's groups had also succeeded in including two women in the SPLM/A delegation to IGAD talks in November 1997, Sittona Osman and Mary Apai. However, some activists argued that those women were not part of the negotiations. As a NESWA executive committee member stated "we tried to involve women in IGAD (talks), but they were kept in the corridors. Thus women are still in an inferior position" (Workshop on the Role of Women in Politics of the New Sudan, Nairobi, Silver Spring Hotel, March 13, 1999). Nonetheless, participation (even in the corridors) built women's confidence and public speaking and conflict resolution skills, and so did their involvement in political struggle within the SPLM/A and its splinter organizations.

Mary Apai, an SPLM/A activist and head of gender desk at the Horn of Africa Centre for Democracy and Development (HACDAD) at the time of initial research, responded to my question on the impact of women's involvement in opposition politics as follows,[3]

> I see that there are changes. Because now we are in decision-making and in the struggle. . . . There is no discrimination! We are treated equally. We are involved in formulating project proposals and in action. . . . I was a member of the 5th IGAD delegation in Nairobi here in 1998 with Sittona [Osman]. We were involved in the technical part as members of the SPLA, as women of the movement. And now I am very happy because I gained the experience . . . [to] formulate a document by myself. This is through the struggle and now [other people listen to us]. (Interview with Mary Apai, Nairobi, March 20, 1999)

In addition to expanding women's experiences, participation unleashed a sense of empowerment that emerged in contradistinction to what they might have experienced, were they still in government-held areas in Sudan. This was evident in Apai's narrative:

> In the struggle here it is up to me, there are no cultures that really oppress us. Religion is there for everybody, if I don't want to pray, nobody would [force me to], if I want to pray nobody would dictate to me how I do that. If I were Muslim the movement would not dictate how many times I should pray. Also there are no religious laws that are governing the movement. The movement is governed by an accumulation of laws that we have formulated through the struggle. But religion is not there! No verses from the Qur'an or the Bible tell us how to govern the people. (Ibid.)

Women's organizations and activists exiled in both Egypt and Kenya used diverse strategies to address exclusion from the structures of opposition parties, and from processes of peace building. Mary Apai's discussion of women's participation in relation to culture, religious freedom, secularism, and governance echoed the debates among women's organizations in both Egypt and Kenya on the second issue that was central to women's activism in exile in the 1990s and early 2000s: ensuring commitment by the opposition in exile to women's human rights without reservations. I discuss this below.

WOMEN'S HUMAN RIGHTS: CONTESTING AND NEGOTIATING ARTICLE 5

As discussed earlier, while in the early years of the NDA, women activists and organizations focused their energies on women's participation and representation; Article 5 dominated much of the public discourse of the exiled opposition throughout the second half of the 1990s. As with the movements that comprised the NDA, women activists and organizations in Egypt had different stands on whether or not to change Article 5. In this section I will address the discourses of resistance that developed around Article 5.

One of the early campaigns seeking the NDA's unreserved commitment to women's human rights was a campaign that a small group, the Feminist Group for Reconstructing Sudan (FGR Sudan), organized in Cairo. The group (which I co-founded) presented a memo to the first NDA Leadership Council meeting after the Asmara conference in January 1996. The group demanded that the NDA deletes "the sentence reading 'provided that [women's] rights do not contradict with religious beliefs'" from the Asmara Resolutions, and suggested an alternative wording for the text.

> The NDA recognizes the active role that women played in the social, economic and political history of the country. It is committed to the endowment of Sudanese women with indiscriminate citizenship rights and duties enshrined in international conventions, including the CEDAW. (FGR Sudan, Memo to the NDA LC meeting, January 4, 1996)

The statement of FGR Sudan welcomed the acknowledgment and commitment to the rights of non-Muslims in the Asmara Declaration, but noted the lack of commitments to women's human rights in Article 5. The memo concluded by arguing that changing Article 5 did not contradict with religious beliefs, but that it contradicted with "the use of dominant religious beliefs to oppress women" (FGR Sudan, January 4, 1996). Despite campaigning among NDA leaders known for commitment to women's human rights, the NDA LC did not discuss Article 5 in the January 1996 meeting (N. Ali 1998).

Other groups and activists also criticized the lack of total commitment to women's human rights despite progress in terms of commitment to equality, human rights, and religious freedom. A member of *Ma'an*, for example, argued that,

> Article 5 is practically at odds with the rest of the Asmara resolutions. . . . I think that this reflects the dominant mentality in the [NDA member] parties towards women, because women's problems have deep roots that cannot be easily resolved, just like the "Southern problem." I believe that even those (NDA leaders) who hold views that support women's issues did not raise the issues pertaining to women. Even if they did, they usually only pay lip service as they consider the struggle over women's issues the responsibility of women. (Ihsan al-Gaddal, Focus Group Discussion with *Ma'an*, Cairo, June 1998)

Following the FGR Sudan, the Sudanese Women's Forum in Cairo organized a similar campaign in early 1996. The SWF collected signatures in Cairo to support a memo asking the NDA to change Article 5. By 1998, women's resistance discourse became strong. The declaration of the Sudanese Women's Alliance's (SWA) organizational meeting, which took place in Asmara, Eritrea, in December 1997, expressed commitment to the NDA's Asmara Resolutions, with the exception of Article 5. In a briefing that SWA organized in Cairo, Egypt, in February 1998, one of the speakers argued that,

> We believe that all of us [women] in our different organizations should push hard so the different political groups recognise CEDAW without reservations when these groups are in opposition and specially that women *support* opposition activities widely. (Cairo, February 1998; tape-recorded)

Before the NDA meeting that took place in March 1998 (the first NDA LC meeting I attended as Sudan National Alliance's representative in the NDA's Executive Office), the SWA organized a wide campaign demanding that the NDA acknowledge CEDAW and change Article 5 of the Asmara declaration accordingly. SWA launched the campaign on March 7, during its celebration of International Women's Day.[4] SWA collected signatures in Egypt, Eritrea, and via the Internet, from Sudanese and non-Sudanese supporters of women's human rights as well as political activists. Members met with NDA leaders who showed commitment to women's human rights and urged them to support the campaign.

A week later, SWA transferred the campaign to Asmara, where women's groups and individual activists were invited to participate in a demonstration that SWA organized prior to the opening session of the NDA meeting. The women held a big banner that demanded that the NDA "recognises CEDAW." Toward the end of the demonstration, the late Widad Siddig, then head of SWA in Eritrea, presented a list of signatures along with the memo, and a copy of CEDAW, to the head of the NDA, Mohamed Osman al-Mirghani. Although there was a good presence of journalists, none (apart of Sudan National Alliance's broadcasting station, *Swt Al-Hurya Wal-Tagdyd* [Voice of Freedom and Renewal]) mentioned the demonstration nor the campaign in their reporting.

In the same NDA meeting, as secretary for women's affairs at SNA, and as the movement's representative in the NDA's Executive Office, I presented a memorandum asking the NDA to acknowledge CEDAW, to change Article 5, and to revise its position on women's participation.[5] Fatima Ibrahim, who attended the meeting as an observer in the NDA's LC, presented a memo asking the NDA to change Article 5 and to promote her to the position of a member instead of an observer in the LC. The NDA discussed both memorandums at the end of the meeting (on the final day at one o'clock in the morning). A third memorandum, from the SWF in Cairo, also demanded the change of Article 5. The London-based newspaper *Al-Fajr* reproduced the three memos shortly after the meeting.

Two other initiatives addressed Article 5 and the position of the NDA toward women's rights. These included a political symposium organized by *Darb Al-Intifada*, an online forum, at the end of 1998, and two preparatory workshops which the women's desk of the Sudan Human Rights Organization (SHRO) London organized in late 1998 and early 1999 respectively, prior to the conference on Human Rights in Transition in Sudan (Kampala), which took place in February 1999. The conference emphasized women's participation and human rights, including within the NDA.

The struggle to ensure commitment by political movements and parties to women's human rights, including those enshrined in CEDAW, without reservation, is not exclusive to Sudan (and South Sudan). Some scholars and movements have argued that the only way to establish legitimacy for and commitment to human rights would be through showing how these do not contradict with local beliefs. These often overlook the strong affinity between religion and local beliefs on one hand, and structures of domination that reduce religion and beliefs into tools for social control on the other hand.[6] As such, it is always easy to delegitimize these claims by arguing that they do not represent "real" Islam or other beliefs.

In line with the above, several commentators and activists urged the NDA to commit to women's human rights without reservations, by arguing that women's human rights and CEDAW were not inconsistent with religion and beliefs in Sudan. In addition to Fatima Ibrahim's articles in the *al-Fajr* and *al-Khartoum* exile newspapers, Mahgoub al-Tigany, head of the Cairo branch of the Sudan Human Rights Organization (SHRO), published an article titled "The National Democratic Alliance and Sudanese Women's Rights" in *al-Khartoum* (August 30, 1998). Al-Tigany argued that none of the articles in CEDAW contradicted Islamic belief. He argued that the "heavenly religions" all ensure "total equality between the two sexes, as this is an obvious truth, protected by values and human dignity" (al-Tigany 1998, 3).

Al-Tigany addressed issues of economic rights (such as inheritance) and political participation by citing the Qur'an. He cited incidents that occurred during the early days of Islam, where women played active public roles, and concluded that the spirit of Islam contradicted, not with CEDAW, but with attempts to enfeeble women and shed light on their abilities (al-Tigany 1998, 3).

While al-Tigany's approach draws upon the analysis of the Republican Brothers, he did not start from the same point of this reformist group. Mahmoud Mohamed Taha and the Republicans argue that shari'a in its current form was not conducive to international human rights and that the verses of the Qur'an which Prophet Muhammad received in Mecca constituted the second message of Islam that was compatible with human rights and liberties (cf. Al-Garrai 1999; Taha 1996). As such, although helpful and supportive of the efforts of women's organizations and activists, al-Tigany's reading was selective and could be refuted by other selective readings that could equally argue that CEDAW was contradictory to religious beliefs.

In March 1998, the NDA finally admitted that Article 5 should be changed,[7] and re-emphasized the importance of women's participation in all NDA activities. The NDA instructed its executive office to follow up on these issues in collaboration with Cairo-based women secretariats of parties and women's groups associated with parties that are members in the NDA. The NDA executive office established two committees to resolve the issue of Article 5 and to prepare a women's charter.

THE NDA COMMITTEES ON WOMEN: NEGOTIATING ARTICLE 5[8]

As a result of persistent campaigning and resistance by women's groups and some of the political parties within the NDA against the NDA's position on women's rights, the NDA formed a committee that consisted of representatives of women's groups associated with parties that are represented in the NDA, in addition to women's secretariats in political parties. The committee held several meetings[9] in which the majority of parties that are member in the NDA presented their positions on Article 5. Some of the women's organizations that wanted to change Article 5 worked on developing a unified position and an alternative text to the article. These included NSWF in Cairo, the SWA, the SWU, *Ma'an*, and the Women's Secretariat in the SNP.

On par with their parties, representatives of both the Umma Party and the DUP held different views on Article 5. The Umma Party's representative in the committee argued that the whole Asmara 1995 document needed revision that could include revising Article 5. The DUP representative objected to the proposed changes and asked "why women's groups wanted to abandon religion."

The groups quarrelled over whether the NDA should commit to signing and ratifying CEDAW without reservations if it assumed power in Sudan. When the committee reached a deadlock, the NDA executive office asked that women's organizations and representatives of political parties draft a charter and present it to the second NDA conference (meeting of the NDA Executive Office in Cairo, June 4, 1998, attended by the author).

The NDA and women's organizations formed a committee to develop a charter for women in Sudan. The committee held several meetings and solicited input from the political parties that were members in the NDA. Women's organizations also submitted content for the charter. The committee also studied CEDAW and incorporated its components into the charter, with the exception of the articles on which Umma and DUP had reservations. These two parties had similar reservations to those of countries in the Middle East and North Africa that ratified CEDAW with reservations. The articles addressed women's equality with men and personal status laws. These countries have argued that these articles contradicted with shari'a laws (UNIFEM [now UN Women]/UNICEF, 1999). The committee agreed that the final draft of the charter should include the diverse views of the political movements and women's groups, including the contested articles, which were bracketed.[10]

Inside Sudan, the National Women's Democratic Alliance, an umbrella organization of women activists and opposition groups, also drafted a charter in response to the NDA LC recommendations in its resolutions of March 1998. The Alliance sent the charter to the leadership of the NDA in exile. The proposed charter emphasized the importance of overthrowing the NIF/NCP. It argued that women's issues were part of the social, economic, and political problems in Sudan and emphasized commitment to conventions that protect women's human rights. In the legal sphere, the charter called for reforming the 1991 personal status laws, devised by the NIF in issues pertaining to marriage and divorce, without suggesting alternative laws.

The mobilization and collective action of diverse women's organizations and representatives of political parties on Article 5 and the women's charter created a space for debate on women's human rights. It was also an opportunity for women's organizations and representatives of political parties with similar ideas to strategize. The result was a progressive charter that prompted the Umma Party (which had initially suggested the development of a women's charter) to put a hold on the final draft that was ready for submission to the NDA LC. This, argued the representative of the Umma Party in the committee, was a request from their membership in Sudan.

The resistance to Article 5 also sensitized the NDA leaders and the communities in exile to the importance and legitimacy of women's human rights. This activism resulted in that those who defended a commitment to women's human rights without reservation gradually assumed a higher moral ground. They were no longer apologetic for supporting women's rights. Article 5 and political "representation," however, became the primary concern of most Sudanese women's groups based in Cairo. As reported to the NDA, "these issues have consumed the energy and time of women's groups, without being able to reach a final consensus on [Article 5], because of the stand of some parties. Given the circumstances our country is facing, this time and energy could have been invested in other equally pressing women's issues had all factions in the NDA responded to women's just claims" (N. Ali 1998).

As the above indicates, the composition of the committees, which consisted mainly of representatives of political parties and women's organizations associated with political parties, was a problem. Expectedly, women took the stands of their parties even where these party interests contradicted with their interests as women. This jeopardized the efficiency of the committee as it created another, parallel body with similar positions to the NDA leadership council. As such, it was not a surprise that women reached the same dead end as the council. One incident is indicative. In the discussions within the committee, some of the members of the SWA and the NSWF tried to appeal to the representative of the DUP as a woman (on the issue of recognizing CEDAW without reservations, showing how this would affect her personally). She threatened to boycott the committee, and later the DUP representative in the NDA Executive Office complained to the NDA Secretary of Organization about the "behaviour of women members of the committee."

Lack of coordination also resulted in duplication of activities, including the drafting of a number of parallel women's charters. Fatima Ibrahim, for example, drafted a charter in her capacity as head of the Sudanese Committee for Women, Youth, and Children's Rights. The chair of the SWF prepared another charter, focusing exclusively on women's right to work. This charter could have complemented the NDA Women's Charter. With the exception of *Ma'an*, the SWA, and some of the contributions to the Internet forum on women, the charters did not explore the causes for the NDA's lack of commitment to women's human rights without reservation.

Another important question is also: where did the women's organizations exiled in Kenya stand in relation to all this, given that most of these organizations worked closely with the SPLM/A, which was a leading member of the NDA?

"ARTICLE 5 IS NONE OF OUR BUSINESS": WOMEN'S ORGANIZATIONS IN NAIROBI AND WOMEN'S HUMAN RIGHTS

While women inside Sudan, and in exile settings other than Egypt, and especially in Eritrea, gradually became involved in resisting the NDA's stand on women's human rights, there was not much interest or knowledge about this issue among women's organizations active in Nairobi. This was despite the involvement of the NSWF and women supporters of the SPLM in Egypt and the women's secretariat of the Sudan National Party (predominantly Nuba) in the Committees on Article 5. The Rapporteur of the committee of the Women's Charter was also from Southern Sudan. Nonetheless most of the predominantly Southern Sudanese women's groups in Nairobi were not aware, nor concerned about this advocacy or about Article 5 until February 1999, when these groups attended the Kampala Conference on Human Rights in the Transition in Sudan. While lack of communication and networking between various women's groups in exile, and the fact that all this predated Facebook and Twitter, could account for this lack of information, it is important to note that some of the Nairobi-based groups considered that the debate on religion and women's human rights was only relevant to the women of Northern Sudan. As one of the SWAN leaders argued, "On our part we told you we do not object to supporting you in this issue. It is important, however, that *you* Northern women agree on a common stand first" (Carla Tongun, in a meeting between women's groups and Dr. John Garang, Kampala, February 1999, attended by the author). The head of the NSWF responded to my question on the organization's position on Article 5 as follows: "I have nothing to say [about this matter]; we explained to you [in the Kampala conference] that this is not our business" (interview with Sittona Osman, Chair, NSWF, Nairobi, March 17, 1999).

These and earlier narratives in this book reveal a conviction among many activists from Southern Sudan that limiting the rights of women on a religious basis was primarily going to affect the Northern Muslim women, although as argued earlier, a lack of commitment to CEDAW without reservations affected all women in Sudan, regardless of religion. The SPLM/A also signed and ratified CEDAW after South Sudan became independent. The reason for this stand was that predominantly Northern women's organizations campaigned to ensure NDA's commitment to CEDAW. Groups active in Nairobi were mainly trying to emphasize their difference from predominantly Northern women's organizations active in Cairo; given our "difficult histories," as a friend and activist said eleven years later while commenting on possibilities for coalition building among women's organizations and activists from North and South Sudan, in the run-up to the South Sudan referendum.

The impact of marginalization, social exclusion, and conflict on women in Sudan's peripheries, and a conviction that women in Northern Sudan, regardless of where they stood in relation to the NIF/NCP regime, did nothing to protest marginalization and violence against their sisters in South Sudan, also accounted for this stand.

In addition to diverse experiences of marginalization and oppression, and the lack of solidarity, organizations in Nairobi, including those seeking gender equality, were working with communities and women directly affected by war. Some wanted to focus their activities on serving this population (interview with the Chair of WODRANS, Nairobi, March 17, 1999; Sittona Osman, Nairobi, March 17, 1999).

This did not mean the Nairobi-based women's organizations focused on immediate needs at the expense of women's human rights and strategic gender interests. On the contrary, the narratives of Southern women indicated they were concerned with the gender-specific effects of war on women (and children). Many of these organizations, for example, wanted to change cultures and customs that discriminate against women. Interviews and reviews of newsletters, short reports, leaflets, and other material that women's groups active in Nairobi produced showed interest in women's human rights and participation, especially in peace negotiations.

During the debates on Article 5 and the Women's Charter, Southern Sudanese women's organizations in Nairobi were working on a Sudanese Women's Social Contract (discussed below). Had predominantly Northern women's organizations and activists, especially those in Cairo, advocated on women's participation in general (including in peace negotiations between the SPLM and the GOS, and including barriers to women's participation other than the NDA), and had they campaigned for women's human rights (including the rights of women affected by war), there would have been more opportunities for coordination and collective action at the time.

Some of the Sudanese women in Egypt faced other barriers to participation, for example. Many women worked long hours as domestic workers. Others faced childcare problems. They lacked the resources to pay for transportation to attend meetings and participate in campaigns. Alawiya Kusheib, secretary for women's affairs in SNP's chapter in Cairo at the time of research, said harsh conditions in Cairo obstructed women from the Nuba Mountains' participation not only in politics, but also in literacy classes and leadership training programs.

> Women here face many problems. First, the children: there are children who are not enrolled in school or who are enrolled but face difficult financial and other circumstances. There are barriers to women's participation in politics. For example the woman has to work to support the family because men cannot find work. Women's work in the houses (as domestic workers) is abundant here so women have to work to fill the place of the husband. . . . The wages usually cover part of the expenses such as rent and minimum household expenses but not all the needs. You see I am the only active woman [in the SNP Women's Secretariat]. There are others but there are many barriers to their participation. Some have to work most of the time, others are occupied by their children's needs, so they do not have time to enroll in any literacy programmes or to attend meetings. (Interview with Alawiya Kusheib, Cairo, August 14, 1998)

Kusheib's narrative points to the intersection of gender, race/regional location, and class in limiting women's capacities and participation. What strategies could women's organizations use to address these factors? Some of the women's organizations in Nairobi that worked closely with UN agencies provided transportation cost to women participating in their programs.

Women's organizations in Nairobi were drafting a Sudanese Women's Social Contract as the NDA committee worked on the Women's Charter. SWAN, which spearheaded the process, organized a workshop where twenty women drafted the contract. Months later, SWAN invited over 300 women from diverse backgrounds to a conference in Nairobi (UNIFEM 1998, 2).

The conference discussed the Social Contract, which focused on legislation and policies that affect women, gender equality, and women's human rights (UNIFEM 1998, 2). Participants in the conference endorsed the contract and asked SWAN to circulate it in and outside Kenya. This was easier than the work on the Sudanese Women's Charter in Cairo, given that participants in the SWAN conference met as women, regardless of political affiliation, and worked on a document that the women wanted to inform the programs of parties they would support in the future.

Just as the groups in Nairobi were not aware of efforts in Cairo to produce a Sudanese Women's Charter, women's organizations in Cairo were not aware of SWAN's efforts to produce a Social Contract for Sudanese women. Groups only became aware of initiatives in other countries when they attended the Kampala Conference on Human Rights in Transition in Sudan in 1999.

THE KAMPALA CONFERENCE ON HUMAN RIGHTS IN THE TRANSITION

The Kampala conference, which a number of organizations convened (those were African Rights, the Southern Sudan Law Society, the SHRO, and Nuba Mountains Solidarity Abroad), brought together NGOs, women's groups, representatives of NDA members organizations, and representatives from the NDA and SPLM-held areas.

The organizers devoted a panel to women and gender, where presenters discussed the situation of Northern and Southern Sudanese women. Speakers highlighted issues of women and war, culture, women's human rights (including Article 5), and women's participation. Participants from six women's organizations[11] ensured that gender equality and women's participation and human rights were present in almost each session of the conference. Consequently, the final declaration of the conference, the Kampala Declaration, included a strong section on women's participation and human rights.

> 1. A national Sudanese Women's Conference should be convened in which the democratic leadership of Sudan should meet together with women and women's organizations. 2. Women should be fully represented in any committee drafting the constitution or the laws including personal laws. 3. Article V of the Asmara declaration requires revision to ensure that women are accorded the full protection of international human rights conventions. (The Kampala Declaration, Kampala, Uganda, February 12, 1999)

Although several NDA member parties considered the Kampala conference and declaration "useful exercises," they nonetheless endorsed the declaration. The conference outcome showed clearly the added advantage of the participation of women leaders knowledgeable about and committed to gender equality.[12] A question that arises would be to what extent did this and other opportunities contribute to collective action among diverse Sudanese and South Sudanese women and women's organizations in exile? How did the intersection of gender, race, social class, and other aspects of identity play out in determining possibilities for coalition building at the end of the twentieth century and at the start of the twenty-first?

RACE, GENDER, AND COALITION-BUILDING

This chapter revealed broadly similar concerns but parallel activisms among Sudanese and South Sudanese women's organizations active in Nairobi and Cairo. It also revealed that predominantly Southern women's organizations based in Nairobi at the time of research saw the concerns of Northern groups based in Cairo as irrelevant to Southern Sudanese women affected by war. This was due to a perceived (and perhaps real) lack of solidarity on the part of Northern women, with communities that have been at war since the 1950s. At the time of initial research, this included a brutal famine in Northern Bahr El Ghazal.

Another problem was connected to constructions of Southern Sudanese women as helpless victims of war, as beneficiaries of the services provided by predominantly Northern groups (if any), and finally as tokens to show respect for diversity.[13]

The SWU in Cairo, for example, has devoted several issues of *Sawt al Mara's* to solidarity with women in Southern Sudan. These newsletters discussed the impact of war on women and children especially after the president of the SWU, Fatima Ibrahim, visited parts of Southern Sudan in 1995, but they did not shed light on resistance among women's organizations.

The former SWF included Southern members in most of their activities. At some point, its chair was from South Sudan. Some of these women were the subject to racist verbal attacks during disputes within the organization, however. For example, during a preparatory workshop for the International Conference on Population and Development, held in Cairo in 1994, differences arose over financial matters with the then head of the organization, who was South Sudanese. This instigated racist comments from several women from the North.

Many Southern Sudanese activists saw racism as a key factor that prevented collective action. As Zeinab Eyega put it,

> I had decided never again to speak to northern [Sudanese] women about racism. I felt it was a waste of energy, because of their denial and defensiveness and because whatever I had to say might better be said by a woman from the north at far less emotional cost to me and probably . . . with a better hearing

from her own. I had also refused to throw myself casually under the banner of "Sudanese women" only to discover that we have serious differences between us, which could collapse our dreams. (Zainab Eyega, "Ignorance by Choice: A Letter to Fatima Ahmed Ibrahim," March 25, 1999, posted on sudanese@list.msu.edu)

Similarly, many of the groups active in Nairobi viewed solidarity by Northern women with suspicion, or as "too little too late." The chair of SWAN, for example, responded to a question on possibilities for coalition building with Northern Sudanese women's organizations and activists as follows:

It is unfortunate that we've not had greater contact with Sudanese women in the North. We have a problem as Southern women with our Northern sisters because for us war is war and death is death and we feel that all of us as nationals and as women should *condemn* all killings, full stop! But it was sad for us that our Northern sisters said nothing about the war. They made no outcry that we heard of about the war when our children or our husbands were being killed in the South. The only time that that *concern* started coming about, was when *Northern men* began to be killed! So for us we have a serious problem and it tells us in principle that the ideology and the socialization of Northern women are probably no different from the socialization of Northern *men*! Which I started out by saying it's a racist ideology, one of inferiority and superiority, where those who consider themselves *Arabs*, not Muslims, *Arabs* feel that the non-Arab is a lesser person who deserves to be, you know, wiped out of the face of the Earth. I am really pointing out that this is not a new phenomenon that came with the NIF. It is a reality of Sudanese history. (Interview with Pauline Riak, Executive Director, SWAN, Nairobi, March 18, 1999)

Riak's narrative emphasized the difference in priorities and in historical experiences of Sudanese and South Sudanese women. She talks about the limits that this history posits to coalition building and collective struggles.

Since I interviewed Riak in 1999, I have cited her powerful statement in several papers and talks. Her words came to my mind when the conflict started in Darfur and when reports about the use of rape to subjugate Darfuri women and communities started to arrive in my email. Quoting Riak in August 2005, I stated that, "Women from the Political North should learn from previous experiences and have a firm stand against gender-based violence (GBV)" and against the conflict in Darfur.

Riak did not speak in blanket terms of Northerners being oppressors.

I see a government in Khartoum with a clique of oppressive people, based on the structures that are there. . . . I know that [among] Northerners in general there are oppressed people and that there are good people and that there're people fighting for a just Sudan, just like us. So I know that these groups exist and they need to be commended inspite of the oppression and the lack of being

able to express their opinions freely. It is difficult for us in Nairobi, [however],
to be in direct contact with those groups because [due to financial difficulties]
we can't even post a letter. (Ibid.)

SWAN had a key objective, however, of uniting Southern Sudanese
women regardless of tribe and political affiliation. In this way, the organization wanted to overcome the impact of factionalism within the SPLM/A on
women in Nairobi, and to reach out to women from marginalized areas of
Sudan, such as the Nuba Mountains. To quote Riak,

Initially, we met socially, to have a laugh together, but once the membership
expanded, the needs became greater, so our objectives are now many. I think
the number one objective is to enhance unity among all Sudanese women
living in Kenya and to sensitize them to patriotic and national consciousness.
(Ibid.)

Some of the interviews were uneasy for me and for the interviewees,
given that many of the conversations covered issues that were considered
taboo by some, and politically incorrect by many who struggled for a New
Sudan. Asking Alawiya Kusheib, secretary of women's affairs in the Cairo
branch of the SNP, whether she saw any barriers to activism and collaboration with predominantly Northern women's organizations outside the marginalized areas of Sudan, she started her response by saying that "mentioning
the different regions" (a concern with difference) was "the talk of the people
of the Old Sudan." Originally from the Nuba Mountains, I asked Kusheib
whether the marginalization of the Nuba Mountains by predominantly Northern governments affected the interaction of Nuba women with predominantly
Northern women's groups or not. Kusheib responded as follows:

You mean the interaction of women from the South and other marginalised
areas with women from the North, right? In the past it was very difficult for
us! The mere fact that a woman from the Nuba Mountains or the South could
deal or work with women from the North was very difficult. Because they
[Northern women] used to think in the past that a woman from the South or the
Nuba Mountain was not worth anything [embarrassed laugh], a third class
human being or so, and as such *they* [Northern women] did not want to deal
with her. At present, however, I think that people have come to understand that
the problem of Sudan is a problem for all Sudanese. Women from the North
and the South should be better enlightened. It is also important to point out that
just as there are marginalised people in the South or Nuba Mountains, there are
marginalised people in the North. If people came to understand this, they can
interact very easily. (Interview with Alawiya Kusheib, Cairo, August 14,
1998)

Asking her how this impacted on possibilities for interaction and solidarity,
she stated,

Of course it had implications, for example, you find a woman from the South or the Nuba Mountains who pulls away from the Northern woman. It is the same for the Northerner, I mean, she would say, this [woman from the South or Nuba Mountains] does not deserve to be taken notice of. She's a *khadim* (slang for female slave), same as what they used to do in the past. I mean [they would say] this is a *khadim* how would we interact with her? This created negative sentiments between the people in the past. (Ibid.)

I asked Kusheib whether she witnessed any changes. She said,

This has not ended completely. For those who came to understand the real problems of Sudanese people, I believe this has ended, but there are others who still need to understand. The intellectuals in the country should raise people's and women's awareness on these matters. (Ibid.)

The issue of difference and the problematic relationships between women from various parts of Sudan came to the forefront of Sudanese exile public discourse after Fatima Ibrahim wrote in an article that Southern women were "backward." Commenting on a discussion that took place in London in November 1998, at one of the preparatory workshops for the Kampala conference, Ibrahim argued that protests to her naming Southern women as backward (because women in parts of South Sudan did not wear clothes) reflected subordination to the "Western understanding of liberation and development." The reason, according to Ibrahim, was that this argument overlapped with the views expressed by a "Western" woman.

In a comment that a university graduate woman in the leadership of a party made in a discussion on women's issues, she said, "The Southern woman is not backward." This comment overlapped with another one by Professor Sondra Hale.[14] . . . Some might think that this was spontaneous or unworthy of notice. But in my opinion, it reflected the western concept on the liberation of women. Professor Hale and this young party member know very well that the extent of education among southern women is much less than that of northern women, the participation of southern women in the modern production sector and political activity is almost none. Polygamy is practised [among] Christians without limits and a widow is inherited by her deceased husband's brother etc. . . . *This proves that the aim is to apply the western concept of women's emancipation: As long as the southern woman is naked and non-Muslim, she is not considered backward.* (Ibrahim 1999)

Ibrahim's article, which parallels what Mohanty (1988) calls the production of Third World woman in some forms of Western feminist scholarship, generated commentary from various activists, especially Southern women. These replies reflected how Southern activist women understood the historical relationship between the North and the South. A group of Southern women in Cairo[15] wrote a reply to the article, which placed Ibrahim's narrative within the wider context of internal colonialism in post-colonial Sudan.

> We do not need to remind ourselves of the brutal war in our country and its consequences. Yet it is impossible to speak about the suffering of the Sudanese masses without pointing to the social and economic backwardness in all parts of the country perhaps with the exception of the center (Khartoum and Gezira region). But . . . we were shocked to be labeled in [Ibrahim's] article as "those who go naked and who are the most *mutakhalifat* (backward)" by Fatima who considers herself a prominent leader in the Sudan and whose leadership role in the SWU and contributions towards liberating Sudanese women cannot be ignored. The meanest part of Fatima's article is where she pointed a finger at Southern Sudanese women, using offending terminology like "naked Southern Sudanese women" and it seems this is not the first time for her to mention this. She insists that Southern Sudanese women are the "most backward" . . . we really felt sorry to hear all this from Fatima who prides herself to be the liberator of Sudanese women. It is true that women in the north had more . . . education than women in the south and we think the reasons are well known. . . . For over forty years the Southern Sudanese have been running for their lives and crossing borders searching for safety. . . . The Southern Sudanese have been the most disadvantaged and maybe that is why they remain the "most backward" in the country. . . . These grassroots women are stuck in the war areas. They have become heads of households. (Cleto Rial et al. 1999)

Cleto Rial et al. further asked the following question:

> Fatima . . . said that our backwardness is the result of colonialism. With all our due respect to all Sudanese: *Does she mean the British colonialism against the Sudanese or the Northern Sudanese colonisation of the South? Has she forgotten that slavery and racism of the North has contributed to our "backwardness"?* . . . what has been said in that column can only remind us of the bitter history between the two parts of the country. *We, Southern Sudanese women, cannot be objectified anymore and we can speak for ourselves.* (Cleto Rial et al. 1999)

This Fanonian discourse on internal colonialism overlaps with the critique that leaders from New Sudan movements articulated in the previous chapter.

Another U.S.-based commentator, Zainab Eyega, drew upon African American feminist scholarship in her response to Ibrahim's column. Eyega started her letter by arguing that: "The history of Northern women's failure to recognize Sudanese women's commonalties as well as our differences and the continued denigration and disrespect of Southern Sudanese is long and discouraging" (Eyega 1999). Eyega gave her letter the title "Ignorance by Choice," which echoes Toni Morrison and her style; it addressed the interplay of race, class, and gender in Sudanese society and the way this has shaped her own experience.

I had hoped that the consciousness of having been "the other" (a woman in a patriarchal society) would have made it easier for you to recognise the racial barriers and differences that exist in the history and struggle of all women and especially among the Sudanese women. As a southern Sudanese woman, Arab racism is a reality within my life as it is not within yours. I ask that you be aware of how the destructive forces of this racism has separated and shaped each of us. The assumption that the northern (Arab) woman is the legitimate and sole representative of all Sudanese women and that the Southern woman or "non-Arab" woman is not-worthy, invisible or an example of "backwardness" further illustrates this racism. I ask that you be aware of the impact of how this narrow mindedness has on our efforts to work together. (Eyega 1999)

The controversy that Ibrahim's article generated raised important questions about the possibilities of establishing alliances between the women of Sudan and South Sudan. This question continues to be valid. It applies not only to possibilities of coalition building between women of Sudan and independent South Sudan, but between women and women's organizations from different parts of Sudan in light of ongoing conflicts, especially in Darfur, South Kordofan State, and the Blue Nile State. I examine this question further in a series of talks I gave in the run-up to the South Sudan referendum (Ali 2010; N. Ali 2011).

Women activists from Southern Sudan I interviewed said it was easier for them to form alliances with women activists from the Nuba Mountains, for example, given that the latter shared similar experiences of conflict and marginalization with them. But it is important not to look at women of South Sudan or of the Nuba Mountains as homogenous groups. Women's socioeconomic privilege, educational background, whether they were in refugee or IDP camps, were displaced into neighboring countries such as Egypt, Eritrea, Ethiopia, or Kenya, resettled in North America, Western Europe, or Australia, or whether they stayed in South Sudan, political affiliation, and other factors affected the priorities they set and the strategies they used to effect change.

Given all these problems, is there any way that women's groups from various parts of the country could work together? I have referred above to the increasing concern with war issues among mainstream women's groups. Building trust will take a long time, however. Women from Northern Sudan, in particular, should exert more effort in terms of broadening the agendas of women's organizations and in terms of defining and redefining women's (and Sudan's) priorities, as well as regional priorities, now that South Sudan has become independent.

In the 1990s and early 2000s, there were a few new predominantly Northern women's organizations that sought to address the above questions. SWA's first organizational meeting which took place in December 1997, elected a Southern Sudanese member as its new chair. In its report of the meeting, SWA made the following statement:

> We started by analysing the position of Sudanese women, not only after the NIF(/NCP) came to power, but before that. We found that even before this regime came to power . . . women were relegated to the position of a social, political, economic and intellectual subordinate. *In that context, women who belonged to certain social groups were subject to differently composed oppression: low income women and women who belong to religiously, culturally and racially disadvantaged areas. . . . We believe that if women in central parts of Sudan have had the privilege of limited access to political participation, the women in the peripheries in Southern, Western,* [and] *Eastern Sudan were totally excluded from this participation and from the process of development.* (Briefing on SWA first organizational meeting, February 1998; emphasis added)

The organization had reached out to women in various marginalized areas of Sudan, including those in non-government-held areas administered by SNA.

Ma'an, too, reached out to Southern Sudanese women in Cairo through inviting Southern Sudanese women to join the organization. Women from the South Sudanese, Beja, and Nuba communities in Cairo enrolled in *Ma'an*'s basic healthcare training program. In the interviews and focus group discussions with *Ma'an* members, interviewees highlighted the importance of working harder to win the trust of women from historically marginalized areas of Sudan. According to Saadia Idris,

> [*Ma'an*] has been able to win the trust of some Southern women who participated in some of our programs and contributed with their opinions. There is a truth, however, that we need to take into consideration: still the Southern sister does not have complete trust that she could realize achievements through [membership in] predominantly Northern groups. This is not because they are not our friends. I have good friends from Southern Sudan. They are like my sisters. When it comes to activism and politics, however, they are cautious. It is not *Ma'an* or the other groups that are going to eliminate mistrust. This requires huge effort [at other levels]. When they see that *we Northerners* are keen on equality and on [South Sudanese] achieving all their rights as real Sudanese, then we can build and achieve [trust]. (Saadia Idris, Focus Group Discussion with *Ma'an*, Cairo, June 1998)

The discourse of *Ma'an* members signaled high awareness of the precarity in which women from historically marginalized parts of Sudan lived, and the resultant distinct priorities.

> We have spoken with loud voices when the Eilefun Massacre happened [in April 1998]. . . . For [Southern women], since 1992 the government closed down the schools of the refugees in Khartoum. We were there and did not say

anything. Because of that even if we tried very hard, [mistrust will persist]. Why? Because they are not integrated into our social fabric. They do feel this and we feel it too. These rifts cannot be built only through political declarations, but there is a need for continuous work. (Ihsan al-Gaddal, Focus Group Discussion with *Ma'an*, Cairo, June 1998)

Groups like *Ma'an* could potentially play important roles, not only in addressing issues of difference, but also (along with women from other parts of Sudan) in producing thinking for the women's movement. Yet these voices were silenced, together with Southern women, by mainstream, official women's organizations. The interviews, and also reports that *Ma'an* and SWA produced, showed how mainstream groups tried to undermine their activities. As one member in *Ma'an* has argued,

> I believe that *Ma'an* perceived itself as a rivulet to support the women's movement organized in political parties, and we believed that this movement should have stretched its hand to *Ma'an*. Unfortunately, and I say this frankly, I say it to the mainstream women's movement, and I say it in a low voice now and will say it in a loud voice when the situation changes: the women's movement dominating women's activism at present does not accept alternative views. It does not accept the Other and this is a truth. It rejects the Other's point of view. Telling in this respect is that we took the initiative and invited [mainstream women's organizations] to participate in our seminars. We found no positive response to our programs. This is reflected in the writings (of the SWU in Cairo), which argue we are an academic group, without them taking the effort to even attend one of our meetings or public activities. Although at present we are handling this cautiously, eventually we are going to speak-out. That this is a problem in the dominant women's movement, so that the public know what is going on and where the problem lies. (Haiat Obeid, Focus Group Discussion with *Ma'an*, Cairo, June 1998)

One dramatic example of the exclusion of these groups is the book *Democracy and Human Rights in Sudan* (al-Tigany 1997). The book included a section on "Sudanese Women," co-authored by Zainab Osman, the former president of the SWF and the former secretary for women's affairs in the DUP, Cairo branch, and Nawal el-Shaykh, a member of the SWU. The two authors solicited accounts from the women's secretariats in the Umma Party and DUP, the latter prepared by Osman, the SWU, and the SWF. The authors justified the limited focus as follows:

> There are women's sections in newly established political groups and newly established women's organizations that were not included in this research because these organizations were formed in exile and also had no existence or *roots* inside Sudan. As such, they do not have practices to be examined anyway. That is why we addressed in this account Women's Secretariats in known, *authentic* existing parties that have historical roots. [Those are] the

Women's Secretariats in the DUP and Umma parties, as well as the deep-rooted SWU. (Al-Hussein and al-Shykh 1997, 183)

Organizations that the chapter excluded included the Union of Beja Women, the Women's Secretariat in the Sudan National Party, the SWA, and *Ma'an*. With the exception of *Ma'an*, all these groups had branches in Sudan, and many of them had branches in the marginalized areas.

The account of al-Hussein and al-Shykh (1997) also excluded the plethora of women's organizations associated with the SPLM/A. The authors justified this by stating that they had included "a short reference on women in the SPLM and that they were not lucky enough to obtain more information about them because of the [war] situation in the western and southern parts of the country." Although a proper branch for the NSWF had not been established in Cairo until February 1998, there were active women in the SPLM office in Cairo, and the women's secretariat in the movement had representatives in the SWF since its establishment.

It is important to note that just as is the case with predominantly Northern women's organizations, the predominantly Southern groups based in Nairobi were also not immune to charges of having narrow agendas in relation to women in the non-government-held areas in Southern Sudan. In the SPLM/A women's conference, held in August 1998, representatives of women's organizations in Kenya and Uganda were called "the women of Kampala" and "the women of Nairobi," implying their detachment from women at the grassroots level. Thus, just as it is important to use intersectional analysis to explore the difference within Sudanese women's organizations, it is important to continue to use this approach, including when approaching women and organizations from marginalized parts of Sudan. Otherwise, we may risk homogenizing different Others (Lazreg 1988; Mohanty 1988). I hope to explore these new layers of difference in future research.

In the 1990s and early 2000s, predominantly Northern and Southern women's groups in Cairo and Nairobi addressed challenges their communities were facing, but also wanted to ensure women's participation in opposition structures and peace negotiations, and to ensure respect for women's human rights in a democratic Sudan.

Most Sudanese women's organizations in Egypt campaigned for the inclusion of women in NDA leadership structures. With exceptions, women's organizations and activists wanted to change Article 5 of the Asmara 1995 declaration, which restricted women's human rights on a religious basis. Similarly, organizations based in Nairobi campaigned for inclusive political structures in the SPLM and for inclusive peace negotiations. These groups produced a Women's Charter to ensure women's rights were safeguarded after the end of the war. Yet organizations were not aware of the activities of their counterparts in Egypt.

The narratives in this chapter offer several lessons on gender, race, intersectionality, and the politics of coalition building. These lessons are not only relevant to Sudan and South Sudan; they can also inform feminist debates on intersectionality and coalition building elsewhere, taking into account that in contexts of conflict and marginalization, gender becomes a defining factor and women become vital for the reproduction of borders between different collectivities (Anthias and Yuval-Davis 1992, 7).

Although the Nairobi-based women's organizations argued that Article 5 was not relevant to them given that communities in Southern Sudan are egalitarian, given their focus on peace building and given the practical needs of women in SPLM-held areas, Nairobi groups worked on issues similar to the issues the groups in Cairo were working on. Yet they were engaged in a process of challenging prevalent social and cultural norms, defying attempts to delegitimize the subordination of women through re-inventing tradition (Yuval-Davis 1997a, 46), and in trying to widen the political space to their advantage.

To build alliances, women's groups need to first create a discourse about the diverse interests and priorities of women from across Sudan. This is difficult to achieve without developing sensitivity to race relations and unequal center/periphery relations within Sudan, and without using intersectionality as an organizing strategy as Chun, Liptz, and Shin (2013) have argued in their study of the experiences of socially marginalized Asian women.

As Yuval-Davis has argued,

> All forms of feminist (and other forms of democratic) politics should be viewed as a form of coalition politics in which the differences among women are recognized and given a voice, in and outside the political "units" and the boundaries of this coalition should be set not in terms of "who" we are but in terms of what we want to achieve. (Yuval-Davis 1997a, 126)

It is important to reach out to the women (and men) at the grassroots levels if the various agendas aiming to change dominant gender relations are to be effective (Connell 1998), whether or not these are integrated into the programs of the opposition. As Molyneux (1988, 129) has argued in the case of Nicaragua, agendas seeking to transform gender relations challenged the dominant power relations and ideologies, including those of subordinate groups. Moments of war, political instability, exile, and transition may transform historical consciousness. With concerted effort, these may also transform notions of national identity (Malkki 1995). Given that constructions of identity as fixed feed upon prevalent definitions of femininity and masculinity, it is important to challenge these constructions, along with definitions of citizenship, human rights, democracy, and fundamental issues that exclude women and reinforce gender inequality. Only then can the women and men of Sudan start to imagine a country that we can all feel we belong to.

NOTES

1. "Professional associations (academic, medical, legal), trade unions, peasant co-operatives, students' and women's organizations, and autonomous organizations of any kind" (Sharabi 1988, 154).

2. Those were: Saadia Abdel Rahim, a journalist and activist in the women's movement, and the late Huriya Hakim, who worked for the Arab Regional TV in Cairo and was also an activist.

3. I published parts of the interview with Mary Apai in Ali 2000.

4. That celebration was held on the 7th because the Women's Forum was organizing an event on the 8th of March.

5. Needless to say, these were not the only issues that occupied me (and other activists) at the time. Other issues of concern included the relationship of the NDA with the Sudanese communities in exile, political repression in Sudan, war, the conditions of women in Cairo, and most importantly, the famine in Bahr Al-Ghazal, South Sudan.

6. See N. Ali (1999).

7. This, however, did not appear in the recommendations of the meeting. When I raised this point in a meeting, the representative of the DUP in the NDA executive office said the DUP did not agree on this recommendation. He argued that this was not the recommendation agreed upon in the meeting. The debate restarted and was finally cut short with the intervention of the SAF representative in the LC who argued that the DUP representative could present the stand of the DUP in the consultations within the executive office of the NDA.

8. This section covers activities up to the NDA's Second Congress. Abdelaziz (2013) provides an elaborate account of the work of the preparatory committee for the NDA Women's Conference.

9. In what follows I draw on a report submitted to the NDA's Leadership Council in September 1998 (N. Ali 1998).

10. The charter was supposed to be discussed in the NDA's second conference, which took place in 2000.

11. Those were the SWA, SWAN, NSWF, NESWA, WODRANS, and Families of the Martyrs of Ramadan. Added to those were the women's secretariat in the DUP, the Women's Office in SHRO, and independent women activists. Representatives from the Pan African Women's Liberation Organization (PAWLO) also participated as observers.

12. The organizers devoted a follow-up conference to women and gender.

13. This analysis is specific to the groups I researched in Cairo. In the past decade, there has been an accelerated change that offered opportunities for genuine and meaningful collaboration in and outside Sudan, but especially in Sudan. We have also witnessed initiatives that Southern Sudanese women led, which included women (and men) from across Sudan and South Sudan).

14. Sondra Hale is a U.S. academic and a socialist feminist with strong connections in Sudan. She has had relations with Sudanese women activists and organizations, and with the CPS since the 1960s (see Hale 2006). The *Journal of Middle Eastern Women's Studies* devoted a special issue to Hale's activism and scholarship on Sudan.

15. This is what they called themselves. One of the women, Sarah Cleto Rial, was then president of SWA. Most of the other authors were members of the NSWF.

Conclusion

Thorny Issues and Perilous Coalitions

Today we no longer say: "Give us more jobs, more rights, consider us your
'equals' or even allow us to compete with you better." But . . . "Let us re-
examine the whole question, all the questions. Let us take nothing for granted.
Let us not only re-define ourselves, our role, [and] our image—but also the
kind of society we want to live in."
"Let us re-examine everything."
(*Manushi: Journal for Indian Women and Society*, January 1979, reproduced
in Kishwar and Vanita 1996, 248–49)[1]

The above excerpt from *Manushi* brings the analysis in this book to a full
circle by suggesting and insisting it is not enough to *ask* political actors to
commit to women's rights and to ensure women's participation without questioning and working to transform the structures, institutions, and the intersecting power relationships that often shape diverse women's experiences of
political and economic exclusion, as well as their experiences of human
rights violations at home, in communities, nationally, and in exile. *Manushi*'s
words of wisdom were relevant to Sudan's exile politics (and politics in
general) in the late 1990s and early 2000s as much as they still are relevant to
Sudan (and to South Sudan) a decade and a half into the twenty-first century.

This book discussed how exiled political parties and movements, with
diverse political agendas and positions on women's human rights and gender
equality, collectively ended up obstructing women's participation in the National Democratic Alliance, the umbrella under which these parties organized
in exile (and in Sudan). Not only did the programs of the alliance lack a clear
gender perspective, movements in the NDA compromised gender equality
and women's human rights in favor of unity and in favor of issues and

questions considered more *fundamental*. These fundamental issues—democracy, secularism, devolution of power, self-determination, just redistribution of Sudan's political and economic resources regardless of region, race, ethnicity, or religion—are *gendered*. They have always affected, and continue to affect, women and men across Sudan and South Sudan in distinct ways.

These issues, which the opposition reached consensus on in the Conference of Fundamental Issues in 1995, were key tenets of the Comprehensive Peace Agreement (CPA), which the Government of Sudan (GOS) and the Sudan People's Liberation Movement (SPLM) signed ten years later in 2005. To a lesser extent, they have informed the Cairo Agreement between the NDA and the GOS in the same year, and the Eastern Sudan Peace Agreement (ESPA), which the GOS and the Eastern Front (EF) signed one year later.

The same *fundamental issues* have also fueled new wars in Darfur in 2003. They emerged again as South Sudan prepared for independence, and have resulted in a re-eruption of conflict in Southern Kordofan and the Bule Nile areas. As was the case with South Sudan, these wars continue to produce precarity and to impact diverse women and men in distinct ways. Displacement, dispossession, and sexual violence against Darfuri women have been well-documented. In Southern Kordofan and the Blue Nile, the conflicts have caused displacement, dispossession, and hunger. Women and girls have had to use tree leaves as sanitary towels during menstruation following the re-eruption of war in the area in 2011. *Do we all belong to this country?* What lessons can opposition parties and movements, women's and civil society organizations, and others learn from the exile politics of the 1990s and early 2000s?

An important lesson for current opposition movements and civil society organizations and think tanks in Sudan and in exile is the importance of involving diverse women (and men) at all levels. Another is the importance of integrating gender equality and intersectional analysis into any plans for the future, especially now that these are sanctioned in successive resolutions of the United Nations Security Council, as discussed earlier in this book.

For women's organizations and activists in Sudan and beyond, this book offers insights that could inform resistance to the exclusion of women from political structures and political processes. One is the importance of carefully examining any structures and processes before endorsing or resisting them. This book has revealed the *heterogeneous* and *contradictory* nature of opposition discourse on gender and women's human rights, given the difference in political programs and gender ideologies of the NDA parties. This book also highlighted the selective approach of the NDA toward international human rights conventions and discourse. On one hand, the alliance relied on international human rights conventions to make its case to the international community against the GOS. Several of the movements organized in the NDA also openly supported women's human rights enshrined in CEDAW.

Nonetheless, collectively, all parties organized in the NDA relinquished women's human rights.

The reason was that gender and women's rights were central in the bargain between sectarian and progressive parties organized in the NDA. Although not pronounced, gender was prominent in defining the coalition between progressive and sectarian conservative groups. It defined the boundaries between historically marginalized areas of Sudan and North/Central Sudan. It also marked the boundaries between the GOS and the NDA in their contest over legitimacy.

References to religion, traditions, and customs perform functions that include maintaining and reproducing the social and economic interests of sectarian parties in Sudan.[2] Having agreed on the separation between religion and politics, removing reservations on women's human rights would have robbed the sectarian parties of one of the key tools of social control. Interviewees from the Umma Party and DUP argued that a commitment to CEDAW without reservations contradicted both Islam and Sudan's local traditions and customs.

What strategies (other than building alliances with progressive political parties) could women's organizations use to resist exclusion and marginalization? One effective strategy for Sudanese women's organizations in Egypt could have been to build stronger alliances with Egyptian women's organizations working to subvert the impact of Islamism in the country, including discourses that discouraged commitment to international human rights conventions such as CEDAW. These challenges persist, and so do opportunities for coalition building with women's organizations in Egypt, Kenya, and beyond, especially in light of the backlash that followed the Arab Spring of 2011 and 2012, and given that extremism has escalated in Nigeria, Syria, Libya, and Iraq (and in European countries) with devastating impact on women, girls, and communities.

There are many sub-regional and regional organizations with which Sudanese and South Sudanese women's organizations committed to women's meaningful participation, respect for women's human rights, and to transforming gender relations could build alliances. During the past decade, activists and practitioners have built important and strategic alliances. The Strategic Initiative for Women in the Horn of Africa, which includes member organizations from across the Horn of Africa, has member organizations from both Sudan and South Sudan. The organization organized numerous programs and advocacy campaigns, including at the level of the African Commission for Human and People's Rights toward law reform and ending discrimination against women in both countries.

There exist several strong networks and coalitions in Africa with whom women's organizations both in Sudan and South Sudan could build alliances and share strategies and knowledge. One such coalition is the Solidarity for

African Women's Rights (SOWAR). SOWAR has been working to promote and protect women's human rights in Africa since its establishment in 2004. The coalition has advocated so African states sign, ratify, and implement the Protocol to the African Charter on Human and People's Rights on the Rights of Women in Africa, adopted by the African Union on July 11, 2003. The coalition has used creative advocacy strategies to convince African governments to sign and ratify the protocol. Discourse of its founders refutes the claims that poverty, conflict, and general precarity in Africa render a commitment to women's human rights and gender equality irrelevant or premature. Faiza M. Jama, director of SOWAR's Secretariat, for example, wrote in 2014 that although Sudan contributed to drafting the protocol, and although the country signed it in 2008, it has not yet ratified it, and that as a result, the country has "remained unaccountable for the continuous and significant abuses of the rights on women and girls in the country" (Mohamed 2014). Jama argued that attempts to ratify and implement the protocol "have stalled significantly attributable to internal conflict, subsequent separation from South Sudan in 2011, and continued political conflict between the Army of Sudan and Sudan Revolutionary Front (SRF)" (Mohamed 2014).

What possibilities exist for collective action at the international level? Several scholars have argued that the rise of extremism in the Middle East, Africa, and elsewhere has been a reaction to neoliberal globalization. Increasingly, feminist and women's rights scholars and activists are proposing and building transnational solidarities to address the impact of globalization on women and girls (cf. Mohanty 2003; Naples and Desai 2002; Jeffrey 1998), as well as other issues of mutual interest. As Jeffrey has argued in the case of South Asia,

> Feminists . . . should engage with the gender implications of the changing integration of national economies into the global economy, of structural adjustment programmes and World Bank conditionalities on social sector spending; of liberalisation policies and changing employment patterns that link people directly into the global economy and encourage consumerism where many cannot afford to play the consumerism game. (1998, 240)

Since the 1980s, Sudan has had to implement conditionalities imposed by international financial institutions by introducing austerity measures. This has involved lifting subsidies from food, gas, and other essential commodities. After the secession of South Sudan, the government decided to lift subsidies from basic commodities as one of many ways to compensate for the loss of about 75 percent of its oil revenue. This led to demonstrations, which the GOS suppressed. Hundreds of protestors (both men and women) have been killed since 2011. Coalition building to address the impact of neoliberal globalization on communities in Sudan and South Sudan is another possible strategy to work collaboratively and transnationally. Such coalitions should also make political decisions to restrict access to food in war-affected areas by GOS, as is the case in South Kordofan at the time of writing, a priority.

It is important that civil society organizations in Sudan and in exile own their agendas, however, and not fall victim to rescue narratives or to initiatives that select one or more victims and portray them as the sole representative of the group affected by atrocities in Sudan. Experiences elsewhere offer good insights. Writing about transnational activism to prevent acid attacks in Bangladesh and to address its impact on victims and survivors, for example, Chowdhury (2011) points to the dangers of erasing local activists' roles and voices, and challenges global feminist tendencies to allow the telling of a partial story.[3] Of course, organizations working at the national level can face similar limitations if they lacked an understanding of the way gender intersects with other aspects of identity, and if they lacked a commitment to challenging oppression that can arise consequently.

Like the exiled opposition, in the 1990s and early 2000s mainstream women's groups had shown a tendency to claim they owned *the* legitimate voice that represented *all* Sudanese women. Not only has this undermined possibilities for collective action between mainstream women's organizations on one hand, and women's organizations led by women from marginalized areas of Sudan on the other hand, it has also created hurdles for collective action among predominantly Northern organizations in exile, especially in the absence of intersectional analysis or at least an understanding of and a commitment to transforming race relations and marginalization in Sudan.

In the 1990s and early 2000s, two parallel women's movements in exile addressed the human rights and political participation of women. While predominantly Northern groups addressed issues of political participation and human rights within the NDA, predominantly Southern groups concentrated on integrating women into the structures of the SPLM/A and dealt with the issue of political participation within the context of war and peace building. Both groups produced documents that defined the role of women, their interests and rights in future Sudan, with one group not necessarily knowing about the activities of the other, until early 1999. Moreover, because of the way predominantly Northern women's organizations articulated their struggles for women's participation and respect for human rights within the NDA, predominantly Southern Sudanese women's organizations considered this agenda as only relevant to Northern Sudanese women. The establishment of the Women's National Democratic Alliance in Eritrea and in the non-government-held areas around the same time added a new and unique voice to these struggles. What could women's organizations active in Sudan and South Sudan learn from this recent history?

Because building trust is difficult in light of Sudan's and South Sudan's difficult histories, collaborations over single issues could be helpful. Given that experience elsewhere has shown the difficulty to assume unity of women's groups on gender alone (Molyneux 1985, 234), alliances could address the gender-specific impact of certain processes or forms of oppression, but groups will need to pay careful attention to how they define these issues and women's roles in them. A successful example is the collective organizing of women from across Sudan and South Sudan in the run-up to the South Sudan Referendum. We defined the boundaries of the coalition not according to *who we are* but in terms of *what we wanted to achieve* (Yuval-Davis 1997a, 120). We wanted to achieve a different outcome, though. The loose coalition included women who wanted Sudan to remain united, and others who wanted South Sudan to secede. So we shifted what we wanted to achieve to a higher level: we agreed to work toward achieving a transparent, free, and fair ballot, with meaningful participation of women at all levels, regardless of the outcome of the referendum, which should reflect the aspirations of the people of South Sudan. This allowed us to work collectively across difference in Sudan, South Sudan, and in exile.

Even where groups and activists reach consensus and a certain level of unity, this should be based on an understanding of this unity as constructed, and as vulnerable to challenges arising from ethnic, racial, class, and other forms of difference (Yuval-Davis 1997a).

Diverse narratives of men and women opposition leaders and activists offer important insights for the literature on intersectionality, and for scholarly narratives on the way women and women's bodies often constitute markers of ethnic, racial, and national difference. Such literature shows that subjugated collectivities often control women and girls in order to mark their difference from Western and colonial societies and their definitions of women's liberation. This literature shows that in communities under occupation, colonialism, comprador regimes, or among contemporary refugee communities in Europe, North America, or in neighboring countries in the same region, the dominant culture is often more egalitarian compared to the cultures of colonized people or refugees. This is often a reason for demonizing feminist efforts to achieve gender equality or commitment to women's human rights enshrined in international human rights conventions (Najmabadi 1991). When focusing the difference gaze and intersectional analysis on internal power relations between collectivities in Northern Sudan on one hand and those in Southern and Western Sudan on the other hand, however, an opposite picture emerges. With the exception of Eastern Sudan, the narratives in this book show that the *marginalized* collectivities constructed their communities as more progressive in terms of gender relations, and on the basis of authentic African matriarchal heritage!

As chapter 5 shows, both male and female activists and leaders from Southern Sudan and the Nuba Mountains interviewed for this research mobilized notions of egalitarian gender norms in their communities in order to mark the boundaries between their collectivities on one hand, and the Northern conservative groups and communities on the other. Many of those leaders argued that while women in Northern Sudan were more modernized because of better access to education and employment, these women, argued interviewees, were not emancipated. Some argued that it is difficult to achieve gender equality in Northern Sudan because women were oppressed in the name of religion and culture.[4] These are much more difficult to change or reform, unlike the case of women in Southern Sudanese and Nuba communities, whose subordinate position is the result of underdevelopment and war.

Cases from other parts of the world suggest that when pitted against the "West," the relationship between gender and nation often results in the subordination of women. Would the reverse in Sudan, where the dominant groups continue to use conservative gender norms to subjugate local collectivities, lead to an opposite result? That is, would it lead to the championing of women's human rights by the *oppressed* collectivities in their quest to mark their difference from dominant groups and to redefine the nation?[5]

This research shows that this is true mainly at the *discursive* level. Despite the relative egalitarianism in Nuba and Southern communities, for example, there exist practices that undermine women's human rights and gender equality. As such, this discourse runs the danger of romanticizing the egalitarianism of local/African cultures. It encourages an understanding of this culture as homogenous and as entirely on par with gender equality and women's strategic interests. This contradicts the realities of women in these areas, who are not only subordinate because of the gender-specific impact of conflict and marginalization at the hands of successive governments in Khartoum, but also because of the prevalence of harmful gender norms and practices, including polygamy, oppressive dowry and marriage customs, partially discriminative customary laws, and restricted land ownership. These norms coexist with egalitarian norms and practices.

These are documented in narratives and texts produced by women activists and groups such as the NSWF, South Sudan Women's Empowerment Network (SSWEN), and other organizations in the South, and in research (Ali 2010, 2011; Jok 1997a, 1997b, and 1998). As such, maintaining such a discourse would suggest a preoccupation with modernization and liberation from Northern dominance as vehicles for obtaining women's strategic interests. Rather, liberatory struggles should work on interrogating and redefining power relations within and outside the household, as well as local cultures, from a gender perspective.

Although Southern women have often resorted to notions of egalitarianism to demarcate their difference when talking about the possibility of establishing coalitions with Northern women's groups, they have been working to transform gender relations internally, and are sometimes resented by sections of their communities for that reason.

Given that in the experience of exile politics in the 1990s and early 2000s New Sudan movements (and the CPS) maintained relatively progressive positions on women's participation and human rights as individual parties, would coalitions between women's organizations and these parties have made a difference? While the answer is no, given the dynamics of NDA's exile politics, women's groups committed to transformation could play a role in integrating gender into current (or future) opposition politics.

A number of questions arise when considering alliance building between women's groups interested in achieving gender-strategic interests on one hand, and political movements on the other. One question is: is building coalitions necessary? If so, then which movements should women's organizations build alliances with? Could these alliances result in transforming gender relations? My answer to the first question is yes. Such solidarities might prove constructive to both the agendas of women's groups and those of the other mixed-gender political movements. They can help women's organizations seeking change address *domination* in all its forms, but without compromising gender equality.

The NDA included parties—mainly constituting the Umma Party and the DUP—that wanted to overthrow the NIF/NCP government, restore multi-party democracy, and introduce reforms that would improve access to the state's political and economic resources by marginalized racial and ethnic groups. The Alliance also included parties that wanted to transform the Old Sudan and establish an alternative order. A strong concern with gender equality was absent in the discourses of both groups. While a progressive stand toward women's human rights was positively related to the discourse of groups seeking transformation and vice versa, with a few exceptions, opposition leaders discussed gender equality only when prompted.

One of the main problems with the way mainstream exiled women's groups have addressed the opposition was that they focused on issues of "representation" and on demands for recognizing women's rights although all issues on the agenda of the opposition were gendered. A focus on representation might result in *male-gendered* and *untransformed* neopatriarchal politics with female participation in it. Molyneux (1998) has argued that this could legitimize the political spaces without changing gender relations.

Current opposition movements (given the nature of their alliances) run the danger of undermining gender equality in the long run. For example, while women have remained active within the SPLM-North after the secession of South Sudan, and while SPLM-North has maintained female representation in its structures, the Alliance into which the movement has entered with a number of Darfuri movements, the Sudan Revolutionary Front (SRF) has suffered from limited participation of women.

Where the movement is allied with other groups, and where women's strategic interests and basic human rights could be compromised in such a bargain, as has been the case with the NDA and as is the current case of the SRF and the National Consensus Forces (NCF), the best strategy would be to have an autonomous network of women's groups that work closely to integrate a concern with gender into the politics of these movements.

The risks involved in this process include possible co-option of women's groups or control over their agenda, especially in the absence of an atmosphere that is less favorable to women's strategic interests, and where the bargaining power of women's groups is low. In the context of exiled women's groups, whether or not the agenda of women's groups were subordinated to that of the political project they were associated with, they were vulnerable to being constructed as such through misrepresentation.

In addition, some of the constituencies of New Sudan groups might relate differently to what women's organizations and activists with transformative agendas might prioritize, especially when leaders and community activists feel that focusing on gender equality could alienate their supporters at the grassroots level, or that commitment to gender equality could challenge gender norms that are key to preserving group identity.

Moreover, although New Sudan groups' commitments to gender equality vary, New Sudan movements have historically represented, and continue to represent, areas and communities that lack the basic needs. These communities are dealing with food insecurity, lack of education and health services, and general social exclusion. These concerns are legitimate, but all these issues are gendered. Ammouna, a U.S.-based Nuba activist, testified at a workshop that the Sisterhood for Peace organized in February 2012:

> As Nuba women, we have organized weekly teleconferences . . . since the war started. In the winter we found out they needed clothes, especially children. . . . Each woman [donated clothes] and made a donation of 80 USDs. We were not able to ship the clothes because it cost US$15,000. We found out that in the Nuba Mountains women needed underwear. When a woman is in her period, she can't use just anything. The women use tree leaves. We were going to buy sanitary pads [but decided to send underpants for women]. We prepared three bags [of clothes] to send through Kenya. As a woman if you heard about anything like that anywhere in the world, won't you contribute to ending it?[6]

Although communities' access to basic needs is important, groups with conservative agendas and individuals seeking to delegitimize feminist and women's rights activism have used it to render a preoccupation with recognizing women's full human rights irrelevant to the specific needs of these societies. Groups with conservative agendas can easily appropriate such a discourse and use it to delegitimize the struggles of women's organizations and movements working to transform gender relations and to ensure commitments to women's human rights in Sudan and South Sudan.

Indeed, it is impossible to transform gender relations in Sudan and South Sudan without women (and men) at the grassroots level constituting a critical mass that is aware of the significance of gender, and that is willing to inform and support efforts for change and transformation, including efforts to achieve gender equality. A commitment to gender equality that takes into account race, ethnicity, social class, disability, sexuality, and other aspects of difference can only strengthen our rethinking of the old neopatriarchal Sudan.

A question that this book has engaged is: how could building coalitions with movements seeking transformation impact efforts to "rethink the whole question" from a gender and feminist intersectional perspective? While movements committed to New Sudan politics can constitute vital allies, the lack of a gender analysis and a feminist critique of the project of the Old Sudan in the programs of these movements and the absence of a unified women's movement that could engage New Sudan politics on equal footing are two of many serious hurdles to the success of such an alliance.

Organizations in exile, such as My Sister's Keeper (MSK) and Sisterhood for Peace (SfP) network, a U.S.-based organization which African American women created, organized women from across Sudan and South Sudan to work on peace building and on a number of issues of concern to Sudanese and South Sudanese. In January 2010, the Sisterhood for Peace addressed "an urgent call for peace in Darfur," which 150 women signed, to Mr. Djibril Bassolé, the Chief Mediator or Darfur on behalf of the United Nations and the African Union. SfP requested to send a delegation of women to participate on the Darfur peace consultations, then taking place in Doha. However, their request was denied. The SfP sent a delegation of eight uninvited women to the consultations.

> [Because] "well–behaved women rarely make history" eight audacious women went to Doha—uninvited and undeterred. They subsequently met with a rather surprised Mr. Bassolé, representatives of all the armed movements and the Government of Sudan, as well as other key stakeholders. By all accounts, the women proved to be constructive, honest brokers. They were even asked to extend their seven-day assignment to ten days. The success of this historic mission demonstrates the unique contributions that diverse Diaspora women can make toward peace building in Darfur and Sudan. (*My Sister's Keeper Newsletter*, Summer 2010)

I have argued throughout the 1990s for the need for an intellectual arm for the women's movement in Sudan and in exile, and for the need to engage issues of gender, race, class, sexuality, and other intersecting aspects of identity. It has been encouraging to see that some of the women's organizations in Sudan, such as the Salmma Women's Centre (which the GOS shut down in July 2014), *Ru'ya*, the Gender Centre, and Ahfad University for Women, among others, have taken this task seriously.

These organizations should continue to seek stronger links with women's organizations and communities at the grassroots level, with women's organizations associated with political movements, and with feminist and women's studies academic programs.

In the 1990s, many of the women's organizations associated with political parties considered theorizing on women, gender, and feminism as irrelevant to the "realities" of Sudanese women. In June 1998, for example, *Ma'an* invited me to discuss contemporary feminist schools in Cairo. A member of *Ma'an* spoke about classical schools of feminist thought. In my talk I discussed critiques by feminists from the Global South of mainstream feminist discourse and new feminisms. After the talk, participants questioned the relevance of the *topic*—and not the *schools*—to the realities and needs of Sudanese women in Sudan and in exile.

The attitudes of many organizations and political activists toward feminisms have been changing in recent years. Over a decade after my talk at *Ma'an*, I relayed the above story to Fahima Hashim, founder of the Salmma Women's Centre, and Zainab el-Sawi, then in charge of the Sudanese Women's Empowerment for Peace (SuWEP) initiative, which the Salmma Centre hosted. Fahima and Zainab invited me to speak about contemporary schools of feminist thought at the Salmma Centre. The audience included a diverse group of both male and female youth associated with the Salmma Centre, activists in the women's movement, and women who hold leadership positions in political parties. The questions reflected knowledge of some of the arguments of feminist schools, and interest in interrogating these arguments further.

Women's rights activists call themselves (and call women like me) *al-gandaryat* (which translates as *genderists*). Activists from younger generations now choose Facebook profile names such as Audre Lord (after Caribbean American writer, radical feminist, and civil rights activist Audre Lorde [1934–1992]). A few are beginning to engage the categories of race or sexuality, in relation to power in Sudan, which is elating.

This book discussed how women's organizations based in Egypt and Kenya responded to the exclusionary practices of the NDA, to exclusion from peace negotiations, and to the lack of commitment to women's human rights. The approaches and focus of each set of organizations reflected the priorities these groups identified at the time. The experiences of these organizations suggest the need for a strong politics of solidarity among diverse women and women's organizations, and especially with women directly affected by war, political oppression, poverty, and marginalization. The need for such solidarities became more acute after the eruption of the conflict in Darfur in 2004, when women's bodies as markers of ethnic and racial difference (Yuval-Davis 1997a; N. Ali 2004) became targets of sexual violence. The war in the Blue Nile and South Kordofan states continue to pose more challenges and to call for further solidarity and action given its impact on women. As an activist and a practitioner, I drew on the narratives of South Sudanese women active in Nairobi, which I document in this book, to argue that Northern Sudanese women in particular should visibly oppose the atrocities against women and communities in all war-affected and marginalized regions in Sudan, and elsewhere in Sudan and South Sudan.

In recent years, Khartoum-based women's organizations, such as *Mubadarat la li-Qahr al-Nisaa* (No to Women's Oppression Initiative), organized several sit-ins, press conferences, and demonstrations, including against the conflict in Darfur and in the Nuba Mountains and South Kordofan State. The organization was launched in solidarity with Lubna Ahmed al-Hussein (interview with Hadia HasabAllah, one of the founders of the initiative, Omdurman, April 2012; conversation with Amel Habbani, one of the founders of No to Women's Oppression, Nairobi, September 17, 2014). A journalist, Lubna, was arrested for wearing "indecent" clothes as defined under Public Order Laws. Hussein distributed invitations to journalists, foreign embassies in Khartoum, and civil society to attend her trial. This generated both local and international solidarity and shed light on the oppression of women under Sudan's Public Order regime.

A YouTube video of a woman being flogged in the backyard of a police station in Omdurman also generated outrage in and outside Sudan, and prompted a solidarity message from no other than African American novelist and Nobel Prize Laureate Tony Morrison, who wrote a piece in honor of "the girl in the video" as the woman came to be known. In "A Letter to a Sudanese Woman" Morrison wrote, "I watched a video of punishment meted out to you—a lawfully mandated public whipping that I understand is not uncommon in your country. I have seen many instances of human brutality, but this one was particularly harrowing." Morrison celebrated the woman's spirit of resistance, and offered a global message of solidarity: "Each cut tearing your back hurts women all over the world. Each scar you bear is ours as well."

Similarly, through events such as Sudan Rising (which is part of a global movement to end gender-based violence), Salmma Women's Center, and Ahfad University for Women worked on reordering the political space, by taking part in the One Million Rising global events each February since 2013. These events brought together hundreds of women of all ages from diverse ethnic groups, wearing clothes of their choice, in collective dancing in a huge public space that is within the walls of Ahfad University for Women.[7] Conversations with Fahima Hashim and Zeinab el-Sawi and narratives about the day on YouTube indicate that while challenging violence as part of V-Day events organized worldwide each year, Sudan Rising challenged, in the words of Fahima Hashim, the restricted public space, lashing of women for violating dress code, and restrictive public order laws that humiliate Sudanese women. If you have access to a computer and the Internet, watch the video on YouTube before reading the epilogue. It will probably cheer you up: https://www.youtube.com/watch?v=-b1w8JsUais#t=162.

NOTES

1. The author wishes to thank Madhu Kishwar, founder of *Manushi*, for permission to reproduce text from "Let Us Re-Examine Everything" in *Manushi: Journal for Indian Women and Society*, January 1979, reproduced in Kishwar and Vanita 1996, 248–49.

2. It was not a coincidence that Umma Party and DUP leaders also justified their stand on CEDAW by saying the CPS took advantage of it to promote its "anti-Islamic" vision of society. The CPS has historically chosen to coexist with local cultures, including those oppressive to women, so as not to "offend the masses" (Hale 1996; El Bakry 1995). The Umma and DUP feared not the CPS's position on religion, but the challenge of CPS's programs to the class interests that both parties represented.

3. Chowdhury draws upon Makau Mutua's (2001) analysis. The latter argues that human rights institutions often sustain an unequal relationship between the Global South and the Global North, including through the construction of Northern actors as rescuers, and Global South actors as victims and villains.

4. As with the discourse of the two sectarian parties, culture and religion are ossified and constructed as fixed by this discourse.

5. The answer is yes, at least at the discursive level, in the case of South Sudan, where for several reasons, which I believe include a desire to mark its difference from the dominant ideology in Khartoum. Post-independence South Sudan has championed women's human rights (see N. Ali 2011). This does not mean South Sudan has achieved gender equality, however. The conflict between different government factions in South Sudan, which started in December 2013, involved abuses against women, including rape. Women in South Sudan also continue to face abuses because of the militarization of society over the past five decades, and because of the dominant culture and norms.

6. Documented by the author and cited in Sisterhood for Peace (2012). PATHWAYS TO SUSTAINABLE PEACE IN SUDAN: WHY WE CAN'T WAIT! *Statement by the Sisterhood for Peace Network on the Conflict in South Kordofan and the Blue Nile*. Boston, My Sister's Keeper, March 1. On file with the author. Also see Ali 2013.

7. The third Sudan Rising event, which took place in February 2015, was a partnership between Ahfad University for Women, the World Health Organization, and the British embassy in Khartoum. It emphasized the role of men in supporting women's rights.

Epilogue

Building Bridges and Re-Examining the Whole Question

It was July 2010. I had just arrived in Juba, South Sudan, from New York, along with six other Sudanese and South Sudanese women who were active in the Sisterhood for Peace movement in North America. Most of us were formerly based in Egypt, Kenya, Ethiopia, or Uganda. My friend and fellow activist Sarah Rial, and Reverend Gloria White Hammond, programs coordinator and co-founder of My Sister's Keeper respectively, were at the airport to welcome us to Juba. We would join about fifty other women, from across Northern and Southern Sudan, who would discuss conflict management and advocacy, political network, and prepare work plans to ensure we engage ongoing processes in Sudan.

At the top of these processes was the South Sudan Referendum. Other important processes included a referendum for the Abyei region, which never took place, popular consultations in South Kordofan and the Blue Nile area, and the Darfur peace process.

Two days later, participants watched the documentary *Pray the Devil Back to Hell*, which documents the struggles of Liberian women to pressurize warring parties to reach a peace agreement and to end the war. After the documentary, I noticed several of the Darfuri women weeping, and saying the documentary reminded them of their own experiences of war. On my way to the refreshments area, I noticed Margaret (not her real name) looking very depressed. I approached her and asked why she hadn't joined the group for refreshments. She looked at me, her eyes sparkling with tears: "what I just saw has reminded me of what we Southern Sudanese had gone through. Do you know that in [my] town, there is a mass grave, and that people sometimes stumble upon skulls?[1] Even here in Juba, there is a mass grave. Security is guarding the area but you can easily see it." I asked how unity between Sudan and South Sudan could ever be "attractive" for a nation that is still living on the brink of mass graves. A nation that has not received a single apology or seen a gesture of remorse or an attempt at reconciliation from any of the key political forces that controlled the state since Sudan achieved political independence.

On the last day of the conference, at breakfast, Theresa, a tall woman with ancient wisdom in her eyes, asked me whether I would consider visiting her area, Abyei, one day. "If you came to Abyei," she says, "you will cry even more than you did for Darfur."

The vision of the New Sudan is still valid to an extent, even though the women and men of South Sudan have overwhelmingly voted for independence. The forces that have vested interest in transformation should continue to work toward achieving such a vision (regardless of what they/we call it) in both the North and the South. The challenges are immense as far as women's rights and meaningful participation are concerned.

In the South, illiteracy is very high, especially among women. Maternal and child mortality are the highest in the world. HIV is increasingly affecting wide sectors of the population, especially women, and poverty is prevalent, especially among women. The women's movement in South Sudan is facing immense challenges, and achieving independence had instigated high expectations. Women's rights concerns could be deprioritized in the face of immense post-independence challenges.

In the North, the challenge ahead is to continue to address the legacy of the Old Sudan, and to achieve the vision of the New Sudan. Addressing this legacy is particularly important if we are to achieve gender equality and respect for women's human rights. Understanding the legacy of the Old Sudan and Sudan's politics since the late 1970s can shed light on current developments in other countries in North Africa who are struggling with Islamist movements.

My research and observations since 2010 on the long-term impact of the violence in South Sudan since the mid-fifties, especially on women and girls, my readings about post-conflict Rwanda and Liberia, and my observation and research regarding gender-based violence in post-Apartheid South Africa—along with reading (and re-reading) the work of scholars such as Cynthia Enloe on gender and militarization—shed strong doubt on the viability of armed struggle as a means of transformation.

As such, while the New Sudan vision and discourse is still relevant to Sudan and South Sudan, and while integrating a clear gender perspective (among other things) can contribute to New Sudan becoming a truly transformational political project, it is important to ask whether militarization can bring about transformation and a new order that ensures social justice and gender equality. As discussed in chapter 1, however, as a scholar activist who spends most of the year in the Global North, and as a Northerner, I do not believe I have the right to question the decision on how to resist marginalization by others, especially movements representing women and men from historically marginalized areas of Sudan. What is needed, perhaps, is a politics of solidarity.

In February 2013 I organized a meeting that brought together women working toward peace and toward achieving women's rights in Sudan and South Sudan to Clark University in Worcester, Massachusetts. Participants came from Sudan, South Sudan, and the United States. We discussed the challenges, opportunities, and priorities for women and communities in the two countries. We discussed ways we could express solidarity and show support for women activists, especially those in war-affected areas such as the Blue Nile State, South Kordofan State, and Darfur who are in Sudan. Two activists from the Blue Nile and South Kordofan, Awatif and Zainab, shared their perspectives on the concerns of the people and women in the two areas, and shared information on the difficulties women in both areas are facing because of the ongoing conflict. A young woman from South Sudan whom I had encouraged several times throughout the meeting to speak, but who had insisted on silence, approached Zainab and Awatif, took off two blue bracelets, and handed them over: "I want you to have these," she said, and started to weep. Solidarity has many meaningful faces.

AN EPILOGUE TO THE EPILOGUE

September 19, 2014
Nairobi, Kenya

An intensive expert consultation organized by the Uganda-based think tank Sudan Democracy First Group (SDFG) has just concluded. During the sessions, working group discussions, and in the corridors, participants underlined the urgency for producing a plan that would guide reform and reconstruction in Sudan, especially for political parties and movements.

Today is the day! I will be sending the draft manuscript of this book to the publisher. I had asked the editor if I could push the submission date back to September 19, so I could take part in the consultation. He agreed—"Go ahead and attend the consultation."

I am getting ready to visit the African Women's Development and Communications Network (FEMNET), and to meet with the organization's head of communications, my friend Nebila Abdulmelik. I contemplate sending the manuscript before leaving the hotel. I read my email and log into my Facebook page. One of my friends has shared part of a piece by Sudanese anthropologist Hayder Ibrahim Ali, founder of the Centre for Sudanese Studies in Cairo in the 1990s. In this piece, Hayder Ali wrote,

I remember when I saw Habermas at the University of Frankfurt in the mid-
1970s, a strange thought descended upon me! What do I have to do with
Habermas when my mother still holds *Zar* (spirit possession) ceremonies, and
when my grandfather in Algureir (a village near Merowe) is still offering
higbat [phylacteries or written amulets], *mihaya* [holy erasure] *and bakhra*
[ritual incensing] (performs traditional healing)? I remember discussions in
Cairo a decade ago, when one of the modernist [*sic*] enthusiasts filled the air
with Foucault, Derrida and deconstructionism, interrupting his talks with visits
to the bathroom to spit out his *saffa* [coarse tobacco]. I used to say it was
impossible for Foucault and the *tumbak* to coexist in this single mouth! In
other discussions about music and Adorno, I used to tell friends that these
topics were larger than us, historically and not theoretically, because Adorno's
grandmother had a piano in her room, on which she played before she went to
sleep.[2]

I decide to hold on to the manuscript, and to send it to the publisher after
returning to the hotel in the afternoon!

Although I disagree with some of H. Ali's witty but sarcastic writing
above, I grappled with thoughts on the relevance of theory to settings like
Sudan for years. In the write-up of the original research on which this book is
based, I wrote a paragraph that I had initially decided not to include in this
book.

I am writing up this research while at many junctures: standing exactly at the
end of a millennium and at the beginning of a new one. A couple of years ago
a very rigorous and interesting book of feminist theory (Haraway 1997) with
the following title was published: *Modest-witness@second.Millenium: Fe-
maleMan_meets_OncoMouse* [a book that has been cited by 3,762 related
publications as of March 1, 2015]. Sometimes I find it most difficult to resist
the seduction of such elegant discourse. But I am also writing up at a moment
when, just a year back, in some areas "back home" [such as Northern Bahr al-
Ghazal], people were massively dying of hunger, and the starvation continues.
In order not to end on such a gloomy note however, I would like to emphasise
that at this juncture, the Old Sudan is being redefined. While this is taking
place, it is imperative to ensure that all forms of unjust relations, including
gender relations, are rethought and transformed. (N. Ali 2000, 41)

Almost a decade and a half later, I have had the opportunity to reflect further
on feminist debates on what constitutes theory and who could be a theorist. I
also had the pleasure of reading and teaching Charles Lemert's (1993) "Social Theory: Its Uses and Pleasures." Lemert wrote that social theory was "a
basic survival skill," which should not be the monopoly of academics or
social theorists.

I can now reflect on the past decade and a half, and on the analysis in this
book—parts of which I shared with numerous activists, practitioners, and
academics—and conclude that social theory can strengthen our quests to

challenge "historically inscribed patterns of discrimination organised around gender" (Lewis 1996), race, sexuality, and regional location in Sudan, South Sudan, and beyond, while also developing a politics of solidarity. Only then could we begin to imagine an alternative Sudan, a *New Sudan* that we feel we can all belong to!

A Luta Continua!

NOTES

1. A high-ranking official in South Sudan's army confirmed Margaret's story to the author in November 2013.

2. I am grateful to Dr. Hayder Ibrahim Ali for permission to reproduce this paragraph in this book. Communication via Skype on February 11, 2015.

Appendix

Institutionalizing the NDA in Exile (1989–1999) and a Selective Chronology of Other Events

September 1989: The NDA established inside Sudan. NDA National Charter drafted and endorsed in October 1989. The Charter identified its objectives as overthrowing the NIF regime, restoring multi-party democratic rule, respect for international norms of individual and collective freedoms, to revitalize the economy and pursue development, the establishment of peace (negotiated in a national constitutional conference), and of a new Sudan. Two Trade Union leaders secretly contacted Fatima Ibrahim and asked her to sign the Charter "on behalf of Sudanese women" and asked her to contact other women's groups. Ibrahim refused to do that and asked to sign on behalf of the Sudanese Women's Union instead. The two activists said they would consult their colleagues get back to her, which did not take place (narrated by one of the two activists in the presence of Ibrahim, Asmara, March 18, 1998). The activists argue that this was due to security reasons whereas Ibrahim argues that this was a conspiracy against her and against the SWU.

March 1990: Meeting between NDA parties and the SPLM/A. "Release on the NDA Charter," Nairobi.
Participant groups: DUP, the Umma Party, the SPLM/A, and the CPS.
Agenda: The SPLM/A's suggested revisions on the NDA Charter. The SPLM/A presented a document that was embodied in the charter, it became a party to the NDA and signed the Charter.
Women: No participants, no reference to women, but SPLM/A noted women's role in production.

July 13–17, 1990: NDA meeting, Addis Ababa. "The First Conference's Final Communiqué."
Participant Groups: As above.
Agenda: Follow-up to the SPLM/A's membership in the NDA, complimentarity of armed and political struggle, the interim (post-NIF) program of action, preparatory procedures for the preliminary national constitutional conference. The NDA chapter in Cairo assigned to carry out preparations for this conference.
Women: No participants, women's strategic interests not addressed.

March 1991: The NDA meeting in Addis Ababa—follow-up to the July 1990 meeting.

January and February 1992: The NDA London meeting. "The Second Conference of the Leaders of the NDA: Final Declaration."
Participant groups: DUP, Umma Party, CPS, Sudan African Congress, Trade Unions, SPLM/A, the "Legitimate Command," and "distinguished National Characters."
Agenda: Program for the interim period, adopting the unified NDA Charter based on the amendments provided by the SPLM/A, the Transitional Constitution, system of rule and strategies of popular mobilization to overthrow the NIF. Issues of identity, development, restructuring of power and wealth, and identifying the relationship between the state and religion postponed until the National Constitutional Conference, to be held in no more than six months after the overthrow of the NIF.
Women: No participants. One reference to women (and children) in the revised NDA Charter, in the context of activating programs for preventive health. The draft transitional constitution made a reference to non-discrimination on the basis of sex in its preamble, and Article 33 stated that "citizens are equal in all rights and duties, and discrimination on the basis of race, sex, religion, political opinion or region is prohibited." Article 25 stated that "men and women are equal in terms of rights and duties, and the family is the basis of society; and is based on interdependence, guided by religion, morality and citizenship. The state should take all precautions to protect the family from factors that might lead to its disintegration and weakening." Article 26 of the constitution stated that the state should protect mothers and children. Women's participation recommended in the Council of Ministers. Article 7.90 on legislative authority recommended that member organizations take into consideration the participation of women. No reference to women in the final communiqué.

April 17, 1993: NDA meeting in Nairobi. "The Nairobi Communiqué."

Participant Groups: The SPLM/A, DUP, USAP, SAC, CPS, "Legitimate Command," and "independent national figures."

Agenda: The outstanding issue of the separation between religion and politics was resolved, armed struggle was adopted as a strategy to overthrow the NIF. Article 1 affirmed that "all international and regional human rights instruments and covenants shall be an integral part of the laws of the Sudan and any law contrary thereto shall be considered null and void and unconstitutional," "laws shall guarantee full equality between citizens on the basis of citizenship."

Women: No participants. Meeting affirmed equal citizenship rights regardless of gender.

June 28, 1994: The Bonn Conference, Bonn, Germany (arranged by Christian Solidarity International).

Participants: Sudanese opposition groups and religious organizations.

Agenda: More pressure on the NIF by the international community. The DUP made reservations on the IGAD Declaration of Principle's right to self-determination.

Women: No adequate information.

September 1994: The Meeting of the Four Forces, Asmara.

Participant Groups: DUP, Umma Party, SPLM/A, and SNA/SAF.

Agenda: The establishment of an NDA broadcasting station in Asmara, preparing for the Asmara 1995 conference.

Women: No participants.

June 1995: Conference for Fundamental Issues, Asmara. "Resolutions of the Conference for Fundamental Issues."

Participant Groups: DUP, Umma Party, CPS, USAP, SPLM/A, SNA/SAF, Trade Unions, "Legitimate Command," and "Independent National Personalities."

Agenda: Ending the war, right to self-determination, the relationship between religion and politics and system of rule during the transitional NIF period, transforming unequal relationships between the center and regions. Anti-NIF armed and political means of struggle. NDA structure established.

Women: No official participants. Article 1.b.5 (Article 5): "The NDA undertakes to preserve and promote the dignity of the Sudanese woman, and affirms her role in the Sudanese national movement and her rights and duties as enshrined in international instruments and covenants without prejudice to the tenets of prevailing religious and noble spiritual beliefs." The structure of the NDA included a woman's bureau appended to the Secretariat of Organization and Administration.

January 12–15, 1996: NDA Leadership Council meeting, Asmara. "Declaration."

Participant Groups: All NDA member organizations and Fatima Ibrahim (as an observer).

Agenda: Follow-up to the Asmara 1995 meeting.

Women: Recommended that the next congress ensure women's representation in the NDA Leadership Council. Recommended that Fatima Ibrahim participate as an observer in the NDA meetings until the issue of women's representation is resolved. The Feminist Group for Reconstructing Sudan presented a memo demanding, among other issues, the change of Article 5 in the Asmara declaration. The Women's Forum in Cairo sent a letter to the meeting nominating Fatima Ibrahim as the representative of women in the LC; their suggestion was not considered.

June 19–22, 1997: NDA Leadership Council meeting, Asmara. "Final Communiqué."

Participant Groups: All NDA member parties.

Agenda: General issues, al-Sadiq al-Mahdi addressed the Leadership Council. The SNA/SAF, Beja Congress, SFDA, SNP, and trade unions were granted seats in the Executive Office.

Women: Article Six in the communiqué acknowledged the role of women in social, economic, and political spheres and renewed commitment to their representation in post-NIF era, called upon NDA party members to observe the representation of women when choosing their representatives in the leadership organs of the NDA. Recommended the formation of a national women's organization that would nominate women representatives in the NDA leadership. The SNA/SAF nominated a woman as its representative in the NDA executive office.

March 18–20, 1998: NDA Leadership Council meeting, Asmara. "Final Communiqué."

Participant Groups: All NDA party members.

Agenda: Review of the NDA performance since 1995, review of the political (including women's) issues and military situation, NDA position on "initiatives for peaceful solution," the situation in the liberated areas, and the preparations for the interim period.

Women: Article H recommended the activation of women's role within all NDA organs, changing Article 5 (the NDA Executive Office asked to look for an alternative text). The Sudan Women Alliance, the Sudan Women Forum, and Fatima Ahmad Ibrahim presented requests to change Article 5 of the Asmara 1995 Resolutions. The SNA/SAF women's secretariat presented a memo and the SWA organized a demonstration prior to the meeting, all the women who participated in the demonstration were invited to attend the opening session of the meeting.

August 15–17, 1998: NDA Leadership Council meeting, Cairo. "The Cairo Declaration."
Participant Groups: All NDA parties.
Agenda: Review of the current situation in Sudan, the war in the Horn of Africa and the Lakes, the famine in Bahr El Ghazal, the NIF constitution, meetings with the Egyptian leadership and administration. Date set for convening the second conference in Asmara.
Women: Section Ten recommended the formation of a national women's organization and the establishment of a Women's Charter that ensures women's rights, the NDA confirmed its commitment to the representation of women in all NDA organs. Fatima Ibrahim was prevented from attending the meeting upon request by the Umma Party and the DUP representatives in the NDA, because the NIF broadcasted a video in which she "uttered abusive language" against the leadership of both parties.

September 1998: NDA Leadership Council meeting, Asmara. "The NDA Leadership Meeting: Final Declaration."
Participant groups: All NDA member organizations.
Agenda: Preparations for the interim period, the role of the Joint Military Command, the impact of the war in the Horn on the NDA.
Women: A committee discussed Fatima Ibrahim's membership and decided that she should attend the meetings after reading an apology regarding her discourse against the two main parties. The issue of women's participation was discussed again, report on the NDA Women's Charter committee presented by SNA/SAF's Women Secretariat and discussed.

May 13, 1999: Sudanese women participants in The Hague Appeal for Peace meeting issue Sudanese Women's Appeal for Peace in the Sudan. Signed by the Civil Society Working Committee, the NDA, National Working Committee, the non-Partisan Working Committee, Nuba Women Working Committee, Southern Women Working Committee, SPDF Working Committee, and SPLM-United Working Committee. Signatories committed to building a culture of peace in Sudan, actively promote peace, and to work to integrate women's perspective into peacemaking efforts at all levels. It also made recommendations to the IGAD, the GOS, and other stakeholders.

June 7–14, 1999: NDA Leadership Council meeting in Asmara. "Release of the NDA Leadership Council Meeting."
Participant groups: As above and the Eritrean Leadership that called for the meeting.

Agenda: Preconditions for a political settlement with NIF as based on the IGAD Declaration of Principles and the resolutions of March 1998 meeting. NDA structure was revised and Leadership Council and Executive Office replaced with a leading council that consisted of the leaders of the parties and specialized committees. The existing NDA secretariats were turned into working groups so as to activate opposition.

Women's issues: Not discussed.

April 13, 2000: Maastricht Declaration of the Sudanese Women's Peace Initiative.

September 2000: The NDA's Second Conference (Mussawwa, Eritrea). Sixteen women participated in the conference.

2002: Second Conference of the Women's Alliance (of the NDA), Kurbaweb, then part of the non-government-held areas in Eastern Sudan.

October 8, 2002: Joint meeting between the Women's National Democratic Alliance (inside Sudan), New Sudan Women's Federation (Nairobi and non-government-held areas in Southern Sudan), and the Sudanese Women's Democratic Alliance (Eritrea and the non-government-held areas in Eastern Sudan). The meeting discussed the resolution of the Massawa conference on holding a women's conference. Memo to the NDA Executive Office demanding that the women's conference take place by the end of 2002, and asking for wider representation in the preparatory committee for the conference. The NDA's Secretary of Organization sent a response to a follow-up memo, saying that the lack of finances was the reason for the delay in holding the conference.

January 2005: Signing of the Comprehensive Peace Agreement between the GOS and the Sudan People's Liberation Movement.

April 2005: Sudanese Women's Priorities and Recommendations to the Oslo Donors' Conference on Sudan.

June 2005: Signing of the Cairo Agreement between the NDA (excluding the Beja Congress and the Free Lions) and the GOS.

October 14, 2006: Signing of the Eastern Sudan Peace Agreement between the GOS and the Eastern Front (the Beja Congress, the Free Lions, and the East Democratic Party).

2010: Establishment of the National Consensus Forces, originally to stand against the ruling National Congress Party in the April 2010 elections. These include the National Umma Party, the Communist Party, the Popular Congress Party, the DUP, New Forces Democratic Movement (*HAG*), Sudan Ba'ath Party, and the Sudanese Congress Party.

July 2011: South Sudan achieved independence, after a referendum in which 98 percent of the population voted for separation.

June 2011: Conflict re-erupted in South Kordofan state.

September 2011: Conflict re-erupted in the Blue Nile State.

November 2011: Armed opposition groups, led by the SPLM-Northern sector, established the Sudan Revolutionary Front (SRF). The SRF is a coalition of Darfuri armed movements, SPLM-North, a faction of the Beja Congress, and members from some of the other opposition parties.

December 2014: SRF, represented by its vice president Minni Arko Minnawi, Sudan's Civil Society Initiative represented by Amin Mekki Medani, National Umma Party represented by Chairperson al-Sadiq al-Mahdi, and National Consensus Forces represented by Chairperson Farouk Abuessa signed Sudan Call Declaration. The declaration is a pledge to "dismantle the one-party state and replace it with a state founded on equal citizenship, through daily popular struggle." Signatories pledged to find a comprehensive solution to Sudan's conflicts, respond to the humanitarian crisis in war-affected areas in Southern Kordofan and the Blue Nile, end corruption and stop economic collapse, revocation of laws restricting human rights and democratic freedom, forming a transitional government, and holding a national constitutional conference through a participatory process. The declaration included a commitment to the participation of women and youth.

December 2014: Eleven women's organizations and networks support the Sudan Call Declaration. These are the Coalition of Political Women, women members of the National Umma Party, New Sudan Women's League, Civil Society Initiative, Sudanese Women's Forum, SuWEP, No to Women's Oppression, Women's Secretariat of the Republican Party, Forum for Women Lawyers, Forum for Women Journalists, and the Families of the Martyrs of 28 Ramadan. The groups call for women's participation in the coordination bodies suggested by the declaration. The groups also demand that "women's issues" be central to efforts for legal reform suggested by the declaration.

Sources: The NDA, Secretariat for Organization and Administration Women in the NDA Documents (June 1998) (compiled by Abdel Magid Wasfy). Declarations and communiqués of the meetings above. Diar (1997), the NDA (1992), the SPLM/A (1990), the NDA (1992), Documents of the London Conference Cairo, February. Key Informant Interviews with NDA Leaders, Sudan Tribune, Sudan Voices, Verwijk (2012), email correspondence, WWW.UMMA.ORG/NDA, and IRIN News.

Bibliography

I. PRIMARY SOURCES

Abdallah, I. (1995). "Questions around the NDA Conference." *Al-Khartoum* 904, June 8.

Abu Al-Bashar, A. (2012). "Maj. Gen. Daniel Kodi Criticizes Sudan Revolutionary Front." *Sudan Vision* 2918. October 3. Retrieved from http://news.sudanvisiondaily.com/details. html?rsnpid=207795 on April 13, 2013.

Abu Eisa, F. (September 1994). "Women's Rights in International Conventions: Reading International Documents Concerning Women's Situations with Reference to the Right to Development." Arabic. *Al-Haq: Periodical of the Union of Arab Lawyers.* Cairo, Egypt.

Abu Kashawa, S. (August 1995). "Reading the Document of the UN Women's Conference." Arabic. *Azza* (36). Khartoum, Sudan.

Africa Watch. (1990). News from Africa Watch. New York.

Al-Hussein, Z. O., and al-Shykh (1997). "The Sudanese Women Forum in Egypt: Continuing the Struggle Abroad." In M. al-Tigany (ed.), *Democracy and Human Rights in Sudan.*

Ali, N. (September 1998). "Report on Article Five and on the Preparation of the 'Charter of Sudanese Women's Rights.'" Presented to the NDA Leadership Council. Cairo.

Ali, N. (February 14, 1999). "Reading 'The Aim Behind the Two Ideas.'" *Al-Fajr.* London.

Al-Inqaz (September 23, 1995). No. 2048.

Al-Khartoum (1995, 21). Cairo, No. 915.

Al-Mahdi, S. (March 1998). *Towards Reform and Renewal of the NDA.* Arabic. Asmara.

Al-Sudan al-Hadith (September 30, 1995). Khartoum. No. 2051.

al-Tigany, M. (August 30, 1998). "The NDA and Sudanese Women's Rights." Arabic. *Al-Khartoum,* daily newspaper, no. 1893.

Ambo Workshop on Sudan: Problems and Prospects. (February 4–7, 1989). Ambo, Ethiopia.

Arman, Y. (August 20, 2014). "New Approach to the National Dialogue in Sudan That Will Stop the Wars, Address the Humanitarian Crisis and Lead to Democratic Transformation." Talk at a round table meeting in Chatam House.

Biro, G. (1994). *Report of the Special Rapporteur on Human Rights in the Sudan.* Geneva, United Nations (reproduced in SHRO 1994).

Bukhari, A. (August 1995). "Our Sister: Why Don't You Defend Yourself?" *Azza* (36) (English language supplement).

Cleto Rial, et al. (February 1999). "An Open Letter to Fatima Ahmad Ibrahim." Posted on sudanese@list.msu.edu.

Deng, F. M. (1989). "What Is Not Said Is What Divides." In A. Ahmed and G. Sørbø (eds.), *Management of the Crisis in the Sudan.*

Deng, F. M. (2010). *New Sudan in the Making? Essays on a Nation in Painful Search of Itself.* Trenton and Asmara: Africa World Press.

Direig, A. I. (1989). "A New Political Structure for the Sudan." In A. Ahmed and G. Sørbø (eds.), *Management of the Crisis in Sudan.*

Eyega, Z. (February 1999). "Ignorance by Choice: An Open Letter to Fatima A. Ibrahim." Posted on sudanese@list.msu.edu.

Fund for Peace (May 1992). "Abuses Against Women in the Sudan." New York.

Garang, J. (1998). *The Vision of the New Sudan: Questions of Unity and Identity.* Edited by E. Kameir. Cairo: COPADES.

Ibrahim, F. (January 3, 1999). "The Aim Behind the Two Ideas." Arabic. *Al-Fajr.*

Ibrahim, M. (April 28. 1997). Interview with Musa Ibrahim. Arabic. *Al-Khartoum.*

Interview with Mr. Mubarak al-Mahdi, NDA SG (Arabic) (September 28, 1998). *Al-Haya* (12991).

Interview with Mr. Mubarak al-Mahdi, NDA SG (September 28, 1998). *Al-Khalij*, daily newspaper (7071).

Interview with Nada Mustafa [Ali] (May 2, 1998). *Al-Khartoum* (1790).

Khartoum State (November 1992). *The Law of Public Order in Khartoum State.*

My Sister's Keeper (2010). *My Sister's Keeper's Newsletter.* Summer. http://www.mskeeper.org/site/index.php?option=com_content&task=view&id=142&Itemid=219 (last accessed on May 21, 2014).

National Democratic Alliance (NDA) (January 1992) *Communiqué of the London Conference.* London.

NDA (1993). *The Nairobi Communiqué.* Nairobi, Kenya.

NDA (1995). "Charter of the National Democratic Alliance." Documents of the Conference of Fundamental Issues. Cairo.

NDA (June 1995). *Conference of Fundamental Issues: Resolution on the Organizational Structure of the NDA Outside [Sudan].* Asmara.

NDA (March 21, 1998). *Communiqué: The NDA Leadership Council (LC) Meeting in Asmara, March 18th–20th.* Asmara, Eritrea.

NDA (August 15–17, 1998). *The Cairo Declaration: Communiqué of the NDA Leadership Council Meeting.* Cairo.

NDA Secretariat for Organization and Administration (May 1998). *Review and Evaluation of the Performance of the NDA outside [Sudan]: June 1995–June 1998.* Arabic. Cairo.

NDA Secretary General's (SG) Office (August 3, 1997). NDA and Women, NDA SG office clarification. Posted on sudanese@list.msu.edu.

NDA Secretary General Office (August 5, 1997). NDA and Women, NDA SG office clarification. Posted on sudanese@list.msu.edu.

NDA Secretary General Office (August 10, 1997). NDA and Women, NDA SG office clarification. Posted on sudanese@list.msu.edu.

National Women's Democratic Alliance (June 1998). *Draft Women's Charter.* Arabic. Khartoum.

Near East Foundation (1996). *A Needs Assessment on Economic Needs and Women's Health of the Displaced Sudanese Community in Egypt.* Cairo.

New Sudan Women Federation (NSWF). *Brochure.* No date.

Osman, S. (November–December 1998). "Women in the Movement: When Six Dynamic Women Met in Addis Ababa in 1985." *The New Woman: A Bi-Monthly Newsletter of NSWF* (8).

Position Statement from the Women's Political Forces and Civil Society Organizations and Groups on the Sudan Call. (2015). Posted on *Sudan Tribune* on January 17.

Professors + Publics: A Roundtable on Academic Activism [Seminar announcement] (2015). Posted on H-Net on February 13. http://www.h-net.org/announce/show.cgi?ID=220399.

Salih, A. (June 20, 1995). "Conference of the Last Opportunity." Arabic. *Al-Khartoum* (914).

Sudan Human Rights Organization in Egypt (1997). *Democracy and Human Rights in Sudan: Commitments of Sudanese Political Parties, Trade Unions and Military Forces.* Edited by M. al-Tigany. Cairo.

SPLM/A Department of Information (1989). "On the New Sudan." In A. Ahmed and G. Sørbø (eds.), *Management of the Crisis.*

SPLM/A (1998). *New Sudan Women's Greater and Effective Participation in Policy and Decision-Making Processes in the SPLM/A.* New Kush (South Sudan).

Sudan Call: A Political Declaration on the Establishment of a State of Citizenship and Democracy (December 3, 2014).

Sudan Catholic Information Office (1999). *Sudan Monthly Report.* Nairobi.

Sudan Cultural Digest Project (SCDP) (1996). "Coping with Dynamics of Culture and Change: The Case of Sudanese in Egypt." Cairo.

Sudan Human Rights Organisation (SHRO) (1994). *Human Rights Violations in the Sudan.* London.

SHRO (1997). "Refugees from Sudan to Neighbouring Countries: Historical Causes and Current Situation." Arabic. *SHRO's non-Quarterly.* Cairo.

SHRO (April 1998). *SHRO Quarterly* (6).

Sudan People's Liberation Movement (1990). *Towards a New Sudan.* Arabic. Cairo.

Sudanese Women Association in Nairobi (October 1998). *Sudanese Women's Social Contract and Negotiating Platform on the Status of Women in Sudan.* Nairobi.

Sudanese Women's Alliance (SWA) (August 1995). "SWA's Position Paper." Paper presented to the first preliminary conference of Sudan National Alliance/Alliance Forces. Asmara.

SWA (December 20–24, 1997). "SWA in Two Years." Unpublished report by the author, presented to SWA's First Organizational Meeting.

The Economist Intelligence Unit. (1994). *Sudan: Country Report.*

The Feminist Group for Reconstructing Sudan. (January 1996). "Letter to the NDA Leadership Council Meeting." Arabic. Cairo, Egypt.

The Kampala Declaration. (February 12, 1999). *Conference on Human Rights in the Transition in Sudan.* Kampala, Uganda.

The Koko Dam Declaration (March 24, 1986). Koka, Ethiopia.

Samuel, J. (November–December 1998). "Interview: Meet a Resourceful Para-Legal Officer, Jasmin Samuel." *The New Woman* (8).

Silverstein, K. (2015). "Why is South Sudan a Hellhole? Blame George Clooney." www.gawker.com/why-is-south-sudan-a-hellhole-blame-george-clooney-1683838565 (last accessed on February 7, 2015).

UNIFEM (now UN Women) (1998). *African Women's Struggle for Peace* 1(2).

Wudu, S. K. (2014). "South Sudan President Fires John Garang's Widow." *Voice of America.* August 20. www.voanews.com/content/south-sudan-john-garang-rebecca-nyandeng-fired/2422912.html (last accessed on February 7, 2015).

II. SECONDARY RESOURCES

Abdel 'Al, M. (2008). "Women's Participation in Political Activities." Arabic. In B. Badri (ed.), *Sudanese Woman: Her Present and Future.* Omdurman, Sudan: Ahfad University for Women. Cairo: Dar Madarik.

Abdelaziz, I. A. (1993). *Women at the Barrel of the Gun/Women under the Gun.* Arabic. Cairo: Gazirat Alward.

Abdelaziz, I. A. (2013). *Women in the Scope of the Rifle: How They Infiltrated the Corridors of the National Democratic Alliance.* Arabic. Cairo, Egypt: Maktabat Gazerat al-Ward.

Abdel Hafiz, K. (March 1998). "On the Position of the (Sudan Communist) Party towards Women: Working among Women in the UK." Arabic. *Afaq Gadidah* (17).

Abdel Halim, A. M. (1994). "Challenges to the Application of International Women's Human Rights in the Sudan." In R. Cook (ed.), *Human Rights of Women: National and International Perspectives.* Pennsylvania: University of Pennsylvania Press.

Abdel Halim, A. M. (1998). "Attack with a Friendly Weapon." In M. Turshen and C. Twagiramariya (eds.), *What Women Do in Wartime: Gender and Conflict in Africa.* London: Zed.

Abdel Halim, A. M. (2006). *Sudanese Women in the United States: The Double Problem of Gender and Culture.* Lewiston, NY: Edwin Mellen Press.

Abdel Halim, A. M. (2009). "Women's Organizations Seeking Gender Justice in the Sudan 1964–1985." *Review of African Political Economy* (121), 389–407.

Abdel Halim, A. M. (2011). "Gendered Justice: Women and Criminal Law in the Sudan." In L. Oette (ed.), *Criminal Law Reform and Transitional Justice: Human Rights Perspectives for Sudan*. Burlington, VT: Ashgate.

Abdel Halim, A. M. (October 2002). "The Time Is Now." *The Sudanese Human Rights Quarterly* (14). http://www.shro-cairo.org/quarterly.htm.

Abd el-Salam, S. (September 1995). "The Media Discourse of Political Islam on the Beijing Conference." Arabic. *Sawasiah* (6), Cairo, Egypt.

Abdulhadi, R. (1998). "The Palestinian Women Autonomous Movement: Emergence, Dynamics and Challenges." *Gender and Society* 12(6).

Abdul-Rahim, M., ed. (1986). *Sudan since Independence: Studies of the Political Development since 1956*. Aldershot, UK: Gower.

Abu El-Yamen, S. H., I. M. Mustafa, and S. Ibrahim. *Analysis of Mortality Levels Trends and Differentials Census Data*. Publication based on 2008 census. Khartoum: Central Bureau of Statistics.

Abu-Lughod, L. (1998). "The Marriage of Feminism and Islamism in Egypt: Selective Repudiation as a Dynamic of Postcolonial Cultural Politics." In L. Abu-Lughod (ed.), *Remaking Women: Feminism and Modernity in the Middle East*. Princeton: Princeton University Press.

Abusharaf, R. M. (2002). *Wanderings: Sudanese Migrants and Exiles in North America*. Ithaca, NY: Cornell University Press.

Abusharaf, R. M. (2009). "Competing Masculinities: Probing Political Disputes as Acts of Violence against Women from Southern Sudan and Darfur." In S. M. Hassan and C. R. Ray (eds.), *Darfur and the Crisis of Governance in Sudan: A Critical Reader*. Ithaca: Cornell University Press.

Abusharaf, R. M. (2009). *Transforming Displaced Women in Sudan: Politics and the Body in a Squatter Settlement*. Chicago: University of Chicago Press.

Acklesberg, M. (1985). "'Separate and Equal?' Mujeres Libres and Anarchist Strategy for Women's Emancipation." *Feminist Studies* 1(11).

Afkhami, M., and E. Friedel, eds. (1997). *Muslim Women and the Politics of Participation: Implementing the Beijing Platform*. Syracuse: Syracuse University Press.

The African Women's Development and Communication Network (FEMNET) (April 25, 2014). "Call for Abstracts: African Women in Power/Politics." http://www.femnet.co/index. php/en/african-women-s-journal/item/280-call-for-abstracts-african-women-in-power-politics (accessed on May 13, 2014).

Africa Watch (November 1994). "Sudan: In the Name of God, Repression Continues in Northern Sudan." Volume 6, no. 9.

Afshar, H. (1998). "Disempowerment and the Politics for Civil Liberties for Iranian Women." In H. Afshar (ed.), *Women and Empowerment: Illustrations from the Third World*. London: Macmillan.

Afshar, H., and M. Manyard (1994). *The Dynamics of 'Race,' and Gender: Some Feminist Interventions*. London: Taylor and Francis.

Ahmed, A., and G. Sørbø (eds.). *Management of the Crisis in the Sudan: Proceedings of the Bergen Forum 23–24 February 1989*. Bergen: University of Bergen Centre for Development Studies.

Ahmed, L. (1992). *Women and Gender in Islam*. New Haven: Yale University Press.

Ahmed, S. I. (June 1997). "Women and Political Participation: Illusion and Reality of Women's Emancipation in the Sudan." Paper presented to the Fourth International Conference of Sudan Studies Association. Cairo.

Ajak, B., et al. (2006). *They Poured Fire on Us from the Sky: The Story of Three Lost Boys from Sudan*. Public Affairs.

Al-Ali, N. (2000). "'We Are Not Feminists': Egyptian Women's Rights Activists on Feminism." In C. Nelson and S. Rouse (eds.), *Globalization and the Indigenization of Knowledge Debate: Comparative Perspectives*. Gainesville, FL: University of Florida Press.

Al-Ali, N. (2002). *Secularism, Gender and the State in the Middle East: The Egyptian Women's Movement*. Cambridge: Cambridge University Press.

Al-Ali, N. (2007). *Iraqi Women: Untold Stories from 1948 to the Present*. London: Zed Books.

Al-Ali, N., and N. Pratt (2009). *What Kind of Liberation? Women and the Occupation in Iraq*. Berkeley: University of California Press.

Ali, A. A., K. Yassin, and R. Omer (2014). "Domestic Violence against Women in Eastern Sudan." *BMC Public Health* 14(1136).

Ali, A. A., et al. (2012). "Prevalence of and Factors Affecting Female Genital Mutilation among Schoolgirls in Eastern Sudan." *International Journal of Gynecology and Obstetrics*.

Ali, H. (1991). *The Crisis of Political Islam: Case of the National Islamic Front in Sudan*. Arabic. Cairo, Egypt: Sudan Studies Centre.

Ali, H. (1996). *Islamic Movements and the Issue of Democracy*. Arabic. Beirut, Lebanon: Centre for Arab Unity Studies.

Ali, N. M. (1993). "Coping Amidst Crisis: The Narratives of Five [Northern] Sudanese Women." MA thesis, Political Science Department. Cairo: American University in Cairo.

Ali, N. M. (1995). "Gender and Politicized Islam in Sudan: Case of a Khartoum-Based Women's Organization." Paper presented to the Workshop on Pathways to Education. Hamburg: UNESCO Institute for Education.

Ali, N. M. (1998). "Survival, Empowerment and the Invisible Economy: Cases from Atbara, Sudan." In R. Lobban (ed.), *Middle Eastern Women and the Invisible Economy*. Gainesville, FL: University Press of Florida.

Ali, N. M. (1999). "Women's Human Rights: Lost between Islamists and Secularists." Arabic. In O. al-Garrai (ed.), *Women's Rights between Islamic Schools and International Conventions*. Arabic. Cairo: CIHRS.

Ali, N. M. (2000). "Meet Mary Apai: Gender, Culture and Conflict in Sudan." *Agenda* 43.

Ali, N. M. (2000). "Thorny Issues and Perilous Conditions: Addressing Women's Human Rights in the Context of Conflict and the Struggle to Restore Democracy in Sudan (1989–2000)." *Al-Raida* (XXI), 103.

Ali, N. M. (February 2001). "On Gender, Conflict and Democracy: Case of the Sudanese Opposition in Exile." Paper presented at the Women, Conflict and Peace-Building Conference. Political Science Department, University of York.

Ali, N. M. (2003). "Gender and Conflict: Case of the Sudan." Paper presented at the East Africa Seminar, Department of Anthropology, University of Oxford, Oxford, UK.

Ali, N. M. (March 16, 2004). "Engaging DfiD's 'Sudan Country Engagement Plan.'" Paper presented at the workshop on gender and post-conflict reconstruction in Sudan. House of Commons, Westminster, London.

Ali, N. M. (November 2004). "Root Causes of the Conflict in Darfur: The Impact on Women, and Recommendations for Action." Paper presented at the Conference on the Root Causes of the Conflict in Darfur. The Hague, Netherlands.

Ali, N. M. (2005). "Endangering Peace by Excluding Women." *Forced Migration Review* (24), 50–51.

Ali, N. M. (April 2005). "Peace, Conflict and Economic Development in Eastern Sudan." Paper presented at the Sudan Focal Point—Europe Meeting. Germany.

Ali, N. M. (July 2005). "Peace, Conflicts and Democratization in Sudan: A Gender Perspective." Arabic. Paper presented to the conference on Sudan, *Between War and Peace: The Role of Civil Society in Peacekeeping and Development*. Vlotho, Germany. Published in *Ruwaq Arabi* (38–39), 183–92.

Ali, N. M. (December 14, 2010). "Sudan: Flogging and Harassment of Women Continue." *The Huffington Post*. http://images.huffingtonpost.com/2013-02-20-floggingandharassmentofwomeninSudan.pdf.

Ali, N. M. (2011). *Gender and Statebuilding in South Sudan*. Washington, DC: United States Institute of Peace.

Ali, S. M. M. (2013). "Women [and] Local Governance Institutions-Building in Post-Conflict Eastern Sudan." Retrieved from http://www.unifr.ch/federalismnetwork/assets/files/Best%20Papers%202011/samia%20paper.pdf.

Ali, T. (1988). "The State Agricultural Policy: A Quest for a Framework for Analysis of Development Strategies." In T. Barnett and A. Abdel Karim (eds.), *Sudan: State, Capital and Transformation*. New York: Biddle.

Ali, T. (1989). *The Cultivation of Hunger: State and Agriculture in the Sudan.* Khartoum: Khartoum University Press.

Ali, T. (1994). *The Cultivation of Hunger: State and Agriculture in the Sudan.* Arabic. Cairo: Sudanese Studies Centre.

Ali, T., and R. O. Mathews (1999). *Civil Wars in Africa: Roots and Resolution.* Montreal and Kingston: McGill-Queen's University Press.

Ali, Y. (1997). "Muslim Women and the Politics of Ethnicity and Culture in Northern England." *Women Living Under Muslim Laws* (20).

Al-Nagar, S., and A. Salih (February 1989). "Women in Production: An Attempt at Curriculum Change." Paper presented to the Workshop on Women's Studies in the Sudan. Khartoum.

Al-Nawrani, T. (2011). "The History of Quotas in Sudan." Arabic. In A. El-Battahani (ed.), *Elections and the Media.*

Al-Rafai, A. (2007). "Political Instability and Nation-Building: Sexual Violence against Female Teenagers in the Occupied Palestinian Territories." In P. Ouis and T. Myhrman (eds.), *Gender-Based Sexual Violence against Teenage Girls in the Middle East.* Beirut: Save the Children Sweden.

Al-Rufai, N. (1989). "Participation of Sudanese Women in the Political Life of the Sudan during the Condominium Administration." Diploma Dissertation. Institute of African and Asian Studies, University of Khartoum.

Al-Sadiq, R (1995). "Women of Omdurman during Mahdiyya." Arabic. *Kitabat Sudaniyya* (6).

Alvarez, S. (1990). *Engendering Democracy in Brazil: Women's Movements in Transition Politics.* Princeton: Princeton University Press.

Amadiume, Ifi (1987). *Male Daughters, Female Husbands: Gender and Sex in an African Society.* London: Zed.

Amadiume, Ifi (1997). *Reinventing Africa: Patriarchy, Religion and Culture.* London: Zed.

Andrijasevic, R., C. Hamilton, and C. Hemmings (2014). "Re-Imagining Revolutions." *Feminist Review* 106, 1–8.

Anis, A. (2001). "Charting New Directions, Reflection on Women Political Activism in Sudan." MA thesis. Halifax: Saint Mary's University.

Anis, A. (2002). "Moving Boundaries: Forms of Resistance and Women's Solidarity in Islamist Sudan." In Y. F. Hassan and R. Gray (eds.), *Religion and Conflict in Sudan.* Nairobi: Paulines Publications Africa.

An-Na'im, A. (1987). "National Unity and the Diversity of Identities." In F. Deng and P. Gifford (eds.), *The Search for Peace and Unity in the Sudan.* Washington, DC: Woodrow Wilson Center Press.

Anthias, F., and N. Yuval-Davis (1992). *Racialised Boundaries: Race, Nation, Gender, Colour and Class and the Anti-Racist Struggle.* London: Routledge.

Appiah, K. A. (2015). "Race in the Modern World: The Problem of the Color Line." *Foreign Affairs* 94(2): March/April, 1–8.

Arabi, A. (2011). "In Power without Power: Women in Politics and Leadership Positions in Southern Sudan." In F. Bubenzer and O. Stern (eds.), *Hope, Pain and Patience: The Lives of Women in South Sudan.* Johannesburg, South Africa: Jacana Media.

Arabi, A. (2012). "In Power without Power: Women in Politics and Leadership Positions in South Sudan." In F. Bubenzer and O. Stern (eds.), *Hope, Pain, and Patience: The Lives of Women in South Sudan.* Johannesburg, South Africa: Jacana Media.

Ascoly, N. (1997). "A Woman's Place in the Nation: Analysing the Discourse of the Nation of Islam." In *Women Living under Muslim Laws*, Dossier 20.

Atanga, L. L. (2009). *Gender, Discourse and Power in the Cameroonian Parliament.* Oxford: African Books Collective.

Badran, M. (1991). "Competing Agendas: Feminisits, Islam and the State." In D. Kandiyoti (ed.), *Women, Islam and the State.* London: Macmillan.

Badran, M. (1994). "Gender Activism: Feminists and Islamists in Egypt." In V. Moghadam (ed.), *Identity Politics and Women: Cultural Reassertions and Feminisms in International Perspective.* Boulder: Westview.

Badran, M. (2001). "Understanding Islam, Islamism, and Islamic Feminism." *Journal of Women's History* 13(1), 47–52.

Badri, A. (November 23, 1999). *The Experience of Ahfad University for Women*. Lecture at the University of Manchester, Manchester, UK.

Badri, A., and I. Abdel Sadiq (1997). *Displaced Women in Khartoum and Northern Kordofan*. Nairobi: UNIFEM.

Badri, B., ed. (2008). *Sudanese Woman: Her Present and Future*. Arabic. Omdurman, Sudan: Ahfad University for Women. Cairo: Dar Madarik.

Badri, B. (2011). "The Next Elections: Challenges and Opportunities for Collective Action." Arabic. In A. El-Battahani (ed.), *Elections and the Media*.

Badri, H. K. (1985). *The Women's Movement in the Sudan*. New Delhi: UNESCO.

Baffoun, A. (1994). "Feminism and Muslim Fundamentalism: The Tunisian and Algerian Cases." In V. Moghadam (ed.), *Identity Politics and Women: Cultural Reassertions and Feminisms in International Perspective*. Boulder: Westview.

Bagadi, H. O. (1989). "A Review of Peace Efforts since April 1985." In A. Ahmed and G. Sørbø (eds.), *Management of the Crisis in the Sudan: Proceedings of the Bergen Forum 23–24 February 1989*. Bergen: University of Bergen Centre for Development Studies.

Barakat, H. (1996). *Contemporary Arab Society*. Arabic. Beirut: Centre for Arab Unity Studies.

Basu, A. (2000). "Globalization of the Local/Localization of the Global: Mapping Transnational Women's Movements." *Meridians* 1(1).

Bashir, M. O. (1969). *Educational Development in the Sudan: 1898–1956*. Oxford: Clarendon.

Bashir, M. O. (1980). "Ethnicity, Regionalism and National Cohesion." *Sudan Notes and Records* LXI(61).

Ben Jelloun, T. (1987). *The Sand Child*. Trans. by A. Shridan. San Diego: Harcourt Brace Jovanovich.

Bennoune, K. (1994). "Algerian Women Confront Fundamentalism." *Monthly Review* 46(4).

Berridge, W. J. (2015). *Civil Uprisings in Modern Sudan: The 'Khartoum Springs' of 1964 and 1985*. Bloomsbury Publishing.

Beswick, S. (2000). "Women, War and Leadership in South Sudan (1700–1994)." In J. Spaulding and S. Beswisk (eds.), *White Nile, Black Blood: War, Leadership, and Ethnicity from Khartoum to Kampala*. Asmara and London: Red Sea Press

Beswick, S. (2001). "'If You Leave Your Country You Have No Life!' Rape, Suicide, and Violence: The Voices of Ethiopian, Somali, and Sudanese Female Refugees in Kenyan Refugee Camps." *Northeast African Studies* 8(3), 69–98.

Beswick, S. (2004). *Sudan's Blood Memory: The Legacy of War, Ethnicity, and Slavery in South Sudan*. Rochester, NY: University of Rochester Press.

Bilal, A. A. (2005). *The Social Question and Civil Society in Sudan*. Arabic. Khartoum, Sudan: Azza Publishers.

Bleuchot, H., C. Delmet, and D. Hopwood, eds. (1991). *Sudan: History, Identity, Ideology*. Reading, UK: Ithaca Press.

Boddy, J. (1989). *Wombs and Alien Spirits: Women, Men and the Zar Cult in Northern Sudan*. Madison: University of Wisconsin Press.

Boddy, J. (2007). *Civilizing Women: British Crusades in Colonial Sudan*. Princeton and Oxford: Princeton University Press.

Bouatta, C., and D. Merabtin (1994). "Social Representations of Women in Algeria's Islamist Movement." In V. Moghadam (ed.), *Identity Politics and Women: Cultural Reassertions and Feminisms in International Perspective*. Boulder: Westview.

Boulo, D. A. (July 5–7, 1994). "The Situation of Displaced Sudanese in Egypt." Paper presented to the workshop organized by Sudanese Women's Forum on "Sudanese Women, Population and Development." Cairo, Egypt.

Browers, M. (2006). "The Centrality and Marginalization of Women in the Political Discourse of Arab Nationalists and Islamists." *Journal of Middle East Women's Studies* 2(2), 8–34.

Bubenzer, F., and O. Stern, eds. (2011). *Hope, Pain and Patience: The Lives of Women in South Sudan*. Johannesburg, South Africa: Jacana Media.

Bujra, J. (1998). "Book Review of S. Geiger's *TANU Women*." *Review of African Political Economy* 76, 297–98.

Bunch, C. (1995). "Transforming Human Rights from a Feminist Perspective." In J. Peters and A. Wolper (eds.), *Women's Rights/Human Rights: International Feminist Perspectives*. New York: Routledge.

Burnet, J. (2008). "Gender Balance and the Meanings of Women in Governance in Post-Genocide Rwanda." *African Affairs* (London) 107(428), 361–86.

Butler, A. (2003). *Feminism, Nationalism and Exiled Tibetan Women*. New Delhi: Kali for Women.

Cameron, Deborah (1998). "Gender, Language and Discourse: A Review Essay." *Signs* 23(4).

Chant, S. (2000). "From 'Woman Blind' to 'Mankind': Should Men Have More Space in Gender and Development?" *IDS Bulletin* 31(2).

Chatterjee, P. (1990). "The Nationalist Resolution of the Women's Question." In K. Sangari and S. Vaid (eds.), *Recasting Women: Essays in Indian Colonial History*. New Jersey: Rutgers University Press.

Chazan, N. (1989). "Gender Perspectives on African States." In J. Parpart and K. Staudt (eds.), *Women and the State in Africa*. Boulder, CO: Rienne Lynner.

Cheriet, B. (1996). "Gender, Civil Society and Citizenship in Algeria." *Middle East Report (MERIP)*. January–March.

Chiriyankandath, J. (1991). "The 1986 Elections: Tradition, Ideology and Ethnicity." In P. Woodward (ed.), *Sudan after Nimeiri*. London: Routledge.

Cho, S., K. W. Crenshaw, and L. McCall (2013). "Toward a Field of Intersectionality Studies: Theory, Applications, and Praxis." *Signs* 38(4), 785–810.

Cho, S., K. W. Crenshaw, and L. McCall, eds. (2013). "Intersectionality: Theorizing Power, Empowering Theory." Special issue. *Signs* 38(4).

Chowdhury, E. H. (2011). *Transnationalism Reversed: Women Organizing against Gendered Violence in Bangladesh*. New York: State University of New York Press.

Chun, J. J., G. Lipsitz, and Y. Shin (2013). "Intersectionality as a Social Movement Strategy: Asian Immigrant Women Advocates." *Signs* 38(4), 917–40.

Collins, Robert (1997). "Africans, Arabs and Islamists: From Conference Tables to Battlefields in the Sudan." Paper presented to the Fourth Triennial Meeting of International Sudanese Studies Association. Cairo, Egypt, June 12–14.

Connell, D. (n.d.). "From Resistance to Governance: How the EPLF/PFDJ Experience Shapes Eritrea's Regional Strategy." Retrieved from http://www.danconnell.net/articles/resistance-governance-how-eplfpfdj-experience-shapes-eritreas-regional-strategy.

Connell, D. (1997). "Update: Political Islam Under Attack in Sudan." *MERIP*, Winter.

Connell, D. (1998). "Strategies for Change: Women and Politics in Eritrea and South Africa." *Review of African Political Economy* 76.

Corcoran-Nantes, Y. (1993). "Female Consciousness or Feminist Consciousness? Women's Consciousness-Raising in Community-Based Struggles in Brazil." In S. Radcliffe and S. Westwood (eds.), *'Viva': Women and Popular Protest in Latin America*. London: Routledge.

Cornwall, A. (2000). "Missing Men? Reflections on Men, Masculinities and Gender in GAD." *IDS Bulletin* 31, 18–27.

Cornwall, A., and D. Eade (2010). *Deconstructing Development Discourse: Buzzwords and Fuzzwords*. Warwickshire, UK: Oxfam G. B.

Cosslett, T., et al., eds. (1996). *Women, Power and Resistance: An Introduction to Women's Studies*. Buckingham: Open University Press.

Coulter, C. (2009). *Bush Wives and Girl Soldiers: Women's Lives through War and Peace in Sierra Leone*. Ithaca, NY: Cornell University Press.

Crenshaw, K. W. (1989). "Demarginalizing the Intersection of Race and Sex: A Black Feminist Critique of Antidiscrimination Doctrine, Feminist Theory and Antiracist Politics." *University of Chicago Legal Forum*, 139–67.

Crenshaw, K. W. (1991). "Mapping the Margins: Intersectionality, Identity Politics, and Violence against Women of Color." *Stanford Law Review* 43, 1241–99.

Currier, A. (2012). "The Aftermath of Decolonization: Gender and Sexual Dissidence in Post-Independence Namibia." *Signs* 37(2).

D'Amico, R. (1982). "What Is Discourse?" *Humanities in Society* 5(3/4), 201–12.

D'Awol, A. M. (2011). "'Sibu ana sibu ana' ('Leave Me Leave Me'): Survivors of Sexual Violence in Southern Sudan." In F. Bubenzer and O. Stern (eds.), *Hope, Pain and Patience: The Lives of Women in South Sudan*. Johannesburg, South Africa: Jacana Media.

Dean, J. (1996). *Solidarity of Strangers: Feminism after Identity Politics*. Berkeley, CA: University of California Press.

DeLuca, L. (2008). "Sudanese Refugees and New Humanitarianism." *Anthropology News* 49(5), 17–18.

DeLuca, L., and L. Eppich (2007). "It Takes Two Hands to Clap: Sudanese Refugee Women Contribute to Conflict Resolution in Sudan." *Anthropology News* 48(6), 38–39.

Deng, P. (April 2, 1998). "Grassroots Have a Voice: An Era of Equal Economic Opportunities and Citizen Participation." *Sudan Dispatch: Journal of Sudanese Development*.

Deng, D. K. (2014). "Memory, Healing and Transformation in South Sudan." *Transitional Justice Working Paper No. 2*. Juba: South Sudan Law Society.

de Waal, A. (1997). *Food and Power in the Sudan*. London: African Rights.

de Waal, A. (2014). "When Kleprocracy Becomes Insolvent: Brute Causes of the Civil War in South Sudan." *African Affairs* 113(452), 347–69.

de Waal, A., and J. Flint (2006). *Darfur: A Short History of a Long War*. London: Zed Books.

Diar, D. (June 1997). "The Sudan National Democratic Alliance (NDA): The Search for Peace, Unity and Democracy." Paper presented to the Fourth International Sudan Studies Association Meeting. Cairo, American University in Cairo.

Djaburi, L. (1998). "The Syrian Women: Reality and Aspirations." In H. Afshar (ed.), *Women and Empowerment: Illustrations from Third World*. London: Macmillan.

Dolan, C. (2014). "Has Patriarchy Been Stealing the Feminists' Clothes? Conflict-Related Sexual Violence and UN Security Council Resolutions." *IDS Bulletin* 45, 80–84.

Economic and Social Council (1997). *Agreed Conclusions 1997/2*. Retrieved from www.un.org/womenwatch/osagi/pdf/ECOSOCAC1997.2.PDF.

Edward, J. (2007). *Sudanese Women Refugees: Transformations and Future Imaginings*. New York: Palgrave.

Edward, J. K. (1996). "Women as Refugees: Change through Displacement among Southern Sudanese Women in Cairo." Unpublished MA thesis. Cairo, American University in Cairo.

Eggers, D. (2006). *What is the What? The Autobiography of Valentino Achak Deng*. San Francisco: McSweeny's.

Ekrine, S., ed. (2013). *Queer African Reader*. Dakar, Senegal: Pambazuka.

El Bakri, Z. (1995). "The Crisis in the Sudanese Women's Movement." In S. Werrienga (ed.), *Subversive Women: Women's Movements in Africa, Asia, Latin America and the Caribbean*. London: Zed.

El Bakri, Z., and E. Kameir (1990). "Women's Participation in Economic, Social and Political Life in Sudanese Urban and Rural Communities: The Case of Saggana in Khartoum and Wad Al-A'sha Village in Gezira." In S. Shami et al. (eds.), *Women in Arab Society: Work Patterns and Gender Relations in Egypt, Jordan and Sudan*. Paris, France: UNESCO.

El Bakri, Z., et al. (1985). "Sudanese Sub-Project: Women in Sudan in the Twentieth Century." In S. Wieringa, *Women's Movements and Organisations in Historical Perspective*. The Hague, the Netherlands: Institute for Social Studies.

El Bakri, Z., et al. (1985). *The State of Women Studies in the Sudan*. Khartoum: DSRC.

El-Battahani, A. (1988). "Nation Building between Democracy and Dictatorship: Theoretical Introductions towards Subsequent Empirical Studies." Arabic. Paper presented to the Eleventh Arkuwit Conference. Khartoum.

El-Battahani, A. (June 1997). "Which Way Sudan? And Whose Sudan Anyway?" Abstract presented to the Fourth International Sudan Studies Association Meeting. Cairo.

El-Battahani, A. (1997a). *Women and Human Rights*. Arabic. Omdurman: Babiker Badri Scientific Association for Women.

El-Battahani, A., ed. (2011). *Elections and the Media: Case Study of the Elections of 2010*. Arabic. Khartoum: University of Khartoum Press.

El-Battahani, A. (2012). "Emergence of Nuba Nationalism: The Dialectic of Class and Ethnicity in the Peripheries of Sudan." *Sudan Journal of Economic and Social Studies* 10(1), 9–52.

El-Battahani, A. (2013). "The Post-Secession State in Sudan: Building Coalitions or Deepening Conflicts?" In G. Sørbø and A. Ahmed (eds.), *Sudan Divided*.

El-Jack, A. (2007). "Gendered Implications: Development-Induced Displacement in the Sudan." In P. Vandergeest, P. Idahosa, and P. Bose (eds.), *Development's Displacements: Ecologies, Economies and Cultures at Risk*. Vancouver: University of British Columbia Press.

El-Jack, A. (September 22, 2010). "'Education Is My Mother and Father': The 'Invisible' Women of Sudan." *Refugee* 27(2).

El-Makki, A. M. (1993). *Political Islam and Neo-Authoritarianism in Sudan: Reflections on the Socio-Economic Foundation*. Ottawa: IDRC.

El-Tahawy, M. (1995). "Women's Education: Closing the Gender Gap." *Middle East Times*, January 15–21.

El-Tom, A. (2011). *Darfur, JEM, and the Khalil Ibrahim Story*. Trenton: The Red Sea Press.

El-Tom, A. (2013). *"Study War No More": Military Tactics of a Sudanese Rebel Movement*. Trenton: The Red Sea Press.

Elzobier, A. (2014). *Political Islam: The Logic of Governance in Sudan*. Bloomington, IN: Authorhouse.

Enloe, C. (1989). *Bananas, Beaches and Bases: Making Feminist Sense of International Politics*. London: Pandora Press.

Enloe, C. (2004). *The Curious Feminist: Searching for Women in the New Age of Empire*. Berkeley: University of California Press.

Enloe, C. (2007). *Globalization and Militarism: Feminists Make the Link*. Lanham, MD: Rowman & Littlefield.

Enloe, C. (2010). *Nimo's War, Emma's War: Making Feminist Sense of the Iraq War*. Berkley: University of California Press.

Enloe, C. (2013). *Bananas, Beaches and Bases: Making Feminist Sense of International Politics*. 2nd edition. Berkley: University of California Press.

Epprecht, M. (2013). *Sexuality and Social Justice in Africa: Rethinking Homophobia and Forging Resistance*. London: Zed.

Erickson, J., and C. Faria (2011). "'We Want Empowerment for our Women': Transnational Feminism, Neoliberal Citizenship, and the Gendering of Women's Political Subjectivity in Post-Conflict South Sudan." *Signs* 36(3), 627–52.

Fabos, A. (2010). *'Brothers' or Others? Propriety and Gender for Muslim Arab Sudanese in Egypt*. Oxford: Berghahn Books.

Fadlalla, A. (2007). *Embodying Honor: Fertility, Foreignness, and Regeneration in Eastern Sudan*. Wisconsin: University of Wisconsin Press.

Fadlalla, A. (2011). "State of Vulnerability and Humanitarian Visibility on the Verge of Sudan's Secession: Lubna's Pants and Transnational Politics of Rights and Dissent." *Signs: Journal of Women in Culture and Society* 37(1).

Fanon, F. (1961). *The Wretched of the Earth*. 1990 edition. London: Penguin.

Falola, T., and N. A. Amponsah, eds. (2013). *Women, Gender, and Sexualities in Africa*. Carolina Academic Press.

Falola, T., and B. Teboh, eds. (2013). *The Power of Gender and the Gender of Power: Women's Labor Rights and Responsibility in Africa*. New Jersey: Africa World Press.

Farah, A. "Women's Need to Acquire Labour Minimizing Technologies in the Agrarian Household in Western Sudan." PhD thesis, Faculty of Agriculture. University of Khartoum, Khartoum, Sudan.

Farr, V. A. (2007). "Notes toward a Gendered Understanding of Mixed Population Movements and Security Sector Reform after Conflict." *Signs* 32(3): 591–96.

Feldman, R. (1983). "Women's Groups and Women's Subordination: An Analysis towards Rural Women in Kenya." *Review of African Political Economy* 27/28.

Ferree, M., and S. Roth (1998). "Gender, Class and the Interaction between Social Movements: A Strike of West Berlin Day Care Workers." *Gender and Society* 12(6), 626–48.

Fielding, N. (1988). *Joining Forces: Police, Training, Socialization and Occupation*. London: Routledge.

Fielding, N. (1993). "Ethnography." In N. Gilbert (ed.), *Researching Social Life*. London: Sage.

Fisher, J. (1990). *Out of the Shadows: Women, Resistance and Politics in South America*. Latin America Bureau.

Fisher, S., and K. Davis, eds. (1993). *Negotiating at the Margins: The Gendered Discourses of Power and Resistance*. New Jersey: Rutgers University Press.

Flax, J. (1990). "Postmodernism and Gender Relations in Feminist Theory." In L. Nicholson (ed.), *Feminism/Postmodernism*. Routledge: London.

Flint, J., and A. de Waal (2008). *Darfur: A New History of a Long War*. London: Zed Books.

Fluehr-Lobban, C. (1994). *Islamic Society in Practice*. Gainesville, FL: University Press of Florida.

Fluehr-Lobban, C. (June 9, 1995). "Cultural Relativism and Universal Rights." *The Chronicle of Higher Education*.

Fluehr-Lobban, C. (2012). *Shari'a and Islamism in Sudan: Conflict, Law and Social Transformation*. New York: I. B. Tauris.

Foucault, M. (1972). *The Archaeology of Knowledge*. Trans. by A. M. S. Smith. New York: Pantheon.

Foucault, M. (1978). *The History of Sexuality: An Introduction*. Trans. by R. Hurley. Harmondsworth: Penguin.

Foucault, M. (1980). *Power/Knowledge: Selected Interviews and Other Writings (1972–1977)*. Ed. C. Gordon. Briton: Harvester.

Fraser, N. (1990). "Talking about Needs: Interpretive Contests as Political Conflicts in Welfare-State Societies." In C. Sunstein (ed.), *Feminism and Political Theory*. Chicago: The University of Chicago Press.

Fraser, N., and L. Nicholson (1990). "Social Criticism without Philosophy: An Encounter between Feminism and Postmodernism." In L. Nicholson (ed.), *Feminism/Postmodernism*. Routledge: London.

Friedman, E. (1995). "Women's Human Rights: The Emergence of a Movement." In J. Peters and A. Wolper (eds.), *Women's Rights/Human Rights: International Feminist Perspectives*. New York: Routledge.

Fuentes, C. R. (1996). "They Do Not Dance Alone: The Women's Movement in Latin America." In T. Cosslett et al. (eds.), *Women, Power and Resistance: An Introduction to Women's Studies*. Buckingham: Open University Press.

Gaitskell, D., et al. (1983). "Class, Race, Gender: Domestic Workers in South Africa." *Review of African Political Economy* (27/28).

Garang, J. (2000). Quoted in IRIN Humanitarian News and Analysis (2000). "Sudan: Sudanese Opposition Leader Calls for Unity." Nairobi, Kenya: IRIN.

Garcia, A. M. (1989). "The Development of Chicana Feminist Discourse (1970–1980)." *Gender and Society* 3(2), 271–38.

Gardner, K. (1998). "Women and Islamic Revivalism in a Bangladeshi Community." In P. A. Jeffrey and A. Basu (eds.), *Appropriating Gender: Women's Activism and Politicized Religion in South Asia*. London: Routledge.

Al-Garrai, O., ed. (1999). *Women's Rights between Islamic Schools and International Conventions*. Arabic. Cairo: CIHRS.

Garrido, L. (1998). "Fighting Both Struggles in Palestine." *Lola: International Feminist Magazine* 8(97–98).

Geiger, S. (1997). *TANU Women: Gender and Culture in the Making of Tanganyika Nationalism: 1955–1965*. Portsmouth, NH: Heineman.

Germani, S. (1994). "The Role, Place and Power of Middle Class Women in the Islamic Republic." In V. Moghadam (ed.), *Identity Politics and Women: Cultural Reassertions and Feminisms in International Perspective*. Boulder: Westview.

Gicaman, R., and P. Johnson (1989). "Palestinian Women: Building Barricades and Breaking Barriers." In J. Bennin and Z. Lockman (eds.), *Intifada: The Palestinian Uprising against Israeli Occupation*. London: Tauris.

Gluck, S. (1994). *An American Feminist in Palestine: The Intifada Years*. Philadelphia: Temple University Press.

Goetz, A. M. (1998). "Women and Gender Equality in Policy: South Africa and Uganda." *Review of African Political Economy* (76), 241–62.

Gordon, A. (1996). *Transforming Capitalism and Patriarchy: Gender and Development in Africa*. Boulder: Lynne Rienner.

Grabska, K. (2010). "Lost Boys, Invisible Girls: Stories of Sudanese Marriages across Borders." *Gender, Place and Culture: A Journal of Feminist Geography* 17(4), 479–97.

Grabska, K. (2014). *Gender, Home and Identity: Nuer Repatriation and Change in Gender Relations among Nuer in Southern Sudan*. Suffolk: James Currey.

Gramizzi, C., and J. Tubiana (2013). *New War, Old Enemies: Conflict Dynamics in South Kordofan*. Geneva: Small Arms Survey.

Gruenbaum, E. (1981). "Medical Anthropology, Health Policy and the State: A Case Study of the Sudan." *Policy Studies Review* 1(1).

Gruenbaum, E. (1991). "The Islamic Movement, Development and Health Education: Recent Changes in the Health of Rural Women in Central Sudan." *Social Science and Medicine* 33(6).

Gruenbaum, E. (1992). "The Islamic State and Sudanese Women." *MERIP* 22(6).

Grzanka, P. R., ed. (2014). *Intersectionality: A Foundations and Frontiers Reader*. Boulder, CO: Westview.

Guenena, N., and N. Wassef (1999). *Unfulfilled Promises: Women's Rights in Egypt*. Cairo: Population Council.

Gupta, A., and J. Ferguson (1992). "Beyond 'Culture': Space, Identity and the Politics of Difference." *Cultural Anthropology* 7(2–22).

Gupta, M. (1997). "What Is Indian about You? A Gendered, Transformational Approach to Ethnicity." *Gender and Society* 11(5), 572–96.

Hajjar, L. (1998). "Between a Rock and a Hard Place: Arab Women, Liberal Feminism and the Israeli State." *MERIP*, Summer.

Hale, S. (1986). "The Wing of the Patriarch: Sudanese Women and Revolutionary Parties." *MERIP* 16(1).

Hale, S. (1992). "The Rise of Islam and Women of the National Islamic Front in Sudan." *Review of African Political Economy* 54.

Hale, S. (1993). "Transforming Culture or Fostering Second Hand Consciousness? Women's Front Organizations and Revolutionary Parties—The Sudan Case." In J. Tucker (ed.), *Women and Arab Society: Old Boundaries, New Frontiers*. Bloomington: Indiana University Press.

Hale, S. (1996, 2006). *Gender Politics in the Sudan: Socialism, Islamism and the State*. London: Westview.

Hale, S. (2001a). "Alienation and Belonging—Women's Citizenship and Emancipation: Visions for Sudan's Post-Islamist Future." *New Political Science* 23(1), 25–43.

Hale, S. (2001b). "Testimonies in Exile: Sudanese Gender Politics." *Northeast African Studies* 8(2), 83–128.

Halim, R. (1997). "Letter to *Agenda*." *Agenda* 32.

Hall, C., et al. (1999). "Editorial: Snakes and Ladders: Reviewing Feminisms at Century's End." *Feminist Review* 61(1–3).

Hall, M., and B. A. Ismail (1981). *Sisters Under the Sun: The Story of Sudanese Women*. London: Longman.

Hall, R. (1998). "Design for Equality: Linking Policy with Objectives in South Africa's Land Reforms." *Review of African Political Economy* 77, 451–62.

Halliday, F. (1996). *Islam and the Myth of Confrontation: Religion and Politics in the Middle East*. London: I. B. Tauris.

Hammersley, M. (1995). *The Politics of Social Research*. London: Sage.

Hamza, A. (June 1993). "Sexist Matriculation Policy in Sudan: Challenges Faced by Sudanese Women." *Women Living under Muslim Laws*. Dossier 11–12–13.

Haraway, D. (1988). "Situated Knowledges: The Science Questions in Feminism and the Privilege of Partial Perspective." *Feminist Studies* 4, 575–99.

Haraway, D. (1997). *Modest_Witness@Second_Millennium.FemaleMan_Meets_OncoMouse: Feminism and Technoscience*. New York: Routledge.

Harding, S. (1987). "Introduction: Is There a Feminist Method?" In S. Harding (ed.), *Feminism and Methodology: Social Science Issues*. Bloomington, IN: Indiana University Press.

Harir, S. (1997). "Recycling the Past in Sudan." Arabic. In S. Harir and T. Tvedt (eds.), *Sudan: Short-Cut to Decay*, trans. by M. An-Na'im and M. Osman. Cairo: Sudanese Studies Centre.

Harir, S. (June 1998). Lecture at the Sudan Culture and Information Centre. Cairo, Egypt. Attended and recorded by the author, N. M. Ali.

Hartsock, N. (1990). "Foucault on Power: A Theory for Women?" In L. Nicholson (ed.), *Feminism/Postmodernism*. Routledge: London.

Hassan, S. M., and C. R. Ray, eds. (2009). *Darfur and the Crisis of Governance in Sudan: A Critical Reader*. Ithaca: Cornell University Press.

Hassan, S. (1993). "The Sudan National Democratic Alliance (NDA): The Quest for Peace, Unity and Democracy." *Issue: A Journal of Opinion* 21(1/2), 14–25. Retrieved from http://www.jstor.org/stable/1166281.

Heath, J., and A. Zahedi, eds. (2011). *Land of the Unconquerable: The Lives of Contemporary Afghan Women*. Berkeley, CA: University of California Press.

Hessini, L. (1996). *Living on a Fault Line: Political Violence against Women in Algeria*. Cairo: The Population Council.

Hill-Collins, P. (1990). *Black Feminist Thought: Knowledge, Consciousness and the Politics of Empowerment*. New York: Routledge.

Holt, M. (1996). "State-Building in the Absence of State Structures: Palestinian Women in the Occupied Territories and Shi'a Women in Lebanon." In S. Rai and G. Lievesley (eds.), *Women and the State: International Perspectives*.

Holt, P. M. (1961). *A Modern History of the Sudan*. London: Weidfield and Nicholson.

Holy, L. (1995). "Theory, Methodology and the Research Process." In R. Ellan, *Ethnographic Research: A Guide to General Conduct*. London: Academic Press.

hooks, b. (1984). *Feminist Theory: From Margin to Center*. Cambridge, MA: South End Press.

hooks, b. (1991a). *Ain't I a Woman?* London: Pluto.

hooks, b. (1991b). *Yearning: Race, Gender and Cultural Politics*. Boston: South End Press.

hooks, b. (1997). "Sisterhood: Political Solidarity between Women." In McClintock et al. (eds.), *Dangerous Liaisons: Gender, Nation, and Postcolonial Perspectives*. Chicago, IL: University of Minnesota Press.

Ibrahim, A. A., and Z. El Bakri (1991). "Woman and Women's Studies in Sudan." Arabic. *Bulletin of Sudanese Studies* 11(2/2), 1–7. African and Afro-Asian Studies Institute, Khartoum, Sudan.

Ibrahim, F. A. (1992). "Women Under Repression in the Sudan." Paper presented at the Sudan Human Rights Workshop. Sudan Human Rights Organisation, Cairo, Egypt, November 16–18.

Ibrahim, F. A. (1996). "Sudanese Women's Union: Strategies for Emancipation and the Counter-Movement." *UFAHAMU* XXIV(ii and iii).

Ibrahim, F. M. (1997). "Class and Race Concepts in the Discourse of the SPLM." Paper presented to the Fourth International Sudan Studies Association Meeting. Cairo: American University in Cairo (June).

Ibrahim, N. F., et al. (1996). "The Feminist Movement in Sudan: An Intervention by the Members of the Sudan Feminist Union, Cairo Branch." In the New Woman Research and Study Centre, *The Feminist Movement*.

Imam, A. (1994). "Politics, Islam and Women in Kano, Northern Nigeria." In V. Moghadam (ed.), *Identity Politics and Women: Cultural Reassertions and Feminisms in International Perspective*. Boulder: Westview.

Imam, A. (1997). "Engendering African Social Sciences: An Introductory Essay." In A. Imam et al. (eds.), *Engendering African Social Sciences*. Dakar: CODESRIA.

Ismail, A. A. (December 1999). "The Dialectic of Center and Periphery and the Problem of Identity in the Sudan." Cairo. Retrieved from http://www.baniamer.com/home/articles.php?action=show&id=20 on June 24, 2015.

Ismail, A. A. (2001). "The Discourse of Neo-mahdism: A Critical Reading." Published on sudaneseonline.com on January 13, 2013.

Ismail, E. T. (1982). *Social Environment and Daily Routine of Sudanese Women: A Case Study of Urban Middle Class Housewives*. Berlin: Reimer.

Itto, A. (2006). "Guests at the Table? The Role of Women in Peace Processes." Retrieved from http://www.c-r.org/sites/default/files/Accord18_19Guestsatthetable_2006_ENG.pdf.

Jacob, S. (1983). "Women and Land Resettlement in Zimbabwe." *Review of African Political Economy* 27/28, 33–50.

Jalalzai, Z., and D. Jefferess, eds. (2011). *Globalizing Afghanistan: Terrorism, War, and the Rhetoric of Nation-Building*. Durham, NC: Duke University Press.

Jamal, A. (1991). "Funding Fundamentalism: Sudan." *Review of African Political Economy* 52.

Jayawardena, K. (1986). *Feminism and Nationalism in the Third World*. London: Zed.

Jayawardena, K. (1995). *The White Woman's Other Burden: Western Women and South Asia during British Rule*. London: Routledge.

Jeffrey, P. (1998). "Agency, Activism and Agendas." In P. A. Jeffrey and A. Basu (eds.), *Appropriating Gender: Women's Activism and Politicized Religion in South Asia*. London: Routledge.

Johnson, D. (1991). "North-South Issues." In P. Woodward (ed.), *Sudan after Nimeiri*. London: Routledge.

Johnson, D. (1998). "The Sudan People's Liberation Army and the Problem of Factionalism." In C. Clapham (ed.), *African Guerrillas*. Oxford: James Currey.

Johnson, D. (2003). *The Root Causes of Sudan's Civil Wars*. Oxford: James Currey.

Jok, J. M. (1997a). "Militarization and Gender Violence in Southern Sudan." Unpublished research paper.

Jok, J. M. (1997b). "Reproductive Suffering: Gender and War in Southern Sudan." Unpublished manuscript.

Jok, J. M. (1998). *Militarization, Gender and Reproductive Health in South Sudan*. Lewiston, NY: Edwin Mellen Press.

Jok, J. M. (2007). *Sudan: Race, Religion and Violence*. Oxford, UK: Oneworld Publications.

Jordan, J. (1985). "Report from the Bahamas." In *On Call: Feminist Essays*. Boston: South End Press.

Joseph, S. (1986). "Women and Politics in the Middle East." *MERIP* 16(1).

Joseph, S. (1996). "Gender and Citizenship in Middle Eastern States." *Middle East Report* 26(1).

Jupp, V., and C. Norris (1993). "Traditions in Documentary Analysis." In M. Hammersley (ed.), *Social Research: Philosophy, Politics and Practice*. Thousand Oaks, CA: Sage Publications.

Kaballo, S. (1989). "The Coup in Khartoum." *Review of African Political Economy* 44.

Kaiser, T. (2008). "Sudanese Refugees in Uganda and Kenya." In G. Loescher et al. (eds.), *Protracted Refugee Situations: Political, Human Rights and Security Implications*. Tokyo and New York: UNU Press.

Kalolo, K. (2012). "Social Movements of Tibetan Women in Exile: Identity Constitution by the Tibetan Women's Association." Term paper presented for the course "Theorizing Women, Gender and Development." Clark University, Worcester, MA (fall semester).

Kandiyoti, D., ed. (1991). *Women, Islam and the State*. London: Macmillan Press.

Kandiyoti, D. (1993). "Identity and its Discontents: Women and the Nation." In P. William and L. Christman (eds.), *Colonial Discourse and Post-Colonial Theory: A Reader*. New York: Harvester and Wheatsheaf.

Kandiyoti, D. (1996). "Contemporary Feminist Scholarship and Middle East Studies." In D. Kandiyoti (ed.), *Gendering the Middle East: Emerging Perspectives*. London: Tauris.

Kandiyoti, D. (1997). "Beyond Beijing: Obstacles and Prospects for the Middle East." In M. Afkhami and E. Friedl (eds.), *Muslim Women and the Politics of Participation: Implementing the Beijing Platform*. Syracuse, NY: Syracuse University Press.

Kandiyoti, D. (1998). "Some Awkward Questions on Women and Modernity in Turkey." In L. Abu-Lughod (ed.), *Remaking Women: Feminism and Modernity in the Middle East*. Princeton: Princeton University Press.

Kandiyoti, D. (2011). "Promise and Peril: Women and the 'Arab Spring.'" *Open Democracy*, March 8. http://www.opendemocracy.net (last accessed on February 10, 2013).

Keck, M. E., and K. A. Sikkink (1998). *Activists without Borders: Advocacy Networks in International Politics*. Ithaca, NY: Cornell University Press.

Keddie, N., and L. Beck (1978). "Introduction." In N. Keddie and L. Beck (eds.), *Women in the Muslim World*. Cambridge, MA: Harvard University Press.

Khalid, M. (1990). *The Government They Deserve: The Role of the Elite in Sudan's Political Evolution*. London: Kegan Paul International.

Khalid, M., ed. (1992). *The Call for Democracy in Sudan (By John Garang)*. London: Routledge.

Khalid, M. (2003). *War and Peace in Sudan: A Tale of Two Countries*. New York: Columbia University Press.

Khalid, T. (1995). "The State and the Sudanese Women's Union, 1971–1983: A Case Study." In S. Wierrienga (ed.), *Subversive Women: Women's Movements in Africa, Asia, Latin America and the Caribbean*. London: Zed.

Kenyon, S. (2004). *Five Women of Sennar: Culture and Change in Central Sudan*. Long Grove, IN: Waveland Press, Inc.

Kenyon, S. (2009). "Zainab's Story: Slavery, Women and Community in Colonial Sudan." *Urban Anthropology and Studies of Cultural Systems and World Economic Development* 38(1), 33–77.

Kishwar, M., and R. Vanita, eds. (1996). *In Search of Answers: Indian Coices from Manushi*. London: Zed.

Kitabat Sudaniya (1992). Volume 1.

Kok, P. N. (1996). "Sudan between Radical Restructuring and Deconstruction of State Systems." *Review of African Political Economy* 70, 555–62.

Koomen, J. (2013). "'Without these Women, the Tribunal Cannot Do Anything': The Politics of Witness Testimony on Sexual Violence at the International Criminal Tribunal for Rwanda." *Signs* 38(2), 253–77.

Krippendorff, K. (1980). *Content Analysis: An Introduction to its Methodology*. London: Sage.

Lazreg, M. (1988). "Feminism and Difference: The Perils of Writing as a Woman on Women in Algeria." *Feminist Studies* 14(1).

Lazreg, M. (1990). "Gender and Politics in Algeria: Unravelling the religious paradigm." *Signs* 14(4).

Lazreg, M. (1994). *The Eloquence of Silence: Algerian Women in Question*. New York: Routledge.

Leatherbee, L., and D. Bricker (1994). "Balancing Consensus and Dissent: The Prospects for Human Rights and Democracy in the Horn of Africa." New York: Fund for Peace.

Lemert, C. (2013). "Introduction: Social Theory: Its Uses and Pleasures." In C. Lemert (ed.), *Social Theory: The Multicultural, Global, and Classic Readings*. Boulder, CO: Westview.

Lerner, G. (1987). *The Creation of Patriarchy*. Oxford, UK: Oxford University Press.

Lewis, D. (1993). "Feminisms in South Africa." *Women's Studies International Forum* 16(5), 535–42.

Lewis, R. (1996). *Gendering Orientalism: Race, Femininity and Representation*. London: Routledge.

Long, N. (1992). "Research Practice and the Social Construction of Knowledge." In N. Long and A. Long (eds.), *Battlefields of Knowledge: The Interlocking of Theory and Practice in Social Research and Development*. London: Routledge.

Macleod, A. E. (1990). *Accommodating Protest: Working Women, the New Veiling and Change in Cairo*. Cairo, Egypt: American University in Cairo Press.

Mahdi, S. H. (2008). "The Position of Women in Political Parties: Obstacles and Visions for the Future." Arabic. In B. Badri (ed.), *Sudanese Woman: Her Present and Future*. Arabic. Omdurman, Sudan: Ahfad University for Women. Cairo: Dar Madarik.

Mahmoud, F. B. (1985). *The Sudanese Bourgeoisie: Vanguard of development?* Khartoum, Sudan: Khartoum University Press.

Mahmoud, F. B. (1988). "The Role of Alienation and Exploitation of Women in the Origins of State Capitalism in Sudan." In N. Toubia (ed.), *Women of the Arab World*. London: Zed.

Mahmoud, F. B. (March 1998). "Remarks on the Subordination and Liberation of Women." Arabic. *Afaq Jadida* 17.

Mahmoud, U. (1993). "The Cultural Question in the New Sudan Discourse." In I. Abdalla and I. Sconyers (eds.), *Perspectives and Challenges in the Development of Sudanese Studies*. Lewiston: Edwin Mellen Press.

Makeer, A. (2008). *From Africa to America: The Journey of a Lost Boy from Sudan*. Mustang, OK: Tate Publishing and Enterprise.

Makki, H. (1982). *The Muslim Brothers Movement in the Sudan, 1944–1969*. Arabic. Khartoum: Centre for Afro-Asian Studies.

Malkki, L. H. (1995). *Purity and Exile: Violence, Memory and National Cosmology among Hutu Refugees in Tanzania*. Chicago and London: The University of Chicago Press.

Malkki, L. H. (1996). "Speechless Emissaries: Refugees, Humanitarianism and Dehistoricization." *Cultural Anthropology* 7(1), 377–404.

Malwal, B. (1991). "The Sudan: Between Unity in Diversity and Division." In H. Bleuchot et al. (eds.) *Sudan: History, Identity, Ideology*. Reading: Ithaca Press.

Mama, A. (1995). *Beyond the Masks: Race, Gender and Subjectivity*. London: Routledge.

Mama, A. (1996). "Women's Studies and Studies of Women in Africa during the 1990s." Dakar, CODESRIA working paper, no. 5.

Mama, A. (1997a). "Postscript: Moving from Analysis to Practice?" In A. Imam et al. (eds.), *Engendering African Social Sciences*. Dakar: CODESRIA.

Mama, A. (1997b). "Sheroes and Villains: Conceptualizing Colonial and Contemporary Violence against Women in Africa." In M. J. Alexander and C. T. Mohanty (eds.), *Feminist Genealogies, Colonial Legacies, Democratic Futures*, 46–62. New York: Routledge.

Manna', H. (1997). "The Political Islamic Movement and Human Rights." In B. Hassan (ed.), *Challenges Facing the Arab Human Rights Movement*. Cairo: Cairo Institute for Human Rights Studies.

Marinkovic, N. (August 2011). "Daniel Kodi in South Kordofan: Peacemaker or Traitor?" Retrieved from http://www.enoughproject.org/blogs/daniel-kodi-south-kordofan-peacemaker-or-traitor on April 13, 2013.

Mayard, M. (1994). "Race, Gender and the Concept of 'Difference' in Feminist Thought." In H. Afshar and M. Maynard (eds.), *The Dynamics of Race and Gender: Some Feminist Interventions*. New York: Taylor & Francis.

Mayer, A. (1997). "Aberrant 'Islams' and Errant Daughters: The Turbulant Legacy of Beijing in Muslim Societies." In M. Afkhami and E. Friedl (eds.), *Muslim Women and the Politics of Participation: Implementing the Beijing Platform*. Syracuse, NY: Syracuse University Press.

Mbilinyi, M. (1989). "This Is an Unforgettable Business: Colonial State Intervention in Urban Tanzania." In J. Parpart and K. Staudt (eds.), *Women and the State in Africa*. Boulder, CO: Rienne Lynner.

McCall, L. (2005). "The Complexity of Intersectionality." *Signs* 30(3), 1771–1800.

McClintock, A. (1997). *Imperial Leather: Race, Gender and Sexuality in the Colonial Context*. London: Routledge.

McNay, L. (1992). *Foucault and Feminism: Power, Gender and the Self*. Cambridge: Polity Press.

McCutchen, A. (2014). *The Sudan Revolutionary Front: Its Formation and Development*. Geneva, Switzerland: Small Arms Survey, Graduate Institute of International Development Studies.

Medecins Sans Frintiere (MSF) (March 8, 2005). "The Crushing Burden of Rape: Sexual Violence in Darfur." Briefing paper. Amsterdam.

Medie, P. A. (2003). "Fighting Gender-Based Violence: The Women's Movement and the Enforcement of Rape Law in Liberia." *African Affairs* 112(448), 377–97.

Meese, E., and A. Parker (1989). "Introduction." In E. Meese and A. Parker (eds.), *The Difference Within: Feminism and Critical Theory*. Philadelphia, PA: John Benjamins Publishing.

Mehdid, M. (1996). "En-Gendering the Nation-State: Women, Patriarchy and Politics in Algeria." In S. Rai and G. Lievesley (eds.), *Women and the State: International Perspectives*.

Mendez, J. B., and N. A. Naples (2014). "Introduction." In N. A. Naples and J. B. Mendez (eds.), *Border Politics: Social Movements, Collective Identities, and Globalization*. New York: New York University Press.

Mernissi, F. (1989). *Doing Daily Battle: Interviews with Moroccan Women*. New Jersey: Rutgers University Press.

Mills, S. (1997). *Discourse*. London: Routledge.

Mishler, E. (1986). *Research Interviewing: Context and Narrative*. Cambridge, MA: Harvard University Press.

Moghadam, V. M. (1993). *Modernising Women: Gender and Social Change in the Middle East*. Boulder: Lynne Rienner.

Moghadam, V. M. (1994). "Introduction: Women and Identity Politics in Theoretical and Comparative Perspective." In V. Moghadam (ed.), *Identity Politics and Women: Cultural Reassertions and Feminisms in International Perspective*. Boulder: Westview.

Moghadam, V. M. (2013). *Globalization and Social Movements: Islamism, Feminism, and the Global Justice Movement*. 2nd edition. Lanham, MD: Rowman & Littlefield Publishers, Inc.

Moghissi, H. (1994). *Feminism and Populism in Iran: Women's Struggle in a Male-Defined Revolutionary Movement*. London: Macmillan.

Mohamed, F. J. (July 11, 2014). "11 Years of the Maputo Protocol: Women's Progress and Challenges." Retrieved from http://www.soawr.org/en/news/item/11_years_of_the_maputo_protocol_womens_progress_and_challenges_faiza_j_moha/ on June 30, 2015.

Mohammed, A. (2003). "Sudan: Women & Conflict in Darfur." *Review of African Political Economy* 30(97), 479–81.

Mohammed, A. A., et al. (2011). "Maternal Mortality in Kassala State: Community-Based Study Using Reproductive Age Mortality Survey (RAMOS)." *BMC Pregnancy and Childbirth* 11(102).

Mohanty, C. T. (1988). "Under Western Eyes: Feminist Scholarship and Colonial Discourses." *Feminist Review* 14(1).

Mohanty, C. T. (1991). "Cartographies of Struggle: Third World Women and the Politics of Feminism." In C. T. Mohanty, A. Russo, and L. Torres (eds.), *Third World Women and the Politics of Feminism*. Bloomington: Indiana University Press.

Mohanty, C. T. (2003). "'Under Western Eyes' Revisited: Feminist Solidarity through Anticapitalist Struggles." *Signs* 28(2), 499–535.

Mohanty, C. T. (2013). "Transnational Feminist Crossings: On Neoliberalism and Radical Critique." *Signs* 38(4), 967–91.

Mojab, S. (2003). "Kurdish Women in the Zone of Genocide and Gendercide." *Al-Raida* XXI(103).

Molyneux, M. (1982). *State Policies and the Position of Women Workers in the People's Democratic Republic of Yemen, 1967–1977*. Geneva: ILO.

Molyneux, M. (1985). "Mobilization without Emancipation? Women's Interests, the State and Revolution." *Feminist Studies* 11(2), 227–54.

Molyneux, M. (1998). "Analysing Women's Movements." *Development and Change* 29, 219–45.

Morris, M. (1979). "The Pirate's Fiancée." In M. Morris and P. Patton (eds.), *Michel Foucault: Power/Truth/Strategy*. Sydney: Feral Publications.

Moser, C. (1993). *Gender Planning and Development: Theory, Practice and Training*. London: Routledge.

Mukhtar, Abdel Rahman (1986). *Autumn of Anger*. Arabic. Khartoum, Sudan: Dar al-Sahafa.

Mutua, M. (2001). "Savages, Victims, and Saviors: The Metaphor of Human Rights." *Harvard International Law Journal* 42, 201–45.

Naber, N. (1997). "Workshop Report: A Workshop on Gender and Citizenship in the Muslim World." *MEWS Review* XII(3).

Nageeb, S. A. (2004). *New Spaces and Old Frontiers: Women, Social Space, and Islamization in Sudan*. Lanham, MD: Lexington Books.

Najmabadi, A. (1991). "Hazards of Modernity and Morality: Women, State and Ideology in Contemporary Iran." In D. Kandiyoti (ed.), *Women, Islam and the State*. London: Macmillan Press.

Narayan, U. (1997). *Dislocating Cultures: Identities, Traditions and Third World Feminism*. New York: Routledge.

Nash, J. C. (2008). "Re-Thinking Intersectionality." *Feminist Review* 89, 1–5.

Naples, N. (2002). "The Challenges and Possibilities of Transnational Feminist Praxis." In N. Naples and M. Desai (eds.), *Women's Activism and Globalization: Linking Local Struggles and Transnational Politics*. New York and London: Routledge.

Naples, N. (2003) *Feminism and Method: Ethnography, Discourse Analysis, and Activist Research*. New York: Routledge.

Naples, N., and J. B. Mendez, eds. (2014). *Border Politics: Social Movements, Collective Identities, and Globalization*. New York: New York University Press.

Naples, N., and M. Desai, eds. (2002). *Women's Activism and Globalization: Linking Local Struggles and Transnational Politics*. New York and London: Routledge.

Nelson, C. (1974). "Public and Private Politics: Women in the Middle Eastern World." *American Ethnologist* 1.

Niblock, T. (1987). *Class and Power in Sudan: The Dynamics of Sudanese Politics (1898–1985)*. New York: SUNY Press.

Niblock, T. (1991). "The Background to the Change of Government in 1985." In P. Woodward (ed.), *Sudan after Nimeiri*. London: Routledge.

Nicholson, L. (1994). "Interpreting Gender." *Signs* 20(4).

Nugud, M. I. (1994). *Slavery in the Sudan*. Arabic. Cairo: Sudanese Studies Centre.

Nyaba, P. (1997). *The Politics of Liberation in South Sudan: An Insider's View*. Kampala: Fountain Publishers.

Oakley, A. (1981). "Interviewing Women: A Contradiction in Terms." In H. Roberts (ed.), *Doing Feminist Research*. Boston: Routledge.

O'Barr, J. (1984). "African Women in Politics." In M. J. Hay and S. Stichter (eds.), *African Women South of the Sahara*. London: Longman.

Okley, J. (1992). "Anthropology and Autobiography: Participatory Research and Embodied Knowledge." In J. Okley and H. Callaway (eds.), *Anthropology and Autobiography*. London: Routledge.

Okome, M. O. (2005). "African Women and Power: Labor, Gender and Feminism in the Age of Globalization." *SAGE Race Relations Abstracts* 30(2), 3–26. doi: 10.1177/0307920105054451.

Opie, A. (1992). "Qualitative Research, Appropriation of the 'Other' and Empowerment." *Feminist Review* 40.

Ostergaard, L. (1992). "Gender." In L. Ostergaard (ed.), *Gender and Development: A Practical Guide*. London: Routledge.

Oyewùmí, O. (1998). *The Invention of Women: Making an African Sense of Western Gender Discourse*. Minneapolis, MN: University of Minnesota

Oyewùmí, O., ed. (2003). *African Women and Feminism: Reflections on the Politics of Sisterhood*. Trenton, NJ: Africa World Press.

Pantuliano, S. (2006). "Comprehensive Peace? An Analysis of the Evolving Tension in Eastern Sudan." *Review of African Political Economy* 33(110), 709–20.

Parpart, J. (1987). "Women and Politics in Africa: Old Failures and New Directions." In J. Parpart (ed.), *Africa in the World Politics*. London, UK: Macmillan.

Peterson, J. E (1989). "The Political Status of Women in the Arab Gulf States." *Middle East Journal* XVIII(1).

Philips, A. (1998). "Introduction." In A. Philips (ed.), *Feminism and Politics*. Oxford and New York: Oxford University Press.

Potter, C. B., and C. B. Romano (2012). *Doing Recent History: On Privacy, Copyright, Video Games, Institutional Review Boards, Activist Scholarship, and History That Talks Back*. Atlanta: University of Georgia Press.

Qau'd, A. (1999). *Religious Totalitarianism and Human Rights: Case of Sudan (1989–1994)*. Arabic. Cairo: Cairo Institute for Human Rights Studies.

Radcliffe, S. (1993). "'People Have to Rise Up—Like the Great Women Fighters': The State and Peasant Women in Peru." In S. Radcliffe and S. Westwood (eds.), *'Viva': Women and Popular Protest in Latin America*. London: Routledge.

Rai, S. M. (1996). "Women and the State in the Third World." In S. Rai and G. Lievesley (eds.), *Women and the State: International Perspectives*. London: Taylor and Francis.

Rai, S. M. (2008). *The Gender Politics of Development: Essays in Hope and Despair.* London: Zed.

Reanda, L. (1999). "Engendering the UN: The Changing International Agenda." *European Journal of Women's Studies* 6, 49–68.

Review of African Political Economy 27(28). Special issue on women.

Rida, A. (1975). *Jaafar Numeiry: The Man and the Challenge; Interviews with Jaafar Numeiry.* Arabic. Alexandria: Al-maktab al-Misry Press.

Roberts, P. (1983). "Feminism in Africa, Feminism and Africa." *Review of African Political Economy* 26/27, 175–84.

Rodney, W. (1982). *How Europe Underdeveloped Africa.* Washington, DC: Howard University Press.

Romano, R. C., and C. B. Potter (2012). "Just Over Our Shoulders: The Pleasures and Perils of Writing the Recent Past." In C. B. Potter and R. C. Romano (eds.), *Doing Recent History: On Privacy, Copyright, Video Games, Institutional Review Boards, Activist Scholarship, and History That Talks Back.* Atlanta: University of Georgia Press.

Roscoe, W., and S. O. Murray (2001). *Boy-Wives and Female Husbands: Studies of African Homosexualities.* London: Palgrave Macmillan.

Rothwell, P. (2012). "Unfinished Revolutions: Gaps and Conjunctions." *Signs* 37(2), 271–74.

Rozario, S. (1996). "Community and Resistance: Muslim Women in Contemporary Societies." In T. Cosslett et al. (eds.), *Women, Power and Resistance: An Introduction to Women's Studies.* Buckingham: Open University Press.

Saad, M. (1972). "Notes on Higher Education for Women in the Sudan." *Sudan Notes and Records* (53).

Sabbah, F. (1984). *Women in the Muslim Unconscious.* New York: Pergamon.

Sacks, K. (1982). *Sisters and Wives: The Past and Future of Sexual Equality.* Urbana: University of Illinois Press.

Said, E. (1993). *Culture and Imperialism.* London: Vintage.

Said, E. (1994). *Orientalism.* First published 1978. New York: Vintage.

Salih, F. M. (September 3, 2010). "On the Dialectic of Identity in Sudan." Arabic. Retrieved from https://ar.wikipedia.org/ on June 24, 2015.

Salih, K. O. (1991). "The Sudan, 1985–1989: The Fading Democracy." In P. Woodward (ed.), *Sudan after Nimeiri.* London: Routledge.

Sanderson, L. (1961). "Some Aspects of the Development of Girls' Education in Northern Sudan." *Sudan Notes and Records* X.

Sanderson, L. (1962). "Educational Development in the Southern Sudan (1900–1926)." *Sudan Notes and Records* XLIII(43).

Sanderson, L. (1968). "The Development of Girls' Education in the Northern Sudan (1989–1960)." *Pedagogica Historica* 8(1–2).

Sangari, K., and S. Vaid. (1990). "Recasting Women: An Introduction." In K. Sangari and S. Vaid (eds.), *Recasting Women: Essays in Indian Colonial History.* New Jersey: Rutgers University press.

Sawicki, J. (1991). *Disciplining Foucault: Feminism, Power, and the Body.* London: Routledge.

Sayigh, R. (1996). "Researching Gender in a Palestinian Camp: Political, Theoretical and Methodological Problems." In D. Kandiyoti (ed.), *Gendering the Middle East: Emerging Perspectives.* London: Tauris.

Scott, E. K. (1998). "Creating Partnership for Change: Alliances and Betrayal in the Racial Politics of Two Feminist Organizations." *Gender and Society* 12(4), 400–423.

Seidman, G. W. (1999). "Gendered Citizenship: South Africa's Democratic Transition and the Construction of a Gendered State." *Gender and Society* 13(3), 287–307.

Shaaeldin, E., and R. Brown (1988). "Towards an Understanding of Islamic Banking in Sudan: The Case of Faisal Islamic Bank." In T. Barnett and A. Abdel Karim (eds.), *Sudan: State, Capital and Transformation.* New York: Biddle.

Shakespeare, P., et al., eds. (1993). *Reflecting on Research Practice: Issues in Health and Social Welfare.* Philadelphia: Open University Press.

Sharabi, H. (1988). *Neopatriarchy: A Theory of Distorted Change in Arab Society*. Oxford: Oxford University Press.

Sharabi, H. (1989). "The Dialectics of Patriarchy in Arab society." In S. Farsoun (ed.), *Arab Society: Continuity and Change*. London: Croom Helm.

Sharabi, H. (1991). "Introduction: Patriarchy and Dependency and the Future of Arab Society." In H. Sharabi (ed.), *The Next Arab Decade: Alternative Futures*. Boulder: Westview.

Sherwood, L. F. (2012). "Women at a Crossroads: Sudanese Women and Political Transformation." *Journal of International Women's Studies* 13(5), 77–90. Last accessed on August 8, 2013.

Shettima, K. A. (1995). "Engendering Nigeria's Third Republic." *African Studies Review* 38(2), 61–98.

Sirag, A. O. (September 1999). "Thoughts about the Forthcoming Democracy." Arabic. *Ruaa* 5.

Smith, D. (1987). *The Everyday World as Problematic: A Feminist Sociology*. Boston: Northeastern University Press.

Smith, D. (1990). *Texts, Facts and Femininity: Exploring the Relations of Ruling*. London: Routledge.

Smith, J. (1994). "The Creation of the World We Know: The World Economy and the Creation of Gender Identities." In V. Moghadam (ed.), *Identity Politics and Women: Cultural Reassertions and Feminisms in International Perspective*. Boulder: Westview.

Smith, L. (2013). *Making Citizens in Africa: Ethnicity, Gender, and National Identity in Ethiopia*. Cambridge: Cambridge University Press.

Sørbø, G. M., and A. G. M. Ahmed, eds. (2013). *Sudan Divided: Continuing Conflict in a Contested State*. New York: Palgrave Macmillan.

Spaulding, J., and S. Beswick, eds. (2000). *White Nile, Black Blood: War, Ethnicity and Leadership from Khartoum to Kampala*. Lawrenceville, NJ: Red Sea Press.

Spellman, E. V. (1988). *Inessential Woman: Problems of the Exclusion in Feminist Thought*. Boston: Beacon Press.

Stanley, L., ed. (1993). *Feminist Praxis: Research, Theory and Epistemology in Feminist Sociology*. London: Routledge.

Stewart, A. (1996). "Should Women Give Up on the State? The African Experience." In S. Rai and G. Lievesley (eds.), *Women and the State: International Perspectives*.

Stewart, K. (1999). "New Perspectives of African Feminism and the History of African Women." Review article. *Women's Studies International Forum* 22(2).

Stone, L. (2011). "'We Were all Soldiers': Female Combatants in South Sudan's Civil War." In F. Bubenzer and O. Stern (eds.), *Hope, Pain and Patience: The Lives of Women in South Sudan*. Johannesburg, South Africa: Jacana Media.

Stowasser, B. (1993). "Women's Issues in Modern Islamic Thought." In J. Tucker (ed.), *Arab Women: Old Boundaries, New Frontiers*. Bloomington: Indiana University Press.

Sudanese Catholic Information Office (SCIO) (October 1999). "SCIO Sudan Monthly Report Oct. 1999." Nairobi, Kenya: SCIO.

Sudan Tribune (September 23, 2014). "The Sudan Revolutionary Forces Is Planning a Conference Similar to the Asmara 1995 Conference." Retrieved from http://www.sudantribune.net/9228.

Sullivan, Z. (1998). "Eluding the Feminist, Overthrowing the Modern? Transformations in Twentieth-Century Iran." In L. Abu-Lughod (ed.), *Remaking Women: Feminism and Modernity in the Middle East*. Princeton: Princeton University Press.

Sword, H. (2012). *Stylish Academic Writing*. Cambridge, MA: Harvard University Press.

Taha, H. (1993). *The Military and Muslim Brothers: The Story of the National Islamic Front and Authority in Sudan*. Arabic. Cairo: Markaz al-Hadara al-Arabiyya.

Taha, M. M. (1996). *The Second Message of Islam*. Trans. by Abdullahi An Na'im. Syracuse: Syracuse University Press.

Tamale, S. (1999). *When Hens Begin to Crow: Gender and Parliamentary Politics in Uganda*. Kampala: Fountain Publishers.

Tamale, S. (2006). "African Feminism: How Should *We* Change?" *Development* 49, 38–41.

Tamale, S., ed. (2011). *African Sexualities: A Reader*. Dakar, Senegal: Pambazuka Press.

Tavakoli-Targhi, M. (1994). "Women of the West Imagined: The *Farangi* Other and the Emergence of the Woman Question in Iran." In V. Moghadam (ed.), *Identity Politics and Women: Cultural Reassertions and Feminisms in International Perspective*. Boulder: Westview.

The New Woman Research and Study Centre (1996). *Women in the Arab World: Interventions and Studies from Four Countries*. Arabic. Cairo: Dar al-Mustaqbal al-Arabi.

Tibi, B. (November–December 1991). "Neo-Islamic Fundamentalism." *Women Living Under Muslim Laws* (9/10).

Tomlinson, B. (2013). "To Tell the Truth and Not Get Trapped: Desire, Distance, and Intersectionality at the Scene of Argument." *Signs* 38(4), 993–1017.

Tønnessen, L. (2011). *The Many Faces of Political Islam in Sudan: Muslim Women's Activism for and against the State*. Bergen: University of Bergen.

Tønnessen, L., and H. Kjøstvedt Granås (2010). *The Politics of Women's Representation in Sudan: Debating Women's Rights in Islam from the Elites to the Grassroots*. CHR, Michelson Institute. CMI Report 2.

Tripp, A. M. (1994). "Gender, Political Participation and the Transformation of Associational Life in Uganda and Tanzania." *African Studies Review* 37(1).

Tripp, A. M., I. Casimiro, J. Kwesiga, and A. Mungwa (2009). *African Women's Movements: Transforming Political Landscapes*. Cambridge, MA: Cambridge University Press.

Tucker, J. E., ed. (1993). *Arab Women: Old Boundaries, New Frontiers*. Bloomington: Indiana University Press.

Turshen, M. (1998). "Women's War Stories." In M. Turshen and C. Twagiramariya (eds.), *What Women Do in Wartime: Gender and Conflict in Africa*. London: Zed.

United Nations Development Programme (2014). "Table 4: Gender Inequality Index." *Human Development Report 2014*. New York.

United Nations Division for the Advancement of Women (1997). "International Standards of Equality and Religious Freedom: Implications for the Status of Women." In V. Moghadam (ed.), *Identity Politics and Women: Cultural Reassertions and Feminisms in International Perspective*. Boulder: Westview.

United Nations Economic and Social Council (UN ECOSOC) (1998). "Commission on Human Rights Report on the Fifty-Fourth Session." E/CN.4/1998.177.

Urdang, S. (1979). *Fighting Two Colonialisms: Women in Guinea Bissau*. London: Monthly Review Press.

Urdang, S. (1983). "The Last Transition? Women and Development in Mozambique." *Review of African Political Economy* 26/27, 8–32.

Urdang, S. (1984). "Women in National Liberation Movements." In M. J. Hay and S. Stichter (eds.), *African Women South of the Sahara*. London: Longman.

Vargas, V. (1995). "Women's Movement in Peru: Rebellion in action." In S. Wierringa (ed.), *Subversive Women: Women's Movements in Africa, Asia, Latin America and the Caribbean*. London: Zed.

Verwijk, M. (2012). "Is Peace Not for Everyone? Narratives on a Struggle for Peace, Equality, and Development in Sudan." MA thesis. University of Utrecht, the Netherlands.

Voll, J. O. (1983). "The Evolution of Islamic Fundamentalism in Twentieth-Century Sudan." In G. Warburg and U. M. Kupferschmidt (eds.), *Islam, Nationalism and Radicalism in Egypt and Sudan in the 20th Century*. New York: Praeger Publishers.

Voll, J. O., ed. (1991). *Sudan: State and Society in Crisis*. Bloomington: Indiana University Press.

Wakson, E. (1987). "National Unity and the Diversity of Identities." In F. Deng and P. Gifford (eds.), *The Search for Peace and Unity in the Sudan*. Washington, DC: Woodrow Wilson Center Press.

Walby, S. (1997). *Gender Transformation*. London: Routledge.

Walker, C. (1994). "Women, 'Tradition' and Reconstruction." *Review of African Political Economy* 61, 347–458.

Wanga-Odhiambo, G. (2013). *Resilience in South Sudanese Women: Hope for Daughters of the Nile*. Lanham, MD: Lexington Books.

Warburg, G. (1985). *Egypt and the Sudan: Studies in History and Politics*. London: Franc Cass.

Warburg, G., and U. M. Kupferschmidt, eds. (1983). *Islam, Nationalism and Radicalism in Egypt and Sudan in the 20th Century*. New York: Praeger Publishers.

Warren, C. (1988). *Gender Issues in Field Research*. London: Sage.

Wenger, M. (1991). "Sudan: Politics and Society." *Middle East Report* 172.

White, S. C. (2000). "'Did the Earth Move?' The Hazards of Bringing Men and Masculinities into Gender and Development." *IDS Bulletin* 31(2), 33–41.

Wierringa, S. (1995). *Subversive Women: Women's Movements in Africa, Asia, Latin America and the Caribbean*. London: Zed.

Wilentz, S. (2009). *The Age of Reagan: A History (1974–2008)*. New York: HarperCollins.

Williams, S. (1991). "From 'Mothers of the Nation' to Women in Their Own Right: South African Women in the Transition to Democracy." In T. Wallace and C. March (eds.), *Changing Perceptions: Writings on Gender and Development*. Oxford: Oxfam.

Willimse, K. (2007). *One Foot in Heaven: Narratives on Gender and Islam in Darfur, West-Sudan*. Brill Academic Publishers.

Willemse, K. (2009). "The Darfur War: Masculinity and the Construction of a Sudanese National Identity." In S. M. Hassan and C. R. Ray (eds.), *Darfur and the Crisis of Governance in Sudan: A Critical Reader*. Ithaca: Cornell University Press.

Win, E. (2007). "Not Very Poor, Powerless or Pregnant: The African Woman Forgotten by Development." In A. Cornwall, E. Harrison, and A. Whitehead (eds.), *Feminisms in Development: Contradictions, Contestations and Challenges*. London: Zed.

Wing, S. D. (2002). "Women Activists in Mali: The Global Discourse on Human Rights." In N. Naples and M. Desai (eds.), *Women's Activism and Globalization: Linking Local Struggles and Transnational Politics*. New York and London: Routledge.

Women's Studies International Forum (1996). Special Issue on "Links across Differences: Gender, Ethnicity, and Nationalism." 19(1/2).

Woodward, P. (1990). *Sudan (1898–1989): The Unstable State*. Boulder: Lynne Rienner.

Woodward, P., ed. (1991a). *Sudan after Nimeiri*. London: Routledge.

Woodward, P. (1991b). "A 'New Sudan?'" In H. Bleuchot et al. (eds.), *Sudan: History, Identity, Ideology*. Reading: Ithaca Press.

Yuval-Davis, N. (1996). "Women and the Biological Reproduction of 'the Nation.'" *Women's Studies International Forum* 19(1/2).

Yuval-Davis, N. (1997a). *Gender and Nation*. London: Sage.

Yuval-Davis, N. (1997b). "Women, Citizenship and Difference." *Feminist Review* 57.

Yuval-Davis, N. (2006). "Intersectionality and Feminist Politics." *European Journal of Women's Studies* 13(3), 193–209.

Yuval-Davis, N., and F. Anthias (1989). *Woman-Nation-State*. London: Macmillan.

Zahir, K. (1998). "Interview with the First Sudanese Female Medical Doctor and the First Female Political Detainee." Arabic. *Afaq Gadida* 17.

Ziai, F. (1997). "Personal Status Codes and Women's Rights in the Maghreb." In M. Afkhami and E. Friedl (eds.), *Muslim Women and the Politics of Participation: Implementing the Beijing Platform*. Syracuse, NY: Syracuse University Press.

Zinn, M., and B. Dill (1996). "Theorising Difference from Multiracial Feminism." *Feminist Studies* 22(2), 321–31.

Index

Abba Island, 105
Abdel Rahman, *al-Umda* (Mayor) Musa, 118
Addis Ababa Agreement, 45–46, 64, 70, 106
Ahfad University for Women, 24, 27, 59, 171, 172, 173n7
Al-Azhari, Ismail, 50, 105
Al-Mahdi, Abdulrahman, 61, 77
Al-Mahdi, Mariam, 62, 73n10
Al-Mahdi, Mohamed Ahmed, 61, 133
Al-Mahdi, Mubarak, 82, 88, 95
Al-Mahdi, *Sayid* Al-Sadiq, 62, 67, 81, 89, 105, 184, 187
Al-Mirghani, *Sayid* Mohamed Osman, 79, 89, 94, 98, 142
Amom, Pagan, 109, 110, 111, 112
Apai, Mary, 139–140
Arman, Yasir, 110
Article 5, 76, 78, 81, 83, 84, 85, 86, 86–88, 88–90, 92, 93, 94, 98, 102n12, 116, 129, 130, 133, 140, 140–141, 141–143, 143, 144, 145, 146–147, 148–149, 149, 158–159, 183, 184
Asmara Conference of Fundamental Issues, 1, 2, 3, 7, 9, 10, 70, 75, 76, 80, 87, 96–78, 97, 98, 121, 131–132, 133, 141, 158, 183, 184
Asmara Resolutions, 5, 10, 70, 75, 76, 79, 83, 84, 85, 87, 88, 94, 99, 141–142, 144–146, 183, 184

Beja Congress, 19n2–19n3, 50, 65, 66, 67, 86, 87, 97, 103, 115, 116, 127, 184, 186, 187
Beja Women, General Union of, 66–67, 116, 118, 127, 158
Blue Nile State, 5, 11, 19n1, 56, 58, 64, 105, 108, 118, 120, 155, 162, 172, 175, 177, 187

CEDAW. *See* Convention on the Elimination of All Forms of Discrimination Against Women
Communist Party of the Sudan (CPS), 29, 45, 50, 63, 64, 68, 69, 71–72, 82, 84, 86, 86–87, 96, 97, 100, 102n14, 124–126, 132, 160n13, 168, 173n2, 181, 182, 183
Comprehensive Peace Agreement, 5, 16, 28, 31, 50, 60, 78, 83, 104, 120, 126, 162
Convention on the Elimination of All Forms of Discrimination Against Women, 11, 26, 52, 76, 83–85, 86–87, 88–89, 106, 128, 141, 142–144, 144–145, 145, 147, 162, 163, 173n2
CPA. *See* Comprehensive Peace Agreement
CPS. *See* Communist Party of the Sudan

Darfur, 11, 19n1, 20n13, 20n17, 27, 30, 33, 56, 58, 64, 65–66, 97, 106, 107, 117,

211

About the Author

Nada Mustafa Ali is a scholar, activist, and policy specialist on gender, development, and human rights, with a focus on Sudan and South Sudan. She teaches in the Women's and Gender Studies Department, and is a faculty fellow in the Center for Governance and Sustainability at the University of Massachusetts, Boston. She has also taught at the New School, Clark University, and at Ahfad University for Women. Dr. Ali held associate or fellow positions at the Five College Women's Studies Research Center, Fordham University, and at the International Center for Research on Women. She has written and published widely on gender and women's human rights, especially in Sudan and South Sudan.

In addition to her academic career, Dr. Ali has worked or consulted for several international organizations and United Nations agencies. She was the Women's Program Coordinator at the Cairo Institute for Human Rights Studies, and the Africa Women's Rights Researcher at Human Rights Watch. She has carried out research for the US Institute of Peace and the Small Arms Survey. She has consulted for the United Nations Development Programme, United Nations Population Fund, UN Women, and a range of international, regional, and local organizations.

Dr. Ali received her PhD in government from the University of Manchester, UK. She has a BA (honors) and an MA from Khartoum University and the American University in Cairo, respectively, both in political science.

CPSIA information can be obtained at www.ICGtesting.com
Printed in the USA
BVOW11*1232180715

409205BV00003B/6/P